Galloon

The history of three townlands in County Tyrone from the earliest times to the present day

Best wishes to Judith

W. J. Bradley

17/11/2000.

First published in May 2000
Typeset and designed by
GUILDHALL PRESS
Unit 4, Community Service Units
Bligh's Lane, Derry BT48 0LZ
T: (028) 7136 4413
F: (028) 7137 2949
info@ghpress.com
www.ghpress.com

ISBN 0 946451 57 5

© William John Bradley May 2000

Cover: Photograph shows Henry Bradley (1899-1976) and his granddaughter Rosemary. The photograph was taken by his daughter, Patricia O'Conaill, in 1973.

All rights reserved. No part of this publication may be reproduced or transmitted in any form or by any means, electronic or mechanical, including photocopy, recording, or any information storage or retrieval system, without permission in writing from the publisher. The book is sold subject to the condition that it shall not, by way of trade or otherwise, be lent, re-sold or otherwise circulated without the publisher's prior consent in any form of binding or cover other than that in which it is published and without a similar condition including this condition being imposed on the subsequent purchaser.

GP Media/Guildhall Press receives financial support from the District Partnership for the Derry City Council Area under the European Special Support Programme for Peace and Reconciliation and from the Londonderry Development Office under the Londonderry Regeneration Initiative. We would also like to thank Derry City Council's Recreation and Leisure Department for generous Community Services Grant Aid.

Gallon

The history of three townlands in
County Tyrone from the earliest
times to the present day

William John Bradley

GUILDHALL PRESS, DERRY

Dedicated to the memory of
Rose and Henry Bradley

ABOUT THE AUTHOR

William John Bradley, Dip A.S. Ed, M.A. was born in Gallon Lower in August 1943. He attended Gallon Primary School from 1947 until 1955. In 1955 he transferred to the Christian Brothers' Grammar School, Omagh where he remained until 1961. He qualified as a teacher at St Joseph's College of Education, Belfast in 1964. In Sept 1964, he took up his first teaching post in Newtownstewart Primary School, and moved to Gallon Primary School as principal in 1967. When the school closed in 1969 he moved to the new St Patrick's Primary School, Newtownstewart, where he taught until 1971. He taught in Rosemount Primary School and St Anne's Primary School, Derry until August 1987 when he was appointed principal of Rosemount Primary School.

He edited *Rosemount, the Village and the School (1991)*, wrote 'The Australian Bradleys' which appeared in *The Parish of Ardstraw East* (1995) and also 'The Landlords of the Newtownstewart and Lislap Estate 1610-1932' in *Ulster Local Studies (Summer 1997)*. He is currently Vice-chairman of the Executive Committee of the Federation for Ulster Local Studies and of the West Tyrone Historical Society.

ACKNOWLEDGMENTS

Sincere thanks to the Ulster Local History Trust for their generous financial support without which this book could not have been published.

Also, thanks are also due to the Community Relations Council, Strabane District Council, Omagh District Council, Hamilton's Food Halls, Newtownstewart and EDCO, Belfast for their financial support.

My deepest appreciation Dr Bill Crawford, without whose generous assistance and unfailing encouragement this book would not have been written.

I would also like to thank Mary McColgan, Teresa McCaffrey, Rose Mullan, Patricia O'Conaill, Philomena Devine, Neil McGuigan, Brian Lacey, Terry McBride, John Dooher, Bernard McColgan, Peggy Morris, John McNamee, Tommy McNamee, Maura Burder, John Flood, Jack Johnston, Mr Billy Dunbar, Hugh Gallagher, Michael Cox, my wife, family, friends who encouraged me in various ways and the staff of Guildhall Press, particularly Joe Mc Allister and Paul Hippsley.

I would also like to thank the Ordnance Survey for permission to reproduce maps; Mr Matthew Stout for permission to reproduce maps which had originally appeared in *Townlands of Ulster*; the director of the Ulster Folk and Transport Museum for permission to reproduce photographs; Dr Noel Kissane and the staff of the National Library of Ireland and the staff of the Public Record Office, Belfast.

CONTENTS

PREFACE

by Dr W H Crawford

When I first mentioned to John Bradley the idea that I had for publishing a volume of essays about the study of townlands in Ulster, he agreed to contribute to the project. A few months later, I received the bulk of the manuscript with the suggestion that I might edit it as I saw fit.

The manuscript contained a wealth of observations and information that John had obtained from growing up in the townland and later serving as the last schoolmaster in Gallon School.

Because I was intent on explaining to local historians how they might marry the knowledge they possessed to the information contained in the Public Record Office of Northern Ireland and other archives, I selected material from John's text to illustrate important points. John's original manuscript, however, deserves to be published because it reveals a very good historical sense of the changes that have overtaken Gallon throughout the centuries and is addressed to his own community.

For almost two and a half centuries Gallon was part of the extensive Blessington estate whose archive is held by the National Library of Ireland. Unfortunately these documents have never been listed and so they cannot be used yet to trace the early history of the estate. Although we did manage to find some clues in documents registered in the eighteenth century in the Registry of Deeds in Dublin, the estate records should tell us much more. From them we should learn when the townlands of Gallon and its neighbourhood were laid out, how they were leased through the generations to either middlemen or occupiers, and how and when their fields were enclosed.

Without correspondence as detailed as that which has survived for the neighbouring Abercorn estate, we have to try to guess at the motives and methods that affected life on this estate. We can gain some impressions from the Statistical Survey of the County of Tyrone that was written by John McEvoy and published by the Dublin Society in 1802 while he was working as supervisor of the forestry programme on Lord Mountjoy's demesne at Rash, just north of the town of Omagh. Nevertheless, until the Blessington estate collection is calendared we shall know very little about the inhabitants of Gallon before the nineteenth century.

In all the essays in Townlands of Ulster[1] we showed how important it was to identify the families that had lived in the townlands first from estate records and later from the government valuation records. Then it was possible to relate members of these families to the houses and the lands that they had occupied and to registers of the churches and schools that they had attended. Scraps of information can be acquired from a great variety of other sources such as newspapers, wills and probates, solicitors' archives, membership lists of organisations, business records of all kinds. Genealogists who engage in such painstaking work find that it can bring great rewards. Even fragments may prove vital to any attempt to reconstruct the past and use it to interpret oral history and tradition.

It should not be overlooked that much of the information that could enrich the history of a townland has been taken away by families leaving the townlands. We need to realise that many emigrants may have important pieces of evidence to contribute even if they themselves cannot appreciate that importance. Consider, for example, the many collections of emigrant letters that have been donated, either as originals or copies, for the use of the general reader in the Public Record Office of Northern Ireland. It is essential therefore to encourage such emigrant families to make contact with the Centre for Emigrant Studies in the Ulster American Folk Park which could link them with interested local families. Gallon itself is fortunate in maintaining strong links with several emigrant families.

Our experience in the preparation of Townlands in Ulster has convinced us that similar studies of many townlands will have to be published, before people realise that a great variety of factors went into the making of the characters of many townlands. There seems to be a serious misconception that townlands are readily categorised: they are either settler or native, central or isolated, fertile or infertile, lowland or upland, with resident or absentee management. Such labels take little or no account of the history of the townland and how its community adapted to ever-changing circumstances. We found that the framework we devised for Townlands in Ulster needs to be extended to take account of more evidence. Generalising from a host of examples that can still be recovered will prove more exciting and creative than any amount of theorising based on a few case studies.

INTRODUCTION

To those who live near Newtownstewart, in County Tyrone, Gallon is taken to include not only the three townlands known as Gallon Lower, Gallon Upper and Gallon Sessiagh (or Sessiagh of Gallon), but also the neighbouring townlands of Glenock (or Glenknock), Shannony East, Tullyherin, Lisnafin and even Legfordrum. Indeed the inhabitants of all these townlands would seldom take issue with anyone who called them Gallon men or Gallon women. However, for the purposes of this book, it is necessary to limit the area of study to the three townlands which will be referred to collectively as 'Gallon'.

The name is spelt 'Gallan' on Ordnance Survey maps, but is usually spelt 'Gallon' by the local inhabitants and that is the spelling which will be normally used in this book.

The three townlands comprising Gallon are typical in many respects of other townlands in the north west of Ireland. The various twists and turns of Irish history have left their marks on the place and its people, notably the Plantation of Ulster, the Great Famine and the more recent flight from the land. This book is intended to introduce the reader to the history of Gallon from its earliest settlement to the present day.

There has been a great dispersal of Gallon people to all parts of Ireland and further afield during the last two hundred years, and it is hoped that the book will be of interest to a wide audience. It is also hoped that the publication of this study will encourage others to carry out research into their local areas while folk memories and relevant documents still survive.

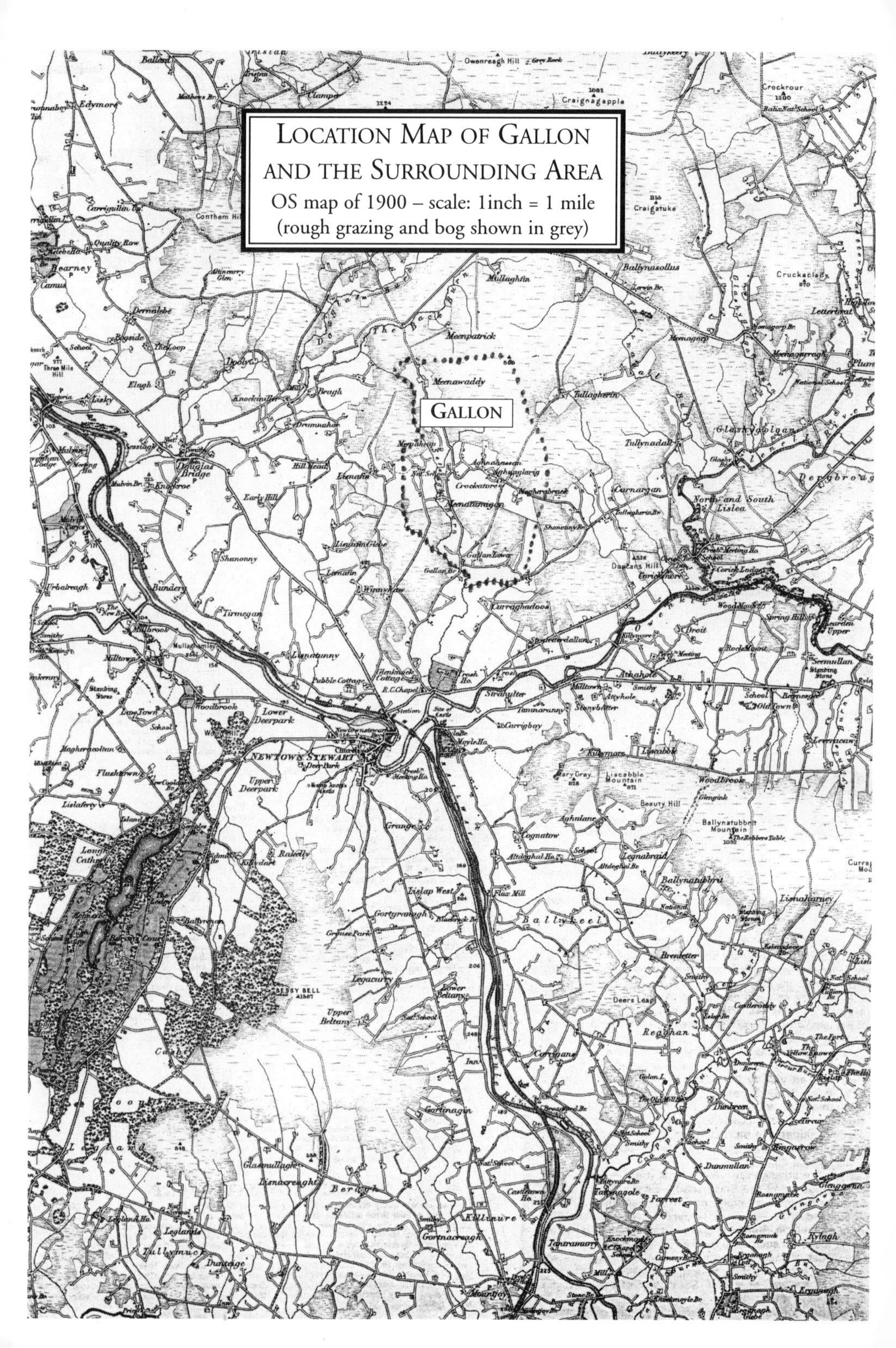

LOCATION MAP OF GALLON
AND THE SURROUNDING AREA
OS map of 1900 – scale: 1inch = 1 mile
(rough grazing and bog shown in grey)
GALLON
Owenreagh Hill
Craignagapple
Crockrour
Craigatuke
Conthem Hill
Cruckaclady
Ballynasollus
Mullaghfin
Meenpatrick
Meenawaddy
Tullagherin
Tullynadall
Carnargan
North and South
Lislea
Corickmore
Curraghadoos
Dooish
Gallan Lower
Shanonny
Bundery
Tirmegan
Lisnatunny
Pubble Cottage
R.C.Chapel
Station
Strahulter
Athahole
Milltown
Stonybatter
Liscabble
Liscabble Mountain
Woodbrook
Beauty Hill
Ballynatubbrit Mountain
Ballynatubbrit
Lower Deerpark
Upper Deerpark
NEWTOWN STEWART
Grange
Lislap West
Flax Mill
Ballykeel
Gortgranagh
Legacurry
Lower Beltany
Upper Beltany
BESSY BELL
Deers Leap
Reaghan
Carrigans
Gortinagin
Glenmullagh
Lisnacreaght
Beragh
Killenure
Gortnacreagh
Dunmullan
Farrest
Tullymuck
Douglas Bridge
Mullaghmoney
Milltown
Lislaferty
Flushtown
Bearney
Edymore
Camus
Dernalebe
Elagh
Knockinillar
Drumnahoe
Early Hill
Shanonny
Urbalreagh
Millbrook
Lisky
Knockroe

CHAPTER 1: LOCATION

The townlands of Gallon Lower, Gallon Upper and Gallon Sessiagh lie north east of Newtownstewart in the parish of Ardstraw East, County Tyrone. Gallon Upper and Gallon Lower are traversed by a county road (known today as Gallon Road) which runs directly from Glenock Catholic Church, on the Newtownstewart – Plumbridge road, to a high point near the television transmitting station at the summit of Koram mountain. Gallon lies within the recently designated 'Sperrin Area of Outstanding Natural Beauty'.

The townlands are therefore about three miles from Newtownstewart, seven miles from Strabane and five miles from Plumbridge. Gallon Sessiagh is served by a road coming off the back road from Newtownstewart to Douglas Bridge. The Sessiagh Road crosses the extensive bogland to the south and comes to an end at a cluster of houses built on the better quality land near the centre of the townland. Gallon Sessiagh can be reached from Gallon Upper and Gallon Lower by the use of private lanes about a mile apart, one lane starting beside Kevin McNamee's house in Gallon Lower, and the other lane near Martin McGuigan's house in Gallon Upper.

The lowest ground is found in the valley of the Crosh and Sessiagh Burns in Lower Gallon, around 250 feet (79 metres) above sea level. The highest point is Gallon Tops, in Gallon Upper, with a height of 809 feet (244 metres). To the north and the east of Gallon are the boglands which occupy much of townlands of Strawletterdallan, Shannony East, Tullyherin, Legfordrum and Lisnafin, while to the south are the more fertile townlands of Glenock and Crosh.

Clusters of dwellings survived until recent times at nine locations in Gallon Upper known as Meenawiddy, Meenaheap, Meenatumigan, Aghnahassan, Aghnaglarig, Black Dyke, Meenavig, Crockatore and Magherabrack.[1] Dwellings in Gallon Lower and Gallon Sessiagh tended to be more scattered, with only one remaining cluster in each of the two townlands.

Gallon Upper's cluster names are used extensively throughout the text; they prove useful in locating the part of the townland under consideration and in differentiating families with the same surnames.

CHAPTER 2: GALLON'S EARLY HISTORY UP TO THE PLANTATION OF ULSTER

THE NEOLITHIC AND EARLY CHRISTIAN PERIOD

The word 'Gallan' in the Irish language means a standing stone. The standing stone which gave the area its name, is located in Gallon Upper, at Crockatore but there is another standing stone in the adjoining townland, Shannony East. Archaeologists ascribe the earliest standing stones to the Early Bronze Age (2500BC-1500BC), although they may have been erected later. The function of standing stones is unclear; they may have been erected to mark graves, pathways or boundaries. Standing stones are sometimes found in circles, such as the well-known stone circle at Beaghmore, near Cookstown, while others have mysterious carvings upon them. Gallon's standing stone has, however, no obviously notable features.

The standing stone at Crockatore from which the townland took its name.

The earliest known inhabitants of Ireland probably entered the country around 7000BC. They were hunters and food gatherers who discovered a countryside almost entirely covered in forests. They preferred to live near rivers and the seashore and are unlikely to have penetrated into the Gallon area.

A new culture arrived in Ireland around 4000BC during the period known as the neolithic era. Unlike the earlier settlers, the newcomers possessed a knowledge of farming. They understood how to plant crops such as oats and barley and they introduced domesticated animals such as cattle and pigs. They brought with them improved tools: polished stone axes, which they used for felling trees, flint tools for harvesting the crops and clay pots for cooking. Because they were not dependent on trapping animals or on fishing, the first farmers were able to move inland and establish relatively permanent settlements. These neolithic farmers are known for the large megalithic tombs of various kinds which they erected as burial sites for their dead.

The neolithic farmers cleared tracts of forested land for cultivation, often by stripping the trees of their barks and thus causing them to die. Due to their ignorance of soil management, they tended to work the tracts of land to exhaustion and then move on to make further clearings in the forests. They appear to have found the soils of the river valleys too heavy to work easily, and tended to settle longer on the lighter soils found on higher ground. They erected elaborate field systems, perhaps to protect their crops from straying cattle or to enclose their animals at certain times of the year.

Brendan McColgan, with the site of the neolithic house & field system in the background.

Most of these field systems have long since been obliterated by more recent farming practices, but occasionally they have been protected by the growth over centuries of blanket bog and are sometimes re-discovered in modern times. Blanket bogs seem to develop in poorly drained locations, where the soil has become acidic though over-cultivation. In such circumstances, sphagnum moss replaces other vegetation and the process of growth and decay of the moss through the centuries leads to the development of a blanket bog which could be many metres deep.

There is overwhelming archaeological evidence of human settlement in Gallon during the neolithic era (4000BC-2500BC). The most obvious evidence is provided by the two portal tombs found in Glenock and in Crosh, two townlands adjoining Gallon. These were probably erected about 2500BC.

> Portal tombs, so called because of the importance of the two stones which flank the entrance to the single chamber, are a simple form of gallery tomb and consist of at least three upright stones bearing one or more capstones.[1]

As well as the standing stone at Crockatore, already described, there is a small stone circle, about 9 metres in diameter and almost totally submerged in the bog in Lisnafin, just across a stream from Meenawiddy, These standing stones may date from the same period as the portal tombs.

Portal tomb at Glenock.

Portal tomb at Crosh.

Further fascinating evidence of Gallon's past emerged in the 1960s, when Bernard McColgan and his father were cutting turf in Meenawiddy (Gallon Upper) and found an ancient hearth and several stumps of wooden posts at a depth of two metres in the bog. Nearby, archaeologists identified the remains of an ancient field system also covered by the bog.

Referring to the well-known field-systems found at Ceide Fields in Co Mayo, Mallory and McNeill write:

> It is difficult to see this planned network of field-systems as anything other than the product of a well-organised society and not the creation of individual farmsteads isolated from one another by thick forests.[2]

Although up to the present no scientific excavation has been undertaken in Gallon Upper, it is likely that the house and field system date from before 2500BC.

A reconstructed neolithic house at the Ulster History Park, Gortin.

Gallon's first inhabitants probably lived in a house such as the one above.

Nowadays, country folk are sometimes puzzled by the stumps of trees that they find buried in bogs. The bog in Gallon Lower, known as the Flough, for example, has many stumps of oak trees that have been unearthed during turf-cutting. It is probable that these tree stumps are many thousands of years old, being the remains of living forests whose trees died or were deliberately killed by the neolithic settlers.

In the adjoining townland of Shannony East, a Bronze Age burial cist was discovered by Thomas McNamee (senior) in 1939. The cist was examined by O Davies and W R Henderson and described as follows:

> When complete, the cist measured 27inches x 24inches... It was carefully floored with slabs... The side stones were levelled up with small corbels and the whole originally covered with a large roughly square cap-stone, measuring 2ft 6ins x 2ft 6ins x 4ins... The bones were uncremated. When they were found, the skull, which was partly broken, lay against one wall, and the other bones were in a heap beside it... The bones belong to a child... probably aged nine to ten years...[3]

Cist tomb found during excavations at Stewart's Castle by the Ancient Monuments Branch, DoE. The archeologist was Ruaidhri O Baoil (1999).

Excavations in August 1999 revealed a well-preserved cist grave in the grounds of Newtownstewart Castle containing the remains of two adults and some burial offerings.

THE COMING OF THE FIRST FARMERS

Traditional historians believe that further waves of invaders settled in Ireland during the prehistoric era. The most influential of these were the Celts, whose civilization spread from central Europe to dominate Ireland and Britain in the three centuries before the birth of Christ.

The Celts brought new farming and metalworking skills to Ireland. They tended to establish communal homes or farmsteads on high ground that they surrounded with circular banks of soil or stones. These structures are known today as cashels and were probably constructed between 400 AD and 1000 AD. There is a good example of a cashel in Crosh, close to one of the portal tombs that have already been mentioned. Another cashel is marked on the earliest Ordnance Survey map of Gallon Upper, near Aghnahassan. All traces of this cashel have, unfortunately, been obliterated in the intervening century.

The cashel (hill fort) at Crosh.

It is likely that the Celts eventually merged with the native civilization, imposing their Gaelic language, druidic religion, brehon laws and customs on the entire country. The folk memory of the earlier settlers remained, however, into our own times, manifested in lingering beliefs among the older generation in the existence of fairies and leprechauns. Mary Ann Bradley, who died in 1947, often described, how, when still a child, she had been walking home through Gallon Upper on a quiet summer's evening when she heard the last group of fairies leave the townland, lamenting in words and music as they headed towards Ballynasollus and Craigatuke mountain.

Because of their more advanced farming and metalworking skills, the Celts were better able to work the heavy soils of the river valleys, so it is likely that the upland areas of Gallon were gradually abandoned and may have remained without permanent residents until the late sixteenth century.

During the fifth century, the area which is now known as North Tyrone, south of Strabane comprised the sub-kingdom of Ui Fiachrach. It had been part of the kingdom of Oirghialla, but later came under the lordship of Cineal Eoghain. Ardstraw was the centre of this sub-kingdom.

According to well established tradition, St Patrick founded a church at Ardstraw, and appointed a local man Macc Erce as bishop. Local people affirm that he stopped on his travels near the present site of Newtownstewart and, not having time to visit Gallon, he satisfied himself by saying 'Gallon lies over there'. Perhaps he felt that the people of Gallon were holy enough already, or were they beyond redemption?

Towards the end of the sixth century, St Eugene (died c. 618) established a monastic church at Ardstraw which soon achieved prominence throughout Ireland. At the synod of Rath Breasail in 1111, it was agreed that a bishopric should be established at Ardstraw. Although no bishops of Ardstraw are mentioned in the annals of the time, it is possible that two of their number were Maol Choluim O Brolchain who was consecrated in Armagh and died in 1122 and Maol Bhride O Brolchain who died in 1139. The bishopric later moved to Maghera and settled eventually in Derry.[4]

The Franciscan Third Order Regulars established a monastery at Pubble, on the banks of the Mourne, near present day Newtownstewart c 1470, and another at Corrick, near the junction of the Owenkillew and Glenelly rivers c. 1480. The monks operated schools and provided care for the sick and the poor, as well as ministering to the local population in the absence of a parish clergy. The local

The site of the monastry at Pubble.

The ruins of the abbey at Corrick.

Gaelic lords were generous patrons of the church, allocating 'glebe lands' to each monastery. The rents paid by tenants on the glebe lands helped to pay for the upkeep of the monks and the monastery.

Crockatore well.

The monasteries at Ardstraw, Corrick and Pubble survived until the collapse of Gaelic power in the early 1600s. Ardstraw monastery was taken over by the reformed Church of Ireland but was eventually abandoned. The monastery at Pubble was also abandoned, but part of its grounds were still used as a cemetery by local Catholic families until 1903 when a new cemetery was opened. Some of the walls of Corrick monastery are still standing, and the grounds are used as a cemetery by a few local families.

MAP OF THE GALLON AREA SHOWING SITES OF ARCHAEOLOGICAL AND HISTORIC INTEREST

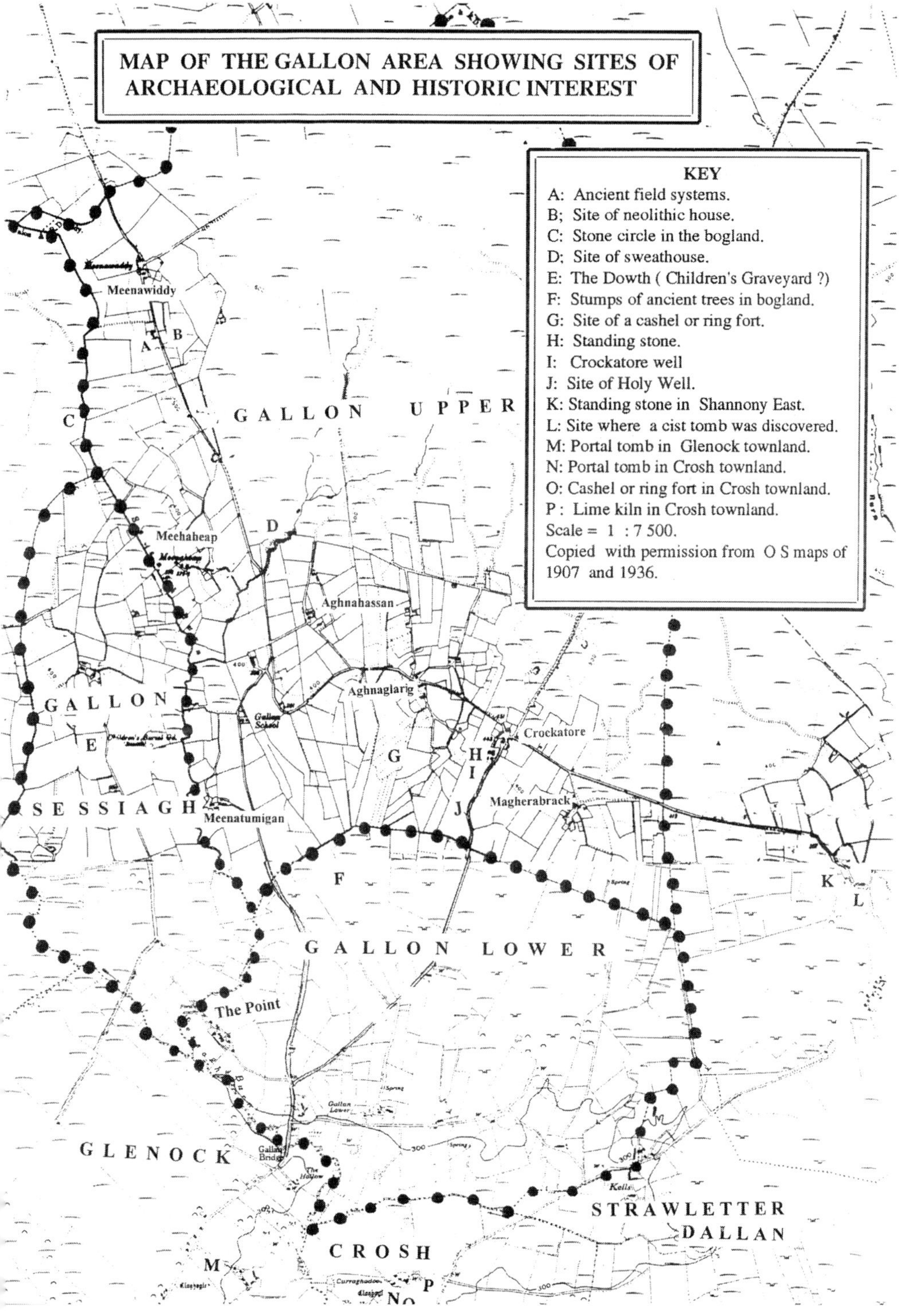
KEY
A: Ancient field systems.
B; Site of neolithic house.
C: Stone circle in the bogland.
D; Site of sweathouse.
E: The Dowth (Children's Graveyard ?)
F: Stumps of ancient trees in bogland.
G: Site of a cashel or ring fort.
H: Standing stone.
I: Crockatore well
J: Site of Holy Well.
K: Standing stone in Shannony East.
L: Site where a cist tomb was discovered.
M: Portal tomb in Glenock townland.
N: Portal tomb in Crosh townland.
O: Cashel or ring fort in Crosh townland.
P : Lime kiln in Crosh townland.
Scale = 1 : 7 500.
Copied with permission from O S maps of 1907 and 1936.
Meenawiddy
A
B
C
GALLON UPPER
D
Meehaheap
Aghnahassan
Aghnaglarig
GALLON
E
Gallon School
Crockatore
G
H
I
J
Magherabrack
SESSIAGH
Meenatumigan
F
K
L
GALLON LOWER
The Point
Gallon Lower
GLENOCK
Gallon Bridge
The Hollow
Kells
STRAWLETTER
DALLAN
CROSH
M
P
Curraghadoo
N O

OTHER SITES OF HISTORIC INTEREST IN GALLON

Holy wells were an important feature of Celtic religious practice, perhaps dating back to pre-Christian beliefs, so it is interesting that Gallon Upper had its own holy well, close to the standing stone at Crockatore. Nowadays the well has fallen into disuse, and is hardly recognisable even as a well, but it was still venerated in living memory, with people visiting the spot in the hope of cures. Crockatore has, however, another carefully maintained spring well, without religious connotations, which is still used as a source of excellent drinking water.

A 'Children's Burial Ground' is marked on the Ordnance Survey map of Gallon Sessiagh. It is known locally as 'the Dowth'. There is some uncertainty about its age and its actual function, but it may have been the site of an ancient church whose grounds remained in use as a place of burial for unbaptised children long after adult burial had been transferred to official graveyards elsewhere. Infant deaths were quite common in former times, particularly during the recurrent famines and outbreaks of plague. There was a belief that unbaptised children need not, or perhaps should not, be buried in consecrated ground. The Children's Graveyard today comprises a circular mound, having a diameter of about 25 metres, which is overgrown with bushes and mature trees.

The Children's Burial Ground in Gallon Sessiagh, locally known as "the Dowth".

A sweathouse.

Local people still have a superstitious dread of interfering with these trees or of even entering the place.

Gallon also had a sweathouse, a primitive type of sauna or steam bath, which was situated on the banks of a tributary of the Sessiagh Burn, still known today as the Sweathouse Burn. Remains of the main portion of the sweathouse can still be seen, built into a dry bank close to the burn. It is circular in shape, about two metres in diameter with a small entrance on the side next to the burn. The roof has long since fallen in and the interior is almost completely filled with soil and rubble.

Treatment in the sweathouse was used as a remedy for rheumatism and similar ailments. Prior to use, a large fire of turf or wood was made inside the sweathouse, heating up the stone walls, and several large stones which had been positioned on the floor. The fire was then extinguished and water was thrown on the warm stones to create steam. Between two and six patients crawled inside, removed their clothes and blocked the small entrance from the inside. They would spend about an hour in the sweathouse, before jumping naked into the cold waters of the burn, drying themselves off and returning home.

The last recorded use of a sweathouse in Ulster was in the 1920s, when the victim of a motoring accident from the South Tyrone area was known to seek relief from the resulting pains by using this remedy. The remains of another building which a local farmer, Vincent McNamee, believes was a sweathouse, can be found on the eastern side of Gallon mountain. The building is about four feet square in shape and about five feet tall.

EVERYDAY LIFE IN THE VALLEY OF THE RIVER MOURNE UNDER THE GAELIC LORDS

Members of the O'Neill family ruled the territory of Tir Owen[5] from the middle of the thirteenth century until the Plantation of Ulster in the early seventeenth century. The 'supremacy of the O'Neills' for much of this period extended over the present counties of Derry, Tyrone and Armagh. As well as the head of the family who usually took the title, 'The O'Neill', a number of lesser kings claimed jurisdiction over various parts of the territory. The valley of the river Mourne and the surrounding area comprised the sub-kingdom of Cineal Moain or Sliabh Sios. One of the most notable local kings was Henry Aimhreidh (Harry Avery) O'Neill who, according to local folklore, built his castle in a commanding position overlooking the southern end of the Mourne valley around 1360. The ruins of this castle are a well-known landmark on a hill just outside Newtownstewart to the present day.

Harry Avery's castle on a hill near Newtownstewart. Although built by a local Irish King the castle is in the Norman style.

In the period 1567-1595, the local ruler, Turlough Luineach O'Neill, 'The O'Neill' built a castle beside the river Mourne near its junction with the Owenkillew to guard a strategic crossing place. The castle was about two miles from Harry Avery's castle and although of some importance, it never became Turlough's main residence; he continued to live at Strabane. Over time a small settlement grew up near Turlough's castle, which became known as Lisglas or Baile Nua, (Newtown, later Newtownstewart).

The exact location of Turlough's castle is not known; it may have been on the north bank of the river Mourne on a mound known today as Pigeon Hill, or it may have been at the bottom of the present Main Street, on the site later occupied by William Stewart's castle. However, excavations carried out at Stewart's Castle in 1999 found no evidence of buildings on that site dating from earlier than 1600.

Turlough's castle was described by a contemporary Englishman, Sir Henry Docwra, in 1601 as follows:

> The castle is six (Irish) miles from Liffer, on the way to Dungannon. It is a pile of strong stone and well built with an iron gate and a chain at the door. It hath before it a large bawn compact with a good high stone wall and in the midst of it is a fair Irish thatched house, able to hold 50 or 60 men in it... a green outside the bawn... bawn with gate.[6]

Hugh O Neill.

Today there is no trace of a castle at Pigeon Hill; perhaps it was demolished by the new settlers in order to provide building materials for the construction of the town of Newtownstewart.

Apart from the ancient road which followed the rivers Strule and Mourne, there were very few roads in Tir Owen in the sixteenth century. Travellers depended on tracks and also used boats to travel on the deeper rivers. Towns as we know them nowadays were few in number. Strabane and Omagh for example, would have consisted of nothing more than a few houses. Most families lived in little circular post-and-wattle houses. There was no chimney; the fire was lit in the middle of the floor and the smoke escaped through a hole in the centre of the roof.

Livestock, especially cattle, were the main source and manifestation of wealth for lords and clan members alike. The clan members owned a few cattle and looked after other cattle for their lord. During the summer months the cattle were moved from the fertile lowlands to fresh pastures on higher ground, such as the slopes of Slieve Trim (Bessy Bell) or Gallon. Temporary dwellings of turf or wickerwork were set up, where the younger members of the family lived through the summer, milking their cows, churning butter and making cheese which would often be stored in the bogs for later use or sent down to the home settlements in the valleys.

In the valleys, small enclosures close to the home settlements were fenced off to grow oats, barley, flax and vegetables. These enclosures were usually cultivated for two consecutive years and then left fallow for perhaps ten years before being cultivated again. Crops were often laid out in 'lazy beds', which consisted of raised plots of earth manured by the use of animal dung. Previously cultivated land was sometimes ploughed using wooden ploughs with iron shoes attached by sally rods to the tails of horses. By modern standards this practice was very inefficient and even cruel.

Oats were ground by hand or in the local mill and flax was spun into linen to make tunics. Pigs and sheep were fattened for meat and the wool was woven into cloth to make a thick woollen cloak known as the Irish mantle.

Woods were still plentiful in the valleys and the hillsides, mostly consisting of deciduous hardwoods such as oak, ash, hazel, holly alder, willow and birch. Oak and ash grew well in the fertile lowlands; alder and willow could grow where the drainage was poor. A wide range of wild animals such as the elk, deer, hare and wolf lived in the woods.

The people living around Baile Nua probably supplemented their diets with salmon and trout, caught in the local rivers, which were among the most bountiful in Western Europe. They drank buttermilk, beer and whiskey; whiskey was believed to have medicinal properties. They also occasionally bled living cows and horses and mixed the blood with butter to make a jelly.

Under the Gaelic system of land tenure, the lord had use of about a third of the land in his territory for his lifetime only and the remaining land was held in common by members of the clan. The common people had to pay taxes to support the armies of their lord, often in the form of livestock. They were also expected to furnish food and shelter for their lord's soldiers and horses when they were in the neighbourhood and to provide labour for the building of castles. However, they were not normally tied to their lords and could move freely to another area if they wished to do so. Tir Owen was under-populated at this time, so the O'Neill lords probably treated their subjects well for fear that they would move away.

Men of learning and culture were highly esteemed by the O'Neills. The McNamees were the official poets to the O'Neills, and one of them, Tadhg, had his own castle at Lough Mary, (near present day Baronscourt) in the fifteenth century.

> The O'Neills... were noted for their great hospitality and in Brian MacAngus McNamee, poet to Turlough Luineach, they had a noted bard. They held their bardic festival annually and welcomed guests from all over Ireland. Traditionally they held this event at the period of the Nativity celebrations.[7]

One of these occasions is described in a poem by Tadhg Dall O hUiginn in which he tells how Turlough entertained him and his fellow poets at Christmas 1577. He recalls that the poets displeased their host by refusing to supply him with panegyrics to his liking. In spite of this Turlough insisted on paying them their due for the poems which they had composed. Turlough's behaviour contrasts favourably with that of Concubhar O Briain, earl of Thomond, who had hanged two poets in 1572!

THE O'NEILL LORDSHIP

Gaelic civilisation flourished in Ireland for several centuries in spite of the fierce rivalries between provincial kings and the frequent threat of external invasion. However, unlike most other countries of Europe, Gaelic Ireland never achieved lasting unity under a single monarchy, making the country more vulnerable to conquest by ambitious foreigners.

As early as 1171, King Henry II of England had laid claim to all of Ireland. Nevertheless, for centuries the English monarchs could only exercise permanent authority in the area around Dublin known as The Pale.

In 1540 King Henry VIII decided to establish his political and religious authority over the entire island of Ireland. He declared himself 'King of Ireland' and initiated a policy of 'Surrender and Re-grant', offering each Irish king a full pardon for past rebellion along with an English title if he would promise to obey English law, renounce the authority of the Pope and impose English laws and inheritance customs in his territory.

Conn Bacach O'Neill, lord of Tir Owen, submitted to King Henry VIII in 1542 and English authority was accepted in his territory, but Henry's policy of reconciliation was not practised by his successors and wars soon broke out between the Irish lords and the English government forces. However, the Irish leaders found it difficult to unite against the common foe and quite often the Irish kingdoms themselves were torn apart by disputes over succession.

Elizabeth I, who became queen of England in 1558, hoped initially to establish her authority throughout Ireland without resorting to force, but the Irish lords felt threatened by the increasing manifestations of English power in their lands.

Turlough Luineach O'Neill, a member of the Sliocht Airt branch of the family, whose territory lay in modern west Tyrone, became lord of Tir Owen in 1567. When he acquired 3,000 Scottish gallowglasses[8] as a dowry with his Scottish wife, Lady Agnes Campbell, Queen Elizabeth feared that he would become too powerful, so she supported Hugh O'Neill of Dungannon in opposition to him. Hugh had lived for a time in England and perhaps the queen believed that he would be more sympathetic to the English cause. Hugh therefore became lord of the eastern portion of Tir Owen, comprising most of modern counties of Armagh and East Tyrone, while Turlough's authority was confined to his original territory in west Tir Owen.

Hugh O'Neill remained loyal to Queen Elizabeth for some years, hoping to be eventually allowed to rule over all of Tir Owen as his ancestors had done. He was eventually goaded into rebellion, however, by the expansionist tactics of the English officials, who wished to impose English administration on Tir Owen too rapidly. He was also angered by the vengeful treatment meted out by Elizabeth's officials to other Irish lords who had not strictly followed the government's wishes.

Between 1594 and 1599, Hugh O'Neill and his allies, Red Hugh O'Donnell, Hugh Maguire of Fermanagh and Hugh McMahon of Monaghan defeated various English armies and succeeded in driving the English out of almost all of Ulster. Eventually, in 1600, Queen Elizabeth sent her most able general, Lord Mountjoy, with a well-trained and heavily equipped army against O'Neill and his allies. Mountjoy adopted a 'scorched earth policy', burning all crops and killing all the cattle which his army encountered in Ulster, causing widespread starvation and famine. Eventually the Irish armies, exhausted and greatly outnumbered, surrendered in 1603.

The terms of surrender offered to Hugh O'Neill and his allies at first appeared to be quite generous; the Irish lords were to be allowed to keep their lands and their titles. However the English officials in Dublin were disappointed by the peace terms, for they had hoped to acquire the lands belonging to the Irish lords. The Lord Deputy, Lord Chichester, began to enforce English law with such severity that Hugh O'Neill and the other leaders of the rebellion felt that they could no longer remain in their native land. On 3 Sept 1607, Hugh O'Neill, Hugh Maguire and Rory O'Donnell fled from Ireland, an event recorded in history as the 'Flight of the Earls'.

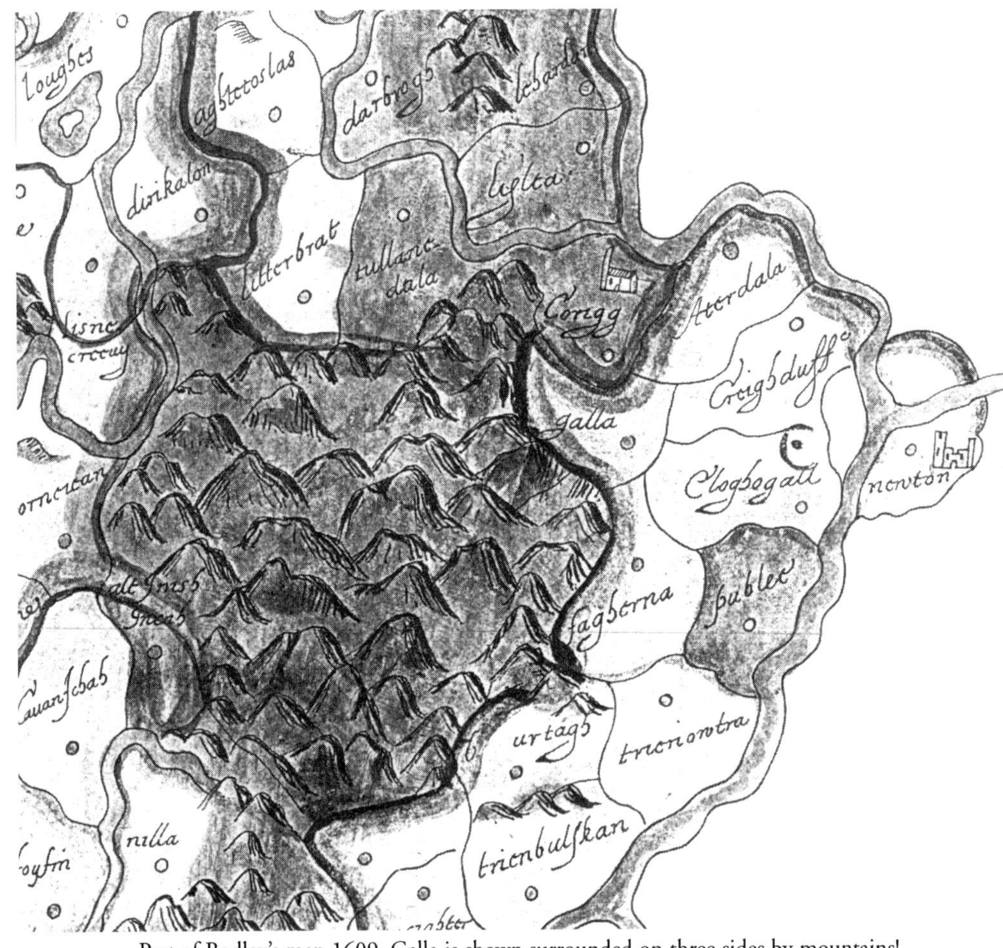

Part of Bodley's map 1609. Galla is shown surrounded on three sides by mountains!

CHAPTER 3: THE ESTABLISHMENT OF THE NEWTOWN AND LISLAP ESTATE AND THE CREATION OF FARMS IN GALLON

THE POLITICAL BACKGROUND

The decision of the Irish Earls of Ulster to abandon their lands in 1607 was interpreted by the English government as an act of treason, and the new king, James I, used this as an excuse to confiscate all their lands. The king believed that permanent peace could be established in Ireland if he 'planted' loyal and well-armed British families on the lands that had previously been ruled by the Irish Earls. Historians refer to this policy as 'The Plantation of Ulster'.

King James allocated estates of 1,000 acres, 1,500 acres and 2,000 acres to favoured English and Scots settlers and soldiers in return for the payment of regular 'crown' rents. Land measures were merely notional, and mountain land was not usually counted, so that most estates were actually as much as ten times larger. (Newton estate actually contained 13,500 acres, while Lislap contained 9,050 acres).

The new landowners were allocated their lands as either 'undertakers' or 'servitors'. Undertakers were English or Scottish gentlemen who were expected to bring British farmers to Ireland and to arm them for their defence. Undertakers were not allowed to take Gaelic tenants, but, because of the obligations placed on them, they were expected to pay a low annual rent of only £5 per 1,000 acres.

Servitors were government officials or soldiers, many of whom were already working in Ireland. They were allowed to take Gaelic tenants, but their rent was to be £8 per 1,000 acres. Some land was also to be allocated to members of the old Gaelic clans whom the government felt they could trust. They were expected to pay a rent of about £11 for each 1000 acres.

All new landowners, whether Undertakers, Servitors or trusted Irishmen, were expected to build a walled enclosure, called a 'bawn', in order to provide protection for the new tenants in case of war with the native Irish.

The first map to show the townland of Gallon (or Galla) was produced by Josias Bodley in 1609 (see map opposite page).

THE NEWTOWN AND LISLAP ESTATE

Two thousand acres around Newtowne and Lislap were allocated in 1610 to James Clapham (otherwise known as Clephame or Chapman), 'an old and faithful servant' of King James. Like other undertakers, James Clapham was expected to bring over from England or Scotland farmers and townsfolk to colonise the lands which he had been granted. These settlers would become tenant farmers, who would pay an annual rent to their new landlord. It was intended that the most fertile land would be cleared of the native Irish occupiers and transferred to incoming English and Scots settlers. The native Irish would have to be satisfied with the less fertile land on the hillsides.

> The several mountaines belonging to the... townlandes, knowne by the names of Slewtrym (Bessy Bell) and Gallagh al' Escheeve (Gallon) are the most fitt and convenient of all the aforesaid lands of Newtowne and Lislap to be graunted and lett to the inhabitants and mere natives of this countrey.[1]

For whatever reason, Clapham did not properly fulfil the conditions of his land grant; he made no serious attempt to replace the existing Irish tenants with English or Scottish settlers.

> It is curious that Clapham should who was regarded as 'faithful' by the King, should act so contrary to his royal master's wishes when he became an undertaker, for the first and almost the only act which Clapham appears to have done was the letting of his entire lands to Irish tenants, for terms varying from five to ten years. This simple process saved him a world of trouble, which the introduction of British settlers incurred, and gave him the largest and quickest returns from his lands in the shape of rents.[2]

Pynnar's Survey of 1619 reported that there were 36 British families and 45 Irish families living on the estate. Among the Irish families noted were many whose names would re-appear among the families living in Gallon: O'Quin, O'Criggan, McAnaly, McNamee, O'Gormley.[3]

Most of these surnames were still common in Gallon until recent times. Torlagh McNemy (McNamee) was listed among the twelve tenants of the Newtowne estate paying Hearth Roll Tax in 1666. This tax was levied only on those with a solid house. Today, McNamee is by far the most common surname found in Gallon.

It would appear that native Irish families continued to hold leases on good land in the Newtowne estate until at least 1628 and possibly even until the end

Tommy McNamee (senior) and family c 1975. McNamees may have lived in the Newtownstewart / Gallon area for at least 400 years.

of the century. By 1630, there were still only 54 adult British males living on the Newtown and Lislap estate.

In 1615, Clapham sold his lands at Newtowne and Lislap to Sir Robert Newcomen for £1400. Newcomen was succeeded in 1629 by his son-in-law, William Stewart.[4]

Meanwhile, William Stewart set about rebuilding the town of Newtowne, renaming it Newtownstewart. He erected a new parish church and built a new three storey castle. However, he was not allowed to enjoy the fruits of his labours for long in peace.

In October 1641 the resentment felt by the native Irish erupted and they attacked the homes of the English and Scottish planters throughout Ulster. Settlers from rural areas fled to Newtownstewart for protection, but had to move on when the rebel leader, Phelim O'Neill, captured the town. However, William Stewart, landlord of the Newtown estate, along with Robert Stewart (who was perhaps his brother), raised a force of loyal settlers, known as the Laggan Army, to oppose the rebels.

Owen Roe O'Neill, a nephew of the great Hugh O'Neill, returned from exile in the Netherlands to lead the insurgent Irish army in Ulster. Not all the dispossessed Irish joined the rebellion however; three grandsons of Turlough Luineach O'Neill: Arthur, Niall and Brian, fought for the government in the hope of being restored to their father's lands in North Tyrone. They were not entirely disappointed in their hopes; when peace was restored they were given lands at Galbally, near Dungannon.

During the ten years of war, rival armies moved backwards and forwards across the country, killing, looting and destroying homes, animals and crops. There was a widespread famine, and plague broke out. It is estimated that one third of the population died. Owen Roe's army won a brilliant victory at Benburb, on the banks of the Blackwater, and for some time almost all of the island was in rebel hands. However, Oliver Cromwell's three year campaign (1649-1652) eventually brought the rebellion to an end.

King James II and his army passed through Newtownstewart on his way to besiege Derry in 1689. The king quartered his soldiers in Stewart's Castle. On his retreat after the unsuccessful siege he ordered that the castle and the parish

Interior view of Stewart's castle at Newtownstewart. The castle was built by William Stewart early in the seventeenth century but burned by King James in 1698 on his retreat from the Siege of Derry. The town's parish church was rebuilt in 1723, but Stewart's castle was abandoned; only its walls remain. The Stewart family moved to a new residence at Rash, near Omagh.

church should be burned so that King William's army, who were in hot pursuit, could not use them for shelter.

THE RE-SETTLEMENTS OF GALLON

The systematic re-settlement of Gallon in historic times probably began in the early seventeenth century, after the lands in the Newtowne estate had been granted to James Clapham in 1610. It is likely that native Irish families made their earlier settlements on the fertile land in Gallon Lower, choosing dry and sheltered sites for dwellings. Their families would have known the area for generations, having used these locations as summer pasture.

The first settlements in Gallon Upper were probably at the locations which are known today as Magherabrack, Crockatore, Aghnaglarig, Aghnahassan, Meenatumigan, Meenaheap and Meenawiddy. As the population rose during the following centuries, these locations grew into clusters of dwellings.

The newcomers to Gallon developed in-fields adjacent to their dwellings for cultivation, and later they broke in more land from the surrounding bogs and mountain pastures.

As soon as the Newtown landlords became established in their estates they granted leases to tenants who would pay rents and undertake to farm in the English style. The landlord's immediate concern would have been to produce revenue from his estate. Initially the entire Gallon area was leased to one individual who acted as a middle-man and collected rents from all those occupying land or houses.

GALLON DIVIDED INTO THREE TOWNLANDS

The landlords soon found it necessary to have maps drawn to show the extent of their properties. Gallon was originally taken to constitute a single townland, (see Bodley's map) but as more and more people settled there, it was decided to split the area into three townlands, according to the natural boundaries: Gallon Sessiagh to occupy the far side of the Sessiagh Burn and Gallon Lower to be separated from Gallon Upper by the extensive bog known as the Flough.

The first reference to Gallon Sessiagh as a townland, separate from the rest of Gallon, is found in a marriage settlement for Mary, Lady Tyrawley, daughter of Viscount Mountjoy, which was drawn up around 1696.[5] The memorial mentions some native Irish living on Viscount Mountjoy's Newtownstewart estate:

Cormac O'Caha, Turlogh O'Cregan, Patrick O'Rory, Toal O'Boyle, Patrick O' Meaghan and Turlogh O'Keage.

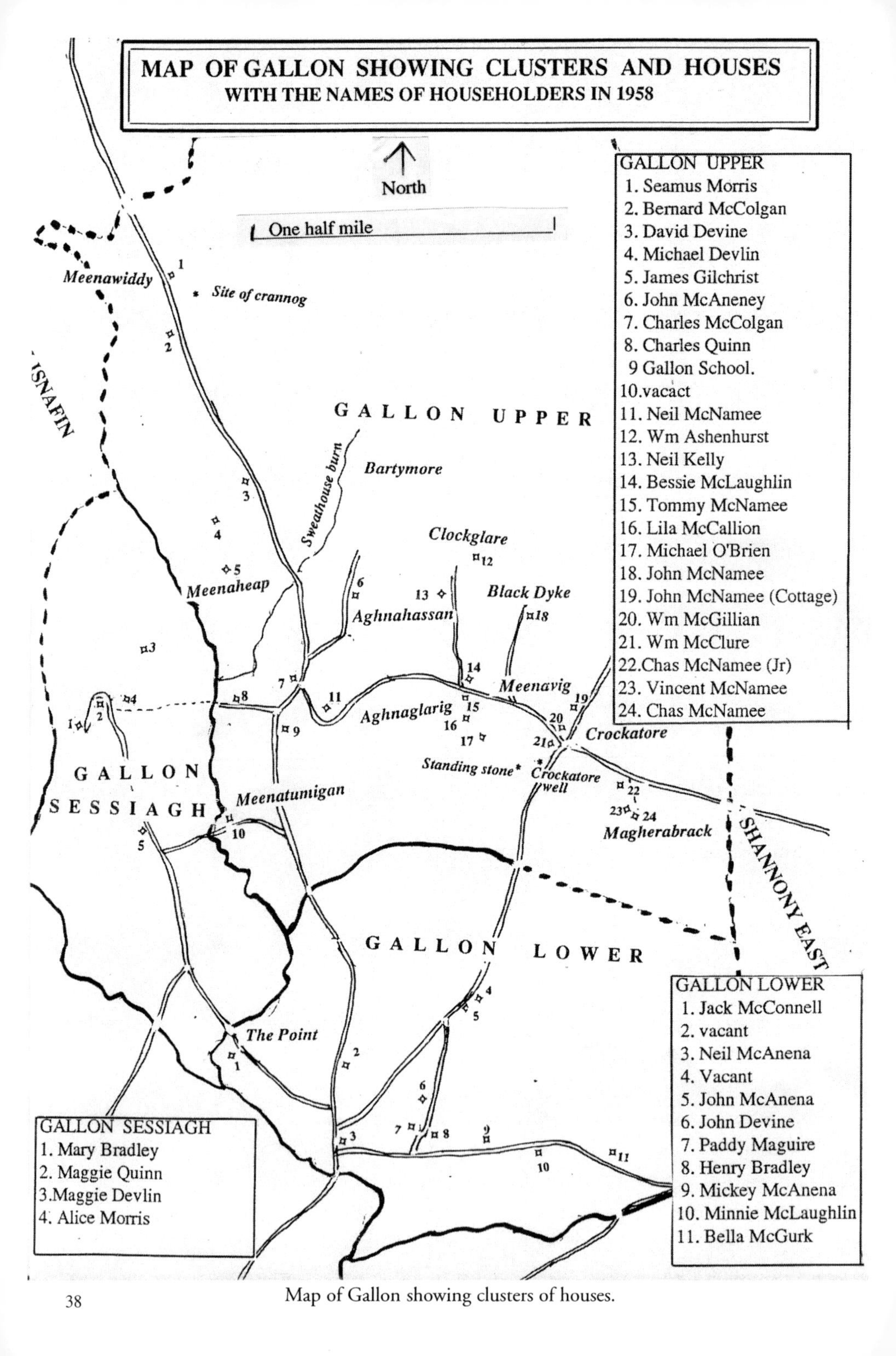

Map of Gallon showing clusters of houses.

A title deed dated 1724 gives details of an agreement between Turlogh O'Cregan of Gallon, Edward Cregan of Gallon and Claud Cregan of Clogher.

> 1 May 1724. Articles made between Torlagh O Crigan of Gallon, Edward Crigan of the same and Claud Crigan of Augher, whereby Torlogh made over his title and interest in the house in Newtownstewart, occupied by Mrs Mulhollon, widow, and his lease of the townland of Gallon to the said Claud and Edward Crigan to be equally shared between them.
>
> Witnessed: John Stewart of Newtownstewart, Cormick McConway of Lardon, George Cristie of Simullan and John McDonnell of Strawletterdallon.
>
> Registered at Clogher 10 Feb 1738 on oath of John McDonnell.[6]

The transaction described in this document may have been a strategy by the O'Cregan / Cregan family (who probably had been Catholics) to retain their interest in the property in case of a 'popish discovery'. Under the Penal Laws, which were still in force during this period, Catholics were not allowed to lease land for a term longer than 31 years and Protestants who informed on them for infringing on the terms of their leases would be entitled to take the leases over.

No one by the name of Cregan has lived in Gallon since before 1850. However, there is a field in Gallon Lower called 'Cregan's Hole', which is a reminder that the Cregans may once have cut turf at that place.

Documents which are held in the Registry of Deeds, (Dublin) show that by 1732, the land within the three townlands, Gallon Lower, Gallon Upper and Gallon Sessiagh had been divided into farms, in readiness for allocation to tenants:

> Wm Colhoun of Crossbale in Co Tyrone, by virtue of letters of attorney from Lord Viscount Mountjoy let to Daniel Conway of Strabane: "All that whole townland of Gallan Upper, Lower and half Sessiagh or what other name or denomination the same is called, known or divided into, as it is now marched and meared. Situate, lying and being in the Mannor of Newtownstewart for the yearly rent of £27 together with 12 pence per pound for receiver's fees, 12/6 as duties per annum as also four cartload of straw and four days work man and horse to be paid on 1st May and 1st Nov. Reserving all mines, minerals woods, quarries for 31 years commencing 1st May 1732.
>
> Witnesses: Patience Colhoun, wife of William, John Howard of Newtownstewart, farmer, Con O'Donnell, Strabane. writer. Registered at Clogher 10 Feb 1738 on oath of John McDonnell.[7]

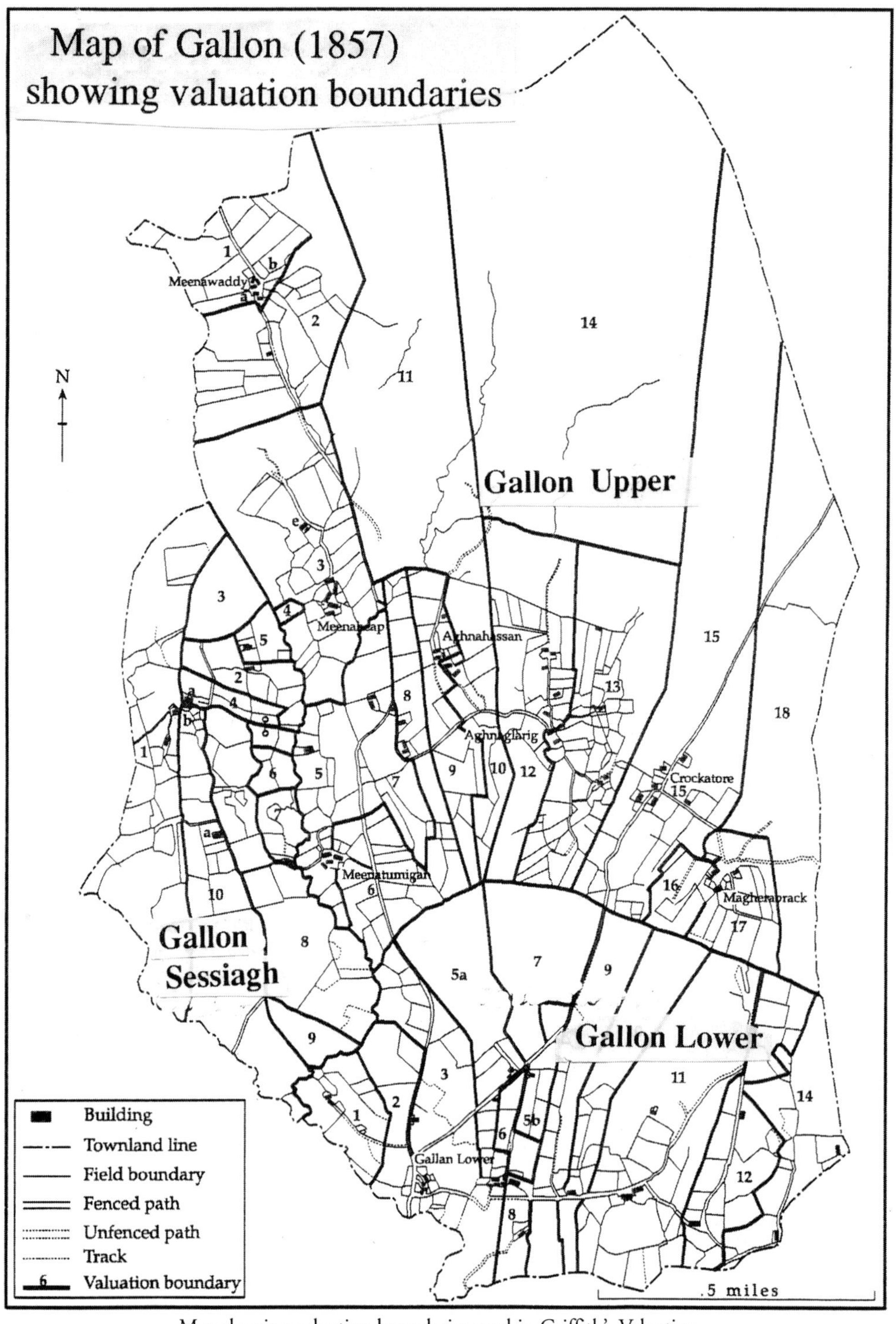

Map showing valuation boundaries used in Griffith's Valuation.

It would appear that Lord Mountjoy leased all three townlands to one individual, Daniel Conway, who was responsible for paying the rent and the tithes. Conway later divided the three townlands into smaller parcels, which he rented out to sub-tenants. He collected the rents from the sub-tenants, making a profit for himself, after he had paid the landlord.

Over the years Gallon's population rose, and soon most of the land which could easily be reclaimed had been incorporated into farms. Tenants began to sub-divide their farms among their sons, in order to provide each of them with a means of livelihood. New family homes were built close to the existing clusters of settlement. These dwellings were likely to be one-roomed structures initially with thatched roofs, mud walls and a single unglazed window. Later the mud walls were replaced by local stone.

As the size of the family increased, the young married man would probably add a second room to his house, and build a chimney. Having a 'good drawing' chimney was considered an important asset to any house; from time to time, chimneys would be 'tumbled' and re-erected in an effort to rid the house of smoke.

Towards the end of the eighteenth century there was a general trend by landlords all over Ireland to eliminate the middlemen who had, on many estates up to that time, rented entire townlands, making profit by collecting rents from the tenants and keeping a percentage before passing on a rent for the entire townland to the landlord. Leases henceforth were granted to individual tenants or groups of tenants and farms were rationalised to ensure that each farm contained a balance of good, medium and poorer land.

The earliest known leases for individual farms on the Newtown and Lislap estate were granted in 1763, when thirty-one year leases were allocated to tenants in the townlands of Carrigans and Killynure. Further leases were allocated in 1766 for farms in Tattynagole, Tully, Glenchordial and Beragh. Twenty one year leases were allocated in 1806 and 1811 for farms in the townlands of Calkill, Gortnacreagh, Castletown and Tattraconnaghty.

There is no record of leases for farms in Gallon before 1828. The tenants mentioned below were probably all Catholics.

Tenants: Hugh McColgan, Gallon Upper, William McColgan, James McColgan, Denis Morris and Patrick McConnell all of the townland of Gallon Upper.
Acres: 52 acres, 1 rood — Rent: £16-1s-11d
Previous tenants: the same — Date: 1/11/1828
Duration: 31 years.

The lives of the Duke of Cumberland, aged about 9, Chas J Power, Mountjoy Forest aged about 7 years and John McColgan, son of Wm McColgan, one of the lessees, aged about 7 years.

Tenants: Francis McLaughlin, Bernard Devlin, (Aghnaglarig) John Kelly, John McRory, Gallon Upper.
Acres: 54a 1r 12p Rent: £7-19-4
Previous tenants: the same Date: 1/5/1829
Duration: 31 years

The lives of the Duke of Cumberland, aged about 9, Chas J Power, Mountjoy Forest aged about 7 years and Charles Kelly, son of James Kelly, one of the lessees, aged about 6 years.

Tenants: Patk Quinn, Andrew Brogan, William Kane of Gallon Lower
Acreage: 19a 0r 32p Rent: £10-18-05
Previous tenants: the same Date: 1/5/18/29
Duration: 31 years

The lives of the Duke of Cumberland, aged about 9, Chas J Power, Mountjoy Forest, aged about 7 years and Andrew Brogan, son of Andrew Brogan, one of the lessees, aged about 7 years.[8]

In the early nineteenth century, leases were generally given for 21 or 31 years, or for the lives of persons named on the lease. If all those who were named were to die before the lease had expired, then the lease could be called in by the landlord and a new lease, (on perhaps less favourable terms) was negotiated. This explains why young children were usually named on leases, rather than older people. The Duke of Cumberland was a 'royal life'. When he died, it would be widely reported. Landlords and their agents kept a close watch over the 'falling in' of leases so that they could grant a new lease at the going rate for land. If people named in a lease had emigrated and died abroad, the landlord and his agent would have difficulty in finding out about their deaths.

By the time of the Griffith's Valuation in 1859, Gallon Upper was divided into eighteen leaseholds, Gallon Lower into fourteen and Gallon Sessiagh into ten. The intention appeared to be that each leasehold should contain roughly equal amounts of arable land. The mountain pastures were divided into three further leaseholds which were shared ('soumed') among groups of tenants living in each of the clusters of dwellings. For some unknown reason, one leasehold in Meenaheap (number 4) contained less than an acre.

THE POPULATION INCREASES

In common with the rest of Ireland, it is probable that there was a considerable growth in the population of Gallon during the eighteenth century, while the tenants made strenuous efforts to increase the productive acreage of their farms by further reclaimation from the bog and mountain pastures.

The early decades of the century however, were marked by cattle disease and harvest failures. There was a severe scarcity of food in 1726/27, and a famine in 1728/29, followed by a further famine in 1741 and many of the recent settlers who had come from England and Scotland, despairing of ever making a decent living in Ireland, emigrated to America. Nevertheless, due to the spread of potato cultivation, the population of Gallon may have remained steady or may even have risen.

It was reckoned that one acre of potatoes could support eight people for a year, and there was sufficient turf for fuel in the nearby bogs, so conditions must have been relatively comfortable for those who were prepared to live a simple life.

THE TITHE APPLOTMENT RECORDS

As well as paying rent to their landlords, tenants in the eighteenth century also had to pay tithes to the Established Church. (Church of Ireland) This caused considerable resentment among Catholics and Presbyterians, especially since the tithe proctors were sometimes inconsistent in the amounts demanded and often insensitive to the difficulties experienced by tenants in bad years.

> Extract from Nathaniel Nisbitt, Lifford to the Earl of Abercorn, London 1 Jan 1751 detailing tithe payments in certain parishes in the counties of Tyrone and Donegal.[9]
>
> Tithe paid by modus (fixed amount) in the parishes of Ardstraw, Urney and Camus:

For a milch cow	9d	For a stripper cow	4d
For a sheep	1d	Easter offering	4d
For a garden	1d	For a turf stack	6d
For a foal	6d	For a marriage	2s
For a burial	1sh 0d	For a christening	1s 6d

Tithes could also be charged on each acre of crops planted, apart from potatoes and grassland.

The 1834 Tithe Applotment Records show that Gallon Upper was divided into eleven leaseholds at that time, Gallon Lower into eight and Gallon Sessiagh into eleven. Each leasehold contained about three farms. One such lease was that held by Henry and Charles Bradley and James McConnell in Gallon Lower. These three tenants shared 86 acres with an annual valuation of £19.2s and a tithe of £1.5s 2d.

The farmers paying tithes for land in Gallon Upper, Gallon Lower and Gallon Sessiagh for 1834 were as follows:

Gallon Upper – Total Tithe: £8. 8sh 7d

E & O Quinn & McCrystal & Devlin (Meenatumigan)
42 acres: £0-14s-9d

Patrick (sen), Patrick(jr) & M Devlin (Meenaheap) 61 acres: £0-14s-8d

John, Manus, Neal (sen) Neal (jr) & Js McColgan 85 acres: £1-3s-5d

Charles McColgan (Aghnahassan) 21 acres: £0-12s-4d

James & John McAnelly (Aghnahassan) 53 acres: £0-9s-7d

A McAnelly & John Brogan(Aghnahassan)
40 acres and 71 acres (mountain): £1-3s-2d

F McLaughlin, John McCrory, B Devlin,
B McCulla, James & Ann Kelly (Aghnaglarig)
31 acres and 86 acres (mountain): £0-15s-5d

Michael, Owen and James McGarvey,
Ed and Michael Hagan (Aghnaglarig)
36 acres and 86 acres (mountain): £0-16s-5d

Michael, Neil (sen), Neil (jr)
McNamee (Crockatore) 8 acres: £0-5s-1d

Brine, Ellen, Owen (sen), Owen (jr), James,
Charles & Bernard McNamee (Crockatore) 23 acres: £0-19s-3d

Neal, Owen, Dennis, David McNamee,
Hugh McCurristel (Magherabrack) 15 acres: £0-14s-7d

Gallon Lower – Total tithe: £5. 15sh 9d

Dennis Morris 6 acres: £0-3s-2d

Phil Quinn and C Brogan 28 acres: £0-11s-2d

P Quinn, A Brogan, William Cassidy 29 acres: £0-13s-3d

Henry & Chas Bradley & James McConnell 86 acres: £1-5s-2d

James Hutchinson 32 acres: £0-9s-1d

John McLaughlin 19 acres: £0-6s-3d

Daniel and James McLaughlin 70 acres: £1-5s-8d

John, Thomas, James, Wm & Chas Hutchinson 58 acres: £1-1s-11d

Gallon Sessiagh – Total Tithe: £2.13sh 0d

John Morris and Dennis McNally	65 acres: £0-15s-4d
Ed Quinn and James Morris	11 acres: £0-1s-4d
Ed Quinn	2 acres: £0-1s-7d
Charles Devlin	14 acres: £0-4s-10d
James McAleer	7 acres: £0-3s-11d
Edward and Owen Quinn	7 acres: £0-2s-6d
Widow Morris and Thomas McMenamin	47 acres: £0-11s-0d
Dennis Morris	5 acres: £0-0s-6d
John Bradley and Brine Morris	28 acres: £0-1s-7d
Denis Morris	8 acres: £0-5s-4d
John Bradley	8 acres: £0-4s-10d[10]

The obligation placed upon Catholics, Presbyterians and Dissenters to pay tithes to support the Church of Ireland caused widespread resentment. The problem was eventually alleviated in the 1838 when the amount of the tithe was reduced by 25% and converted to a charge on the land which was payable by the landlord.

During the eighteenth and early nineteenth century, the making of illicit whiskey, known as "poteen", was widespread in rural Ireland; Gallon was no exception. In those days, there was no organised police force, so the excise men, who had a responsibility for eliminating illicit distillation, were normally accompanied by soldiers in carrying out their unpopular duties – searching for illicit stills and hidden supplies of poteen.

According to a local legend, one of these excise men was so enthusiastic that he went ahead of the military convoy and was seen by neighbours entering a house in Meenawiddy, but never seen to leave it again. Searches by the military of the entire district proved fruitless; local people believe that the excise man found his last resting place under the clay of that kitchen floor in Meenawiddy.

The Ordnance Survey Memoirs for Ardstraw (1834) comment on illicit distillation in the parish:

> The morals of the peasantry are not so good as might be wished. Drunkenness and party spirit still abound to a considerable extent, but cock fighting and private distillation are on the decrease and almost totally confined to the dregs of the people.[11]

After the Great Famine, the price of 'parliament whiskey' was reduced and became more readily available. These factors, and the scarcity of good barley, led to a decline in poteen making.

By the nineteenth century, more and more tenant farmers were holding their farms on twenty one year leases, often with automatic right to renew. Some tenant farmers sub-let around an acre of land to cottiers under the system known as 'conacre'. According to McEvoy,[12] the cottier would have half an acre of oats, half a rood of flax, half a rood of potatoes, the grazing of a cow, and the right to cut turf. They usually paid the farmer in work instead of cash. Sometimes they made additional money by weaving, especially in the winter months.

In 1859 there were twenty two households in Gallon with less than 4 acres of land. These were either sub-tenants or cottiers. The 'Ulster Custom' became generally accepted in Tyrone by this time and improved the conditions of tenants considerably. Under the Ulster Custom, reliable tenants were allowed to pass on their farms to their sons, or, if they chose to move away, were entitled to be given money in recognition of improvements which they or their predecessors had carried out on the farm; i.e. to 'sell' their rights as tenants. The Ulster Custom was never recognised in law, but its *de facto* existence in Ulster helped to prevent much of the agrarian agitation which occurred in southern Ireland during this period.

GRIFFITH'S GRAND JURY VALUATION (1859)

By the middle of the nineteenth century, the government was looking for sources of local taxation that could be imposed on an equitable basis. It was decided to base this taxation upon the value of all property, whether land or buildings. Richard Griffiths was given the task of overseeing the assessment and recording of the valuations in Ireland. The result of this exercise was published in 1859 and is known as the Griffith's Grand Jury Valuation. It provides the most comprehensive record of the landholders and householders in Gallon at that time.

Care must be taken however, when studying the sizes of farms since often the largest farms consisted mainly of mountain pastures which was relatively unproductive. Furthermore, in many instances leaseholds were sub-divided among a number of individuals.

The extent of sub-division varied considerably; Denis Morris's leasehold in Meenawiddy was not sub-divided, while the two leaseholds in Aghnaglarig containing just over 100 acres of arable land were shared between ten tenants and four sub-tenants.

PARISH OF ARDSTRAW.

No. and Letters of Reference to Map.	Names. — Townlands and Occupiers.	Names. — Immediate Lessors.	Description of Tenement.	Area.	Rateable Annual Valuation. — Land.	Rateable Annual Valuation. — Buildings.	Total Annual Valuation of Rateable Property.
	GALLAN, LOWER. (*Ord. S.* 10 & 17.)						
1	William Hill,	Daniel Baird,	House, office, and land,	15 3 30	5 5 0	0 15 0	6 0 0
2	Patk. M'Ananey (*Jas.*),	Same,	House, office, and land,	14 3 30	5 5 0	0 10 0	5 15 0
3 a	Patrick Brogan, (*See No.* 4.)	Same,	House, office, & land,	30 0 20	5 0 0	0 10 0	5 10 0
	John Brogan, (*See No.* 4.)		Land,		5 0 0	—	5 0 0
4 a	Andrew Brogan,	Same,	House, office, and land,	3 1 0	2 0 0	0 10 0	2 10 0
– b	John Brogan,	Same,	Ho.,off.,& gar.(*pt. of*),	0 2 20	0 5 0	0 10 0	0 15 0
– –	Patrick Brogan,		Garden (*part of*),		0 5 0	—	0 5 0
5 A a	Jacob Bradley,	Same,	House, office, & land,	46 2 0	9 10 0	0 15 0	6 0 0
– B – b	John Bradley,		House and land,	3 1 0	1 0 0	0 5 0	2 0 0
	Michael M'Garvey,		Ho., office, & land,			0 10 0	4 0 0
– c	Patk. Brogan (*cottier*),	Free.	House and garden,	0 2 0	0 3 0	0 7 0	0 10 0
– d	Hugh Towler,	Michael M'Garvey,	House,	—	—	0 5 0	0 5 0
– f	Edward M'Connell,	Daniel Baird,	Land,	0 1 20	0 5 0	—	0 5 0
6	Michael M'Ananey,	Same,	House, office, and land,	10 0 20	3 10 0	0 10 0	4 0 0
7	Michael M'Ananey,	Same,	Land,	20 1 20	0 10 0	—	0 10 0
	John M'Ananey,				0 10 0	—	0 10 0
8	John M'Ananey,	Same,	House, office, & land,	7 3 30	5 18 0	0 17 0	7 5 0
5 A e				0 3 10	0 10 0	—	
9	Elizabeth Hutchinson,	Same,	House, office, and land,	28 2 15	5 18 0	0 17 0	6 15 0
10	Patk. M'Ananey (*Neal*),	Same,	House, office, and land,	28 0 6	3 10 0	0 10 0	4 0 0
11 a	Daniel M'Loughlin,	Same,	House, offices, & land,	70 1 30	7 10 0	1 5 0	8 15 0
b	Michael M'Namee,	Reps. Jn. M'Loughlin,	House, office, & land,		7 10 0	0 15 0	8 5 0
– c	John Coll,	Daniel M'Loughlin,	House,	—	—	0 5 0	0 5 0
12 a	John Hutchinson,	Daniel Baird,	House, office, and land,	33 2 10	12 0 0	1 5 0	13 5 0
– b	John M'Namee,	John Hutchinson,	House,	—	—	0 10 0	0 10 0
– c	Hannah M'Crodden,	Same,	House,	—	—	0 5 0	0 5 0
– d	John M'Namee,	Same,	House,	—	—	0 10 0	0 10 0
13	William Hutchinson,	Daniel Baird,	House, office, and land,	9 3 0	5 18 0	1 17 0	7 15 0
14	Samuel Hutchinson,	Same,	Land,	18 1 0	1 15 0	—	1 15 0
			Total,	343 1 21	88 17 0	14 3 0	103 0 0
	GALLAN, UPPER. (*Ord. S.* 10 & 17.)						
1 a	Denis Morris,	Daniel Baird,	House, offices, and land,	34 1 10	10 5 0	1 5 0	11 10 0
– b	Thomas Tansey,	Denis Morris,	House,	—	—	0 10 0	0 10 0
– c	Patrick Keenan,	Same,	House,	—	—	0 5 0	0 5 0
2 a	Peter Morris,	Daniel Baird,	House, office, and land,	41 0 5	7 15 0	1 0 0	8 15 0
3 a	John Devlin,	Same,	House, office, & land,	60 3 8	13 0 0	0 15 0	5 5 0
–	Denis Morris,		Land,			—	4 10 0
–	Bernard M'Namee, (*See No.* 16.)		Land,			—	4 0 0
4 — 3 b	Peter Brogan,	Same,	House and garden,	0 0 20	0 2 0	0 7 0	0 15 0
			Land,	0 3 20	0 6 0	—	
3 c	Patrick M'Kenna,	Denis Morris,	House,	—	—	0 10 0	0 10 0
– d	Thomas Traney,	Bernard M'Namee,	House and garden,	0 0 12	0 1 0	0 4 0	0 5 0
– e	Patrick Devlin,	Denis Morris,	House,	—	—	0 10 0	0 10 0
5 a	Owen Quinn,	Daniel Baird,	House and land,	22 1 20	6 0 0	0 10 0	3 10 0
b	John Quinn,		House and land,			0 10 0	2 10 0
c	Daniel Morris,		Office and land,			0 5 0	1 5 0
6 a	James M'Conway,	Same,	House, office, & land,	21 0 10	7 0 0	0 10 0	2 5 0
b	Edward Rogers,		House, office, & land,			0 10 0	5 15 0
7 a	Charles M'Colgan, (*See No.* 8 & 11.)	Same,	House, offices, and land,	20 2 30	8 5 0	1 5 0	9 10 0
– b	National School-house,	(*See Exemptions.*)					
8 a	James M'Analley, (*See No.* 11.)	Daniel Baird,	House, office, & land,	18 1 30	7 15 0	0 15 0	4 10 0
b	Charles M'Analley, (*See No.* 11.)		House and land,			0 10 0	2 10 0
	Charles M'Colgan, (*See No.* 11.)		Land,			—	2 0 0
9 a	Charles M'Analley, (*See No.* 11.)	Same,	House, office, & land,	19 3 20	4 0 0	0 15 0	4 15 0
b	Michael M'Analley, (*See No.* 11.)		House, office, & land,		4 0 0	0 15 0	4 15 0
10 a	James Brogan, (*See No.* 11.)	Same,	House, office, & land,	20 2 0	4 0 0	0 15 0	4 15 0
b	John Brogan, (*See No.* 11.)		House, office, & land,		4 0 0	0 15 0	4 15 0
– c	Patrick Brogan,	Same,	House and garden,	0 2 10	0 5 0	0 10 0	0 15 0

Extract from Griffith's valuation.

No. and Letters of Reference to Map.		Names. Townlands and Occupiers.	Names. Immediate Lessors.	Description of Tenement.	Area.	Rateable Annual Valuation. Land.	Rateable Annual Valuation. Buildings.	Total Annual Valuation of Rateable Property.
		GALLAN, UPPER—*continued.*			A. R. P.	£ s. d.	£ s. d.	£ s. d.
11		Charles M'Colgan,	Same,	Mountain,	114 1 0	3 4 0	—	0 16 0
		James M'Analley,						0 8 0
		Charles M'Analley,						0 4 0
		Charles M'Colgan,						0 4 0
		Charles M'Analley,						0 8 0
		Michael M'Analley,						0 8 0
		James Brogan,						0 8 0
		John Brogan,						0 8 0
12	a	James Kelly, (*See No.* 14.)	Same,	House, office, & land,	44 1 20	12 0 0	0 10 0	3 10 0
	b	Neal M'Namee, (*See No.* 14.)		House and land,			0 10 0	2 0 0
		Patrick M'Garvey, (*See No.* 14.)		Land,			—	1 10 0
	c	Susan M'Loughlin, (*See No.* 14.)		House and land,			0 5 0	1 15 0
	d	Eliza M'Cullagh, (*See No.* 14.)		House and land,			0 10 0	2 0 0
	e	Bernard M'Cullagh, (*See No.* 14.)		House and land,			0 10 0	3 10 0
13	a	Patk. M'Garvey, sen., (*See No.* 14.)	Daniel Baird,	House, office, & land,	62 1 0	12 5 0	1 0 0	4 5 0
	b	Rose M'Garvey, (*See No.* 14.)		House, office, & land,			0 15 0	6 15 0
	c	Patk. M'Garvey, jun., (*See No.* 14.)		House, office, & land,			0 10 0	1 15 0
	d	Michael M'Garvey, (*See No.* 14.)		House and land,			0 10 0	2 5 0
–	e	Francis M'Bride,	Patrick M'Garvey, sen.,	House,	—	—	0 10 0	0 10 0
–	f	William Ward,	Michael M'Garvey,	House,	—	—	0 5 0	0 5 0
–	g	Anne Martin,	Patrick M'Garvey, sen.,	House,	—	—	0 5 0	0 5 0
–	h	Henry Loane,	Rose M'Garvey,	House,	—	—	0 5 0	0 5 0
14		James Kelly,	Daniel Baird,	Mountain,	238 0 0	3 2 0	—	0 8 0
		Neal M'Namee,						0 4 0
		Patk. M'Garvey, sen.,						0 4 0
		Susan M'Loughlin,						0 4 0
		Eliza M'Cullagh,						0 4 0
		Bernard M'Cullagh,						0 8 0
		Patk. M'Garvey, sen.,						0 8 0
		Rose M'Garvey,						0 15 0
		Patk. M'Garvey, jun.,						0 3 0
		Michael M'Garvey,						0 4 0
15	a	Michl. M'Namee, sen,	Same,	House, office, & land,	122 1 0	10 10 0	0 15 0	4 5 0
	b	James M'Namee,		House, office, & land,			1 0 0	2 15 0
	c	John M'Namee,		House, office, & land,			1 0 0	4 10 0
	–	Michl. M'Namee, jun.		Land,			—	1 15 0
–	d	William Beytagh,	Michael M'Namee, jun.,	House,	—	—	0 15 0	0 15 0
–	e	Neal M'Namee,	Michael M'Namee, sen.,	House and garden,	0 1 0	0 3 0	0 7 0	0 10 0
–	f	Bridget M'Namee,	John M'Namee,	House,	—	—	0 5 0	0 5 0
16	a	Bernard M'Namee, (*See No.* 18.)	Daniel Baird,	House, office, & land,	12 3 20	3 15 0	0 15 0	3 10 0
	b	Charles M'Namee, (*See No.* 18.)		House, office, & land,			0 10 0	1 10 0
17	a	Daniel M'Loughlin, (*See* 18.)	Same,	House and land,	15 3 25	3 5 0	0 10 0	3 15 0
	b	Hugh M'Namee, (*See No.* 18.)	Same,	House and land,		0 10 0	0 10 0	1 0 0
	c	James M'Namee, (*See No.* 18.)	Same,	House and land,		1 10 0	0 5 0	1 15 0
	–	William M'Ananey, (*See No.* 18.)	Reps. John M'Loughlin	Land,		1 5 0	—	1 5 0
–	d	Ellen M'Namee,	Daniel Baird,	House and garden,	0 1 0	0 2 0	0 3 0	0 5 0
18		Bernard M'Namee,	Same,	Mountain,	81 2 20	1 12 0	—	0 12 0
		Charles M'Namee,						0 4 0
		Daniel M'Loughlin,						0 7 0
		Hugh M'Namee,						0 2 0
		James M'Namee,						0 4 0
		William M'Ananey,	Reps. John M'Loughlin					0 3 0
				Total of Rateable Property,	952 3 0	129 17 0	26 11 0	156 8 0
				EXEMPTIONS:				
7	b	. . . . . .	Daniel Baird,	National school-house,	—	—	0 15 0	0 15 0
				Total, including Exemptions,	952 3 0	129 17 0	27 6 0	157 3 0

Extract from Griffith's valuation.

No. and Letters of Reference to Map.		Names.		Description of Tenement.	Area.	Rateable Annual Valuation.		Total Annual Valuation of Rateable Property.
		Townlands and Occupiers.	Immediate Lessors.			Land.	Buildings.	
					A. R. P.	£ s. d.	£ s. d.	£ s. d.
		SESSAGH OF GALLAN—*con.*						
1		William M'Clintock, .	James & George Aiken,	House, offices, and land,	65 2 10	8 15 0	1 5 0	10 0 0
2		Anne Devlin, . .	Same, . .	House and land, .	11 1 0	3 0 0	0 10 0	3 10 0
3		Anne Devlin, .	James & George Aiken,	Mountain, . .	11 2 8	0 5 0	—	0 5 0
		James M'Aleer, .				0 5 0	—	0 5 0
4		James M'Aleer, . .	Same, . .	House, office, and land,	7 2 20	2 0 0	0 10 0	2 10 0
5		John M'Callan, . .	Same, . .	House and land, .	4 2 20	0 10 0	0 10 0	1 0 0
6		Owen Quinn, . .	Same, . .	Land, ...	3 2 0	0 15 0	—	0 15 0
7		John Quinn, . .	Same, . .	Land, ...	5 2 5	1 0 0	—	1 0 0
—	a	Patrick Quinn, . .	John Quinn, . .	House and garden, .	0 1 25	0 5 0	0 5 0	0 10 0
8		John Morris, . .	James & George Aiken,	House, office, and land,	44 3 5	7 15 0	0 15 0	8 10 0
9		William Hill, . .	Same, . .	Land, ...	6 0 15	0 10 0	—	0 10 0
10	a	Owen M'Colgan,	Same, .	House, office, & land,	44 2 25	4 0 0	0 15 0	4 15 0
	b	Daniel Morris, .		House, office, & land,		4 0 0	0 15 0	4 15 0
				Total, . .	205 2 13	33 0 0	5 5 0	38 5 0

Extract from Griffith's valuation.

LAND OWNERSHIP IN GALLON BASED ON GRIFFITH'S VALUATION (1859)

Number of households holding various amounts of land.

	none	> 1 acre	1-5 acres	6-10 acres	11-15 acres	16-20 acres	21-40 acres	40-60 acres	Total farms
Gallon Upper	11	4	4	10	2	3	1	4	28
Gallon Lower	5	1	1	1	2	6	7	0	18
Gallon Sessiagh	0	1	2	2	1	0	2	2	10
Totals	16	6	7	13	5	9	10	6	56

Three tracts of mountain; 238 acres divided among 10 farmers, 114 acres divided among 16 farmers, and 81 acres divided among 6 farmers, have been excluded from these calculations.

Sixteen households had no land, and a further 6 households had less than one acre. These landless families had only a fragile toehold in Gallon, and the Valuation Reports[13] from 1860 until 1910 show how they gradually moved away, settling perhaps in the towns or emigrating.

Those individuals who had no land are usually known as "cottiers". Before the Great Famine farmers would sometimes have allowed them to live rent-free provided that they helped out with the work on the farm. After the Great Famine, there was a significant move away from tillage towards pasture, which required much less labour and many cottiers found that they no longer had any role to play in the countryside and emigrated or moved to the towns.

The Valuation Reports also show how some households with small farms lost all their land but ended their days living on in Gallon, often occupying houses which belonged to larger farms.

A PROSPEROUS FARMER: DENIS MORRIS OF MEENAWIDDY IN 1850s

According to the Tithe Applotment Records (1834), Dennis Morris had no land in Gallon Upper, he had six acres in Gallon Lower and five acres in Gallon Sessiagh. Yet, according to Griffith's Valuation, Denis had acquired 34 acres in Gallon Upper by 1859 with a share in another 60 acres.

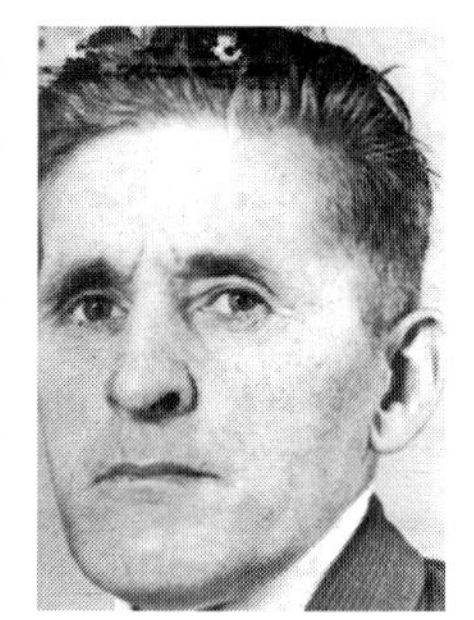
Denis Moris (1917-1985).

In the middle of the nineteenth century, Dennis Morris had two farms and several cottier houses; the valuation placed on his farm house and outbuildings were among the highest in the area. One can see from the Valuation Reports how he incorporated one of the cottier houses into his own house to make it larger, and allowed other houses to lie vacant, perhaps using them as farm buildings.

The Morris children were sent away to Derry for their secondary education: four of them later achieved prominence in the Catholic church. The numerous Morris headstones in Pubble graveyard are a manifestation of this family's status in the area at that time.

In the years immediately after the Great Famine (see Chapter 7) there was widespread disillusionment with life in rural Ireland, manifest especially among the landless country folk, but also extending to the sons and daughters of farmers. An example of the latter was Henry Bradley whose father and mother, Jacob and Madge Bradley had a comparatively substantial farm of 17 acres in Gallon Lower. Before the trauma caused by the famine, Jacob may have been content to stay at home to inherit the family farm. Instead, he emigrated to Australia in 1858 where he was joined some time later by his sister Margaret. Henry's great grand children: Erica, Ruth and Harry Bradley, have visited Gallon on a number of occasions in the 1990s to meet their Irish cousins.

According to Griffith's Valuation of 1859 there were 36 households in Gallon Upper and Gallon Lower holding at least six acres, but by 1930 this number had been reduced to 25, as the table below shows:

Peggy Morris, John Bradley and Alice McElwee (nee Morris)
outside the family home at Meenawiddy.

The gravestone of Dennis Morris (1781-1879) in Pubble graveyard.

LAND OWNERSHIP IN GALLON UPPER & GALLON LOWER IN 1930

	1-5 acres	6-10 acres	11-15 acres	16-20 acres	21-40 acres	40-60 acres	Totals
Gallon Upper	4	3	4	3	7	2	23
Gallon Lower	0	0	0	1	5	0	6

Records are not available for Gallon Sessiagh for 1930.

Farm consolidation between 1859 and 1930 was most evident in Gallon Lower, where the number of farms reduced from 18 to 6. In Gallon Upper the number of farms reduced from 28 to 23 in the same period.

The table below shows the occupiers of farms in Gallon at five different stages; (a) according to the Tithe Applotment Records of 1834; (b) Maturin Baird's Estate Map of c 1850; (c) Griffith's Valuation of 1859; (d) Sale of Maturin Baird's Estate 1930 (e) 2000.

Wedding of Mary & Neil McNamee. The best man was Charles McNamee, the bridesmaid Sadie Connolly.

LANDHOLDERS OF GALLON 1858-2000

	TITHE APPLOTMENT 1834	Acres	D BAIRD'S MAP 1850?	Acres	GRIFFITH'S VALUATION 1858?	Acres	OWNER IN 1935 (D Baird's sale)	OWNER IN 2000
Meenawiddy			GALLON UPPER					
1a	J, M, N& J McColgan	84	Dennis Morris	83	Denis Morris	54	Denis etc Morris	Hugh McElwee
2			Dennis Morris	20	Peter Morris	41	Bernard McColgan	Bernard McColgan
			B McNamee	21			Hugh McAleer	James Doohan
3a	Pat, Pat, M Devlin	62	John Devlin	20	John Devlin	20	Arthur Devlin	Arthur Devlin
5a			Mary & Owen Quinn	21	Owen Quinn	7	Charles Quinn	Rosemary Devine
5b					John Quinn	7	Neil McAnena	Mark McNamee
5c					Daniel Morris	7	Neil McAnena	Mark McNamee
6a			J McConomy	6	James McConway	10	Neil McAnena	Mark McNamee
6b			J McRory	16	Edward Rogers	10	Neil McAnena	Mark McNamee
7a	Charles McColgan	21	Charles McColgan	21	Charles McColgan	25+16m	Mary McColgan	Charles McColgan
8a	Js & Jn McAnelly	53	J & J McAnally	18	James McAnalley		Margt McNally	Mark McNamee
9a	A McAnelly & J Brogan	40	C & M McAnally	20	Charles McAnalley	15+16m	Mary A McNamee	Kieran McNamee
9b					Michael McAnalley	10+16m		Kieran McNamee
10a			James & John Brogan	20	James Brogan	10+16m	Thomas Brogan	Pat McAnena
10b					John Brogan	10+16m	John J Brogan	Pat McAnena
10c					Patrick Brogan	0.5		Pat McAnena
Aghnaglarig								
12a	F McLaughlin, J McCrory		J Kelly	8	James Kelly	6+26m	Neil Kelly 1.5	Tess Patton
12b	B Devlin, B McCulla	31			Neal McNamee	5+26m	Patrick McGarvey	Tommy McNamee
12c	J & A Kelly		Late F McLaughlin	8	Susan McLaughlin	5+26m	Patrick McGarvey	Tommy McNamee
12d			B McCullagh	8	Eliza McCullagh	5+26m	Patrick McGarvey	Tommy McNamee
12e					Bernard McCullagh	12+26m	Patrick McGarvey	Tommy McNamee
13a	M, O, J McGarvey	36	JT & M McGarvey	32	Patrick McGarvey	16+26m	John McGarvey	John McNamee
13b	E & M O'Hagan		J Higgins		Rose McGarvey	30+26m	Sarah McGarvey	Tommy McNamee
13c					Patrick McGarvey Jr	6+26m	Patrick O Brien	Sadie McNamee
13d					Michael McGarvey	10+26m	Michael McGarvey	Tommy McNamee
Crockatore								
15a	M, N & N McNamee	7	M R McNamee	9.5	Michael McNamee sen	45+25m	John McGarvey	Wm & B McNamee
15b					James McNamee	15	Bernard McNamee	Wm & B McNamee
15c	B, E, O, O, J, C McNamee	22	John McNamee	10	John McNamee	25	Bernard McNamee	Wm & B McNamee
16a	N, O, D, D McNamee	15	M J & B McNamee	7	Bernard McNamee	8+16m	Robert Monteith	Vincent McNamee

16b	& H McCurristel		C McNamee	2	Charles McNamee	4+16m		Vincent McNamee
17a			D McLaughlin	4	Daniel McLaughlin	8+16m	John McNamee (MrsH)	Vincent McNamee
			D & J McLaughlin	5				Vincent McNamee
17b			Rose McNamee	1	Hugh McNamee	1+16m		Vincent McNamee
17c			Pat McGarvey	3.5	James McNamee	3.5+16m	Robert Monteith	Vincent McNamee
17d					Wm McAneney	3	Charles McAnena	Hugh Coyle
			GALLON LOWER					
1	P Brogan, A Brogan	29	William Hill	15	William Hill	16	Robert Hill	Kathleen Hegarty
2	& Wm Cassidy		Wm McLaughlin	15	Patrick McAneney (Jas)	15	Neil McAnena	John McNamee
3a	Ph Quinn & C Brogan	28	Brogan	29	Patrick Brogan	15	Neil McAnena	John Bradley
					John Brogan	15	Neil McAnena	J Bradley / J McNamee
4a	Denis Morris?	6	A Brogan	3	Andrew Brogan	3	Neil McAnena	J McNamee
4b			James Brogan	0.5	James Brogan	0.5	Neil McAnena	J McNamee
5a	H & Chas Bradley &	86	Jacob Bradley	17.5	Jacob Bradley	22	Henry Bradley	John Bradley
5b	Jas McConnell		Late C Bradley	28	John Bradley	9	Sarah Maguire	John Bradley
5b					Michael McGarvey	18	Sarah Maguire	John Bradley
5c			Patrick Brogan Sen	0.5	Patrick Brogan	0.5		John Bradley
6					Michael McAneney	10	James McAnena	John McAnena
7			Michael McAnenny	20	John McAneney	24	Michael McAneny	John Bradley
9		+	Jane Hutchinson	32	Elizabeth Hutchinson	28	Maria Hill (Fulton)	Olive Wauchob
10	Jn McLaughlin	20	Pa McAnenny	20	Patrick McAneney (Neal)	28	Joseph McAnena	John McAnena
11a	Dan & Jas McLaughlin	70	John & Daniel	72	Daniel McLaughlin	35	Andy John Graham	Johnny Graham
11b			McLaughlin		Reps J McLaughlin	35	W Hunter	W Hunter
12a	James Hutchinson	32	John Hutchinson	32	John Hutchinson	33	Bella McGurk	Rep. McGurks
13	Jn, T, Js, Wm, Ch	57	Wm Hutchinson	9	Wm Hutchinson	9	Wm Hutchinson	Olive Wauchob
14	Hutchinson		Samuel Hutchinson	19	Samuel Hutchinson	18	Mary & Eliz Hill	Johnny Graham
			GALLON SESSIAGH					
1	J Morris & D McNally	64	No information		William McClintock	65	J J Bradley	Rose Bradley
2	Charles Devlin	13	available		Anne Devlin	11	J.J.Devlin	Leo Maguire
3	John Bradley?	8	(Gallon Sessiagh's		A Devlin & J McAleer	11.5	Henry McAleer	Mark McNamee
4	James McAleer	7	landlord was G Aiken		James McAleer	7.5	Henry McAleer	Mark McNamee

5	Denis Morris?	8	not Baird, but	James McCallan	4.5	Henry McAleer	Leo Maguire
6	Edward Quinn	2	Aiken)	Owen Quinn	3.5	Neil McAnena	Mark McNamee
7	Ed & Owen Quinn	7		John Quinn	5.2	Neil McAnena	Mark McNamee
8	Jn Bradley&Br Morris	28		John Morris	44	Morris	W J Morris
9	Denis Morris	6		William Hill	6	Robert Hill	Kathleen Hegarty
10a	Widow Morris &	47		Owen McColgan	22	Chas McColgan	Chas McColgan
10b	Thos McMenamin			Daniel Morris	22	J J Quinn	Kieran McNamee

Note: 25 + 16m = 25 arable acres plus 16 of mountain.

Guidance on interpreting Griffith's Valuation

1. The numbers and letters beside each householder's name refers to the leases marked on the map.
2. Acreages are given to the nearest complete acre. Where a householder holds less than an acre, the symbol < is used.
3. The valuation of buildings is given in shillings (20 shillings = £1.00). The buildings would normally mean the dwelling house, but could also include outbuildings where these existed. The traditional thatched two roomed house attracted rent of approximately 10 shillings per year. One of the highest rents for houses was paid by Denis Morris (the house owned in 2000 by Hugh McElwee).
4. Tenants held their farms and / or houses directly from the landlord. Some tenants sub-let houses or small amounts of land to sub-tenants or to cottiers.

CHAPTER 4: THE LANDLORDS OF NEWTOWN AND LISLAP (1610-1932)

THE LANDLORDS

The dates indicate when the landlords took possession of the estate.

James Clapham	1610
Sir Robert Newcomen	1618
Sir William Stewart (1st Baronet)	1629
Sir William Stewart, Lord Mountjoy (3rd Baronet)	1654
Sir William Stewart (4th Baronet)	1692
Sir William Stewart, Earl of Blessington (5th Baronet)	1745
Elizabeth and Luke Gardiner (later Viscount Mountjoy)	1769
Charles John Gardiner, later Earl of Blessington	1798
In chancery (due to bankruptcy of Earl of Blessington)	1829
Daniel Baird and James & George Aiken (and others)	1846/7
Daniel Maturin Baird (and others)	1862
Charles Edgar Maturin Baird (and others)	1899
Lands vested and sold to the tenants	1932

THE STEWARTS

The Newtowne and Lislap estate had been granted to James Clapham (otherwise known as Clephane or Chapham) by King James I in 1610. Clapham sold the property to Sir Robert Newcomen in 1618. In 1629, Newcomen's son-in-law, Sir William Stewart (1st Baronet) succeeded to the ownership of the estate. The Stewarts who had been granted other properties at Rathmelton, County Donegal, had originally come from Galloway. Stewart purchased lands at Rash, near Omagh from George Arundel in 1638, thus further extending his estate.

Sir William Stewart died in 1654, being predeceased by his son, Sir Alexander, who had been killed at the battle of Dunbar in 1650. Alexander's son, Sir William Stewart (3rd Baronet) inherited the Newtown and Lislap estates on the death of his grandfather and was awarded the title Lord Mountjoy in 1683. (The family of the Elizabeth I's general, the original Lord Mountjoy, had died out).

Sir William was the Protestant leader of the army of King James stationed at Derry just before the Siege in 1689. He was absent from Ireland during the crisis which led to the overthrow of James II in 1691 and was later killed at the battle of Steinkirk in 1692. His son, also Sir William (4th Baronet) married

Hon Anne Boyle, daughter of Viscount Blessington with estates in Wicklow, Kildare and Hampshire. From this time onwards the family lived in England at their Silchester home. Their only son, Sir William Stewart (5th Baronet) became 3rd Viscount and Earl of Blessington in 1745; however, he died without direct heirs in 1769.

THE GARDINERS

The Mountjoy estates passed to a cousin, Elizabeth Montgomery, who had married Luke Gardiner, a wealthy Dublin merchant with extensive properties in Dublin city and Kilkenny. Luke Gardiner was created Viscount Mountjoy in 1795.

Gardiner was sympathetic to the plight of Catholics under the remaining provisions of the Penal Laws, and had framed 'Gardiner's Relief Act' in 1778, which permitted Catholics to take leases lasting up to 999 years. He introduced another bill in 1782, which extended further rights to Catholics, including the removal of restrictions on Catholic education.[1] He was an enthusiastic property developer, and promoted the building of Mountjoy Square, Blessington Street, Gardiner Street and may other streets in the north side of Dublin City. He also proved to be an enlightened landlord, encouraging his tenants to modernise their farming methods and improve their holdings. His nurseries at Rash, near Omagh, (later known as Mountjoy Forest) provided trees and shrubs for the planting of hedges around fields. Mountjoy Forest eventually occupied 4,000 acres on the east and west banks of the Strule River two miles north of Omagh.

Recognising the value of lime as a fertiliser, Gardiner encouraged its use on the tenants' farms and he established kilns where they could purchase lime at nominal prices. He engaged as his land agent a foremost expert on agricultural methods, John McEvoy, who was to provide detailed descriptions of the work carried out at Mountjoy Forest in the Statistical Survey of County Tyrone (1802).[2]

Gardiner was loyal to the government of the day, and opposed the rising by the United Irishmen in 1798. He raised a company of volunteers among the Catholic tenants of his Dublin properties. He was killed while leading his company into action against the rebels at the battle of New Ross in 1798. His son Charles John Gardiner inherited his father's properties in Tyrone, Dublin and Kilkenny. The Tyrone estates comprised sixty-eight townlands, containing about thirty two-thousand statute acres.

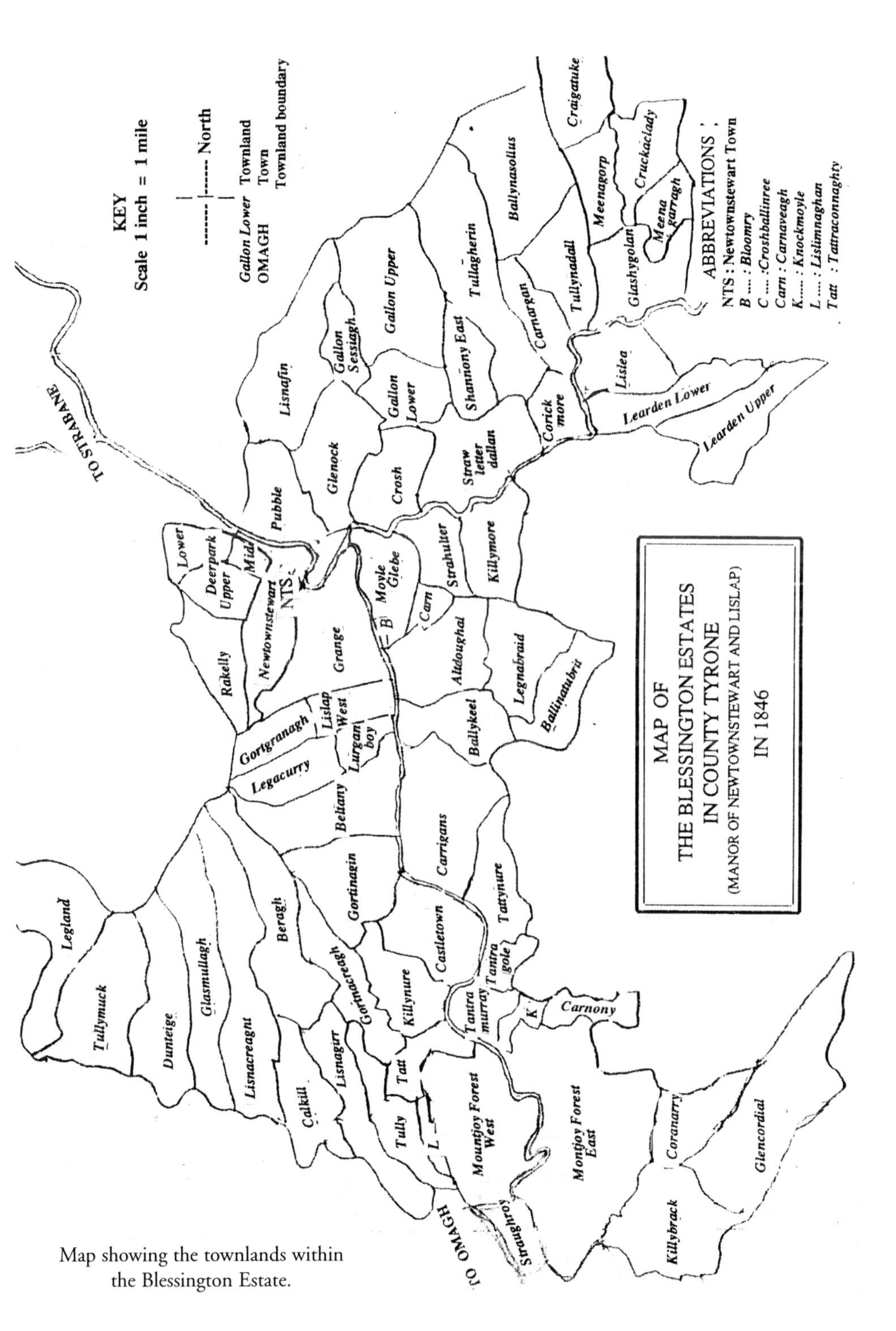

Map showing the townlands within the Blessington Estate.

THE EARL OF BLESSINGTON

Charles John was created Earl of Blessington in 1816 and had at this time, an annual income from his estates and properties of £30,000. He spent substantial amounts of money improving his Tyrone residence 'Old Mountjoy' and began the construction of a new residence on the west bank of the river Strule about four miles north of Omagh.

Lord Blessington married Margaret (Marguerite) Farmer in 1818, a lady of humble birth but stunning beauty, and brought her on a visit to Tyrone. He incurred considerable expense in making his Tyrone home, attractive to his new bride, even erecting a new playhouse especially for the visit. In spite of his efforts however, Marguerite did not enjoy country living and disapproved of any further expenditure on his Tyrone estates.

Marguerite's main ambition was to be accepted into polite society in Dublin and London. However, because of her humble birth and unconventional life-style, the Blessingtons found themselves snubbed by the gentry in both capitals. Henceforth, Lord Blessington and his wife, along with their extensive entourage, travelled extensively in mainland Europe, settling eventually in Paris in 1828. Their extravagant lifestyle led to the collapse of the family inheritance, and when Lord Blessington died in 1829,[3] the Blessington estate was found to be bankrupt. In order to survive in her reduced circumstances, Lady Blessington began to write. Her first book 'The Magic Lantern' had appeared anonymously in 1822, and a novel 'Cassidy' under her own name appeared in

Right: Lord Blessington.

Far right: Marguerite, Lady Blessington; "The most beautiful woman in Ireland".

A Old Mountjoy, former Tyrone home of Lord Blessington.

1833. She continued to write fiction and personal reminiscences until her death in Paris where she had fled to escape from her creditors in 1849.[4]

The Blessington properties in County Tyrone were offered for sale in 1846 and 1847 to pay off the accumulated debts. A Derry merchant, Mr Daniel Baird, purchased the townlands of Gallon Upper, Gallon Lower, Glenock, Newtownstewart and Deerpark among others. Messrs James and George Aiken bought Gallon Sessiagh.

THE BAIRDS AND AIKENS

R H Nolan prepared maps of Daniel Baird's newly acquired estate in 1852. These maps give valuable information about land ownership in Gallon at that time. It is interesting to note that the information provided in Nolan's maps does not correspond exactly with Griffith's Valuation (see below). This may be due to the interval between the collection of the data (up to 8 years) or to changes made to tenancy agreements by the new landlord.

When Daniel Baird died in 1862, he bequeathed his lands to his grandson, Daniel Maturin. In 1875, Daniel Maturin took the surname Baird and inherited the lands. His son Charles Edgar Maturin-Baird succeeded him in 1899. In 1932 under the Irish Land Purchase Acts, Maturin-Baird's lands were vested and sold to the tenants, on payment of an annuity for 50 years towards the cost of compensating the Maturin-Baird family.

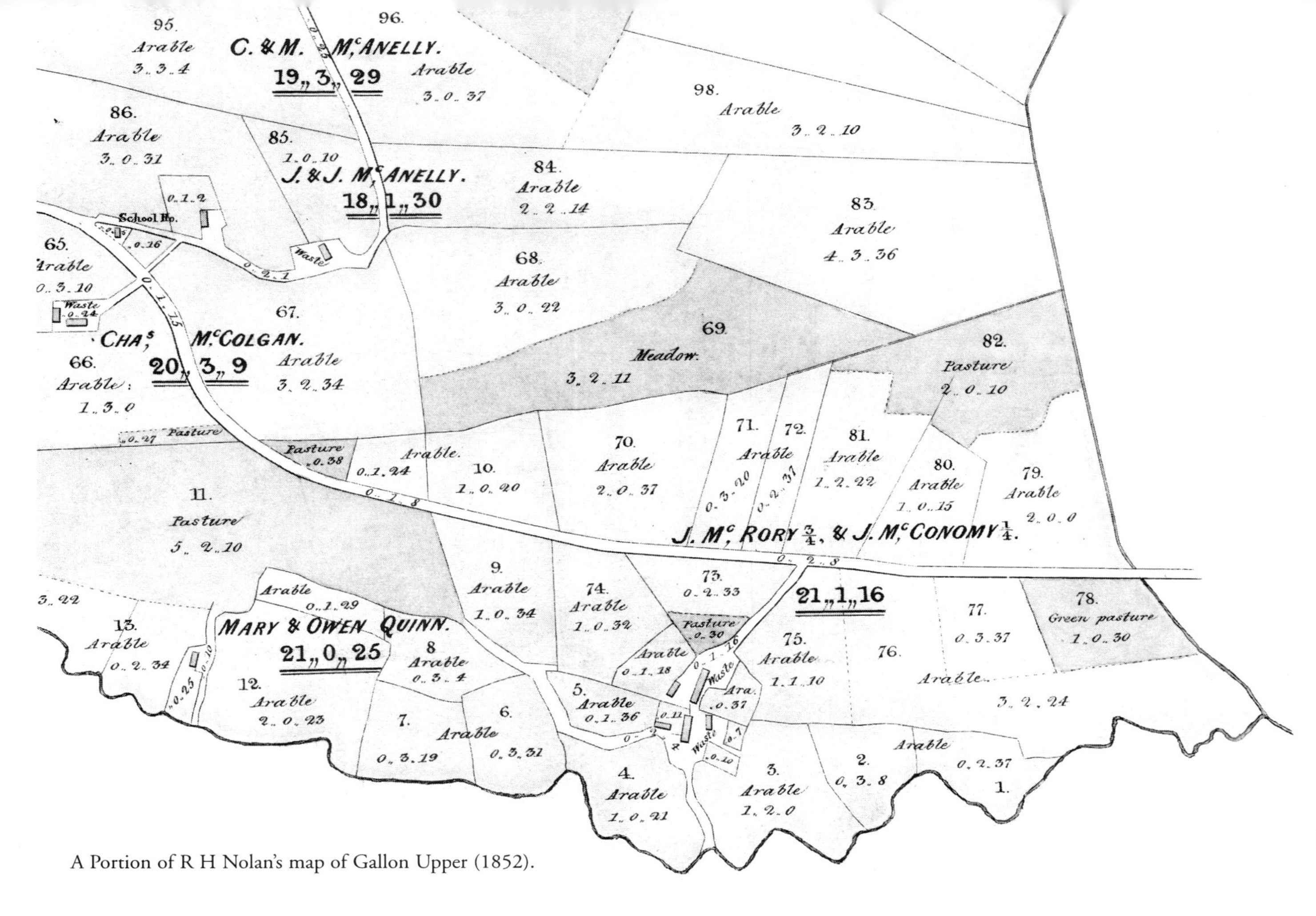

A Portion of R H Nolan's map of Gallon Upper (1852).

So, after more than three hundred years as tenants, Gallon's farmers at last became owner-occupiers. A list of those Gallon farms on the Maturin-Baird Estate, which were bought out in 1932, is given in Appendix F.

CHAPTER 5: THE DEVELOPMENT OF FARMING IN GALLON

LAND QUALITY

The largest of the three townlands is Gallon Upper, which has 952 acres, and the smallest is Gallon Sessiagh, with 205 acres, while Gallon Lower has 543 acres. The land is drained by the Sessiagh Burn, which separates Gallon Sessiagh from Upper and Lower Gallon, and the Crosh Burn, which runs through the lowest land in our study. The two burns meet to form the Glenock Burn, which flows into the Owenkillew River near the Catholic Church at Glenock. Glenock Church is a well-known landmark, which is clearly visible on the right hand side of the road on the approach to Newtownstewart from Omagh.

The most fertile land in Gallon Lower is along the Crosh and the Sessiagh Burns and is composed of Brown Podzols.[1] The land is mostly under grass at present, but in the past produced good crops of potatoes, oats or barley. The upper part of Gallon Lower, adjoining Gallon Upper, comprises over 100 acres of bogland, known locally as "The Flough". The remainder of Gallon Lower consists of surface water gley. Around one third of Gallon Sessiagh consists of peat, but with some surface water gley in the central part of the townland. Gallon Upper lies on the south facing slopes of Gallon Mountain(809 feet). More than half the land in Gallon Upper is peat, and the remainder is composed of surface water glay. There is, however, a small island of brown podzol around Aghnaglarig in Gallon Upper. It has been noted earlier that this area was one of the leaseholds in Gallon Upper which had been sub-divided among a number of tenants by 1858.

POTATOES, OATS AND BUTTERMILK

When Gallon was first settled on a permanent basis, it is likely that the people produced oats, barley and flax and kept sheep, cattle and pigs. Each holding would aim to be self-sufficient, because markets in those years had not yet developed locally.

At the outset, fields and pasture were probably not clearly demarcated. However, by the end of the eighteenth century, some landlords had realised that greater efficiency could only be achieved by enclosing fields and reorganising the farms to make them more self contained.

The tenants were expected to erect ditches and to plant hedges around the newly established fields. Those farms adjoining Gallon mountain were given a share of the mountain, which they might use for grazing sheep and cattle. The right to cut turf ("turbary") on payment of a rent, was also allocated to certain farmers.

Fences in Gallon Lower are generally solid earthen structures, with ditches and dykes (earth ramparts). The dykes are planted with hawthorn on many farms. Sycamore and ash trees are popular around houses. In the lower parts of Gallon Upper, ditches and dykes are also common, but the absence of trees or bushes in the ditches is notable. Many of the fields in Gallon Upper have stone wall fences. Iron gates, made in the forge at Newtownstewart, replaced timber gates in the early years of this century but have been superseded in modern times by mass-produced tubular gates wide enough for modern machinery.

A notable feature of Gallon Upper is the fact that many of the individual fields have retained their unique names. Most of these names are derived from Irish, such as Turnaflochan, Crockban, Forthkeen, Strawduch, Banshiks, and Criggers. Criggers is interesting in that, until recently it consisted of four small fields, about one third of an acre each in size. This may be an example of how farms were sub-divided, often to the extent of dividing fields.

The Irish language had ceased to be the dominant language of Gallon by 1850, so the field names have remained in the memories of the local people for more than 150 years. There are other fields with English names, suggesting that they are broken in from the mountain in more recent times, after English had become the generally spoken language.

The reclamation of land from the mountain was an important feature of farm work in Gallon from the seventeenth to the nineteenth century. The technique known as "paring and burning" was probably used.

> ...the "scraws" or top sods of an inch or an inch and a half thick were pared off, turned upside down until partially dry, and then "footed" or built into small piles until they were completely dry, when they were then burned. The land from which the sods had been removed was made into ridges, and the ashes of the sods were spread over these. Potatoes were planted on top of the ashes, and covered with mould from the furrows.[2]

Most arable farming was done by spade, with crops planted in ridges to assist drainage. This would be especially important on the flat land on either bank of the Canal Sheugh and the Sessiagh Burn. Hay and corn crops were cut using

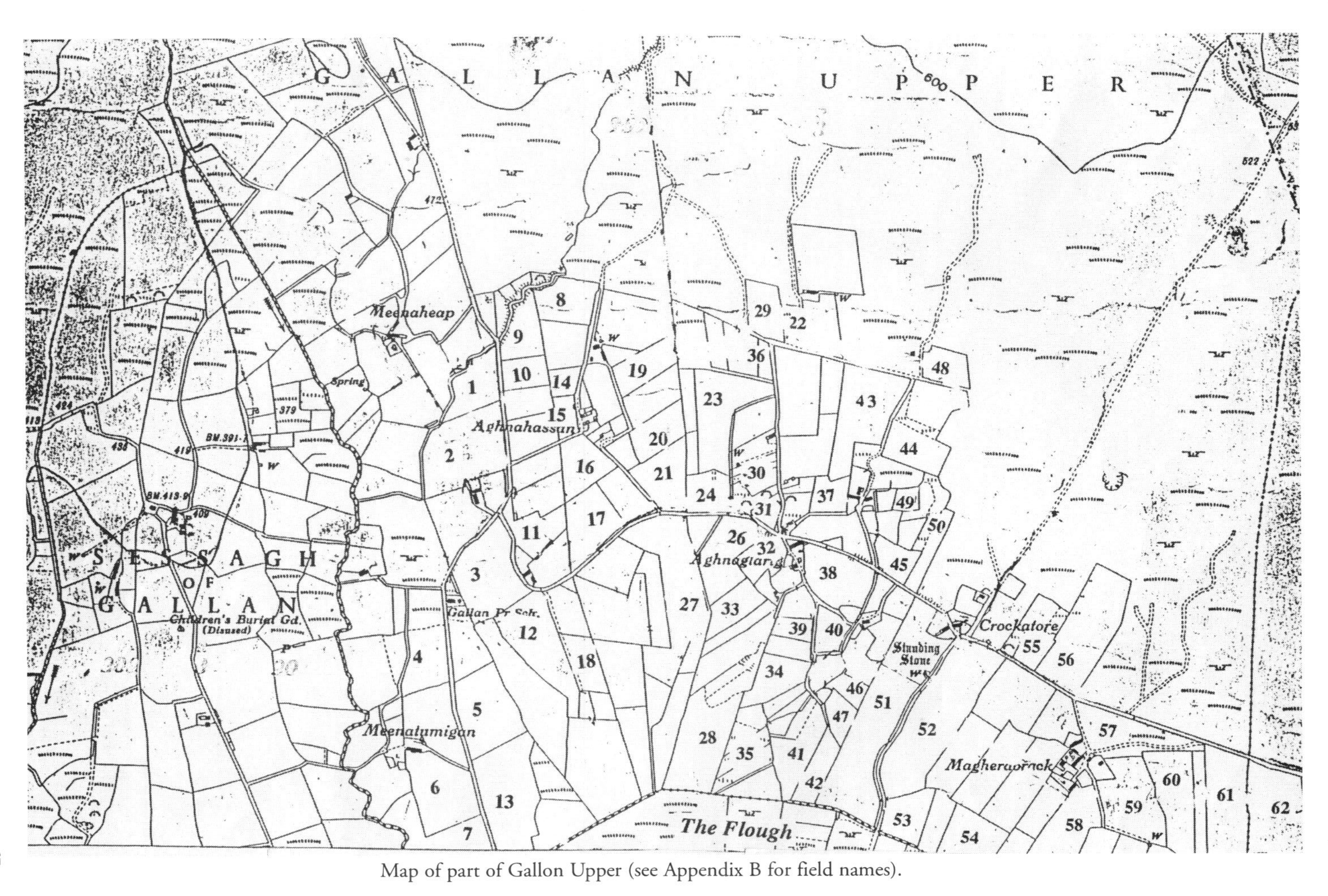

Map of part of Gallon Upper (see Appendix B for field names).

the sickle or reaping hook. The grain was threshed by flail when required by the farmer or his livestock.

Potatoes were first grown in Ulster in the early 1600s but had not made any significant impact upon the eating habits of the inhabitants of North Tyrone until after 1740. Writing about a famine in the Strabane area in the 1740s, John Dooher explains:

> What is clear in these reports is that the potato played a relatively minor role in the diet of the people in the 1740s and that oatmeal seems to have been the major source of food for many families. It was perhaps the experiences of these years that convinced many that an alternative source of food was required and thus led to an over-emphasis on the potato in some parts of the country.[3]

However, oats and other crops were still essential to provide food during the 'hungry months' of July and August when the previous year's crop had been eaten and the new crop was not yet ready for digging. The value of the potato as food is described by Mitchell and Ryan:

> Although 75% of the tuber is water, the food value of an acre of potatoes is greater than that of an acre of any grain crop. The potato yields starch, amino acids and Vitamin C and the consumption of 3 kg (6 lbs) per day provides an adequate diet. In Ireland, 0.4 ha (1 acre) can be expected to yield about 9 tons, enough to feed six adult men for one year and more than adequate to support a relatively large family.[4]

It is likely that, by the end of the eighteenth century, potatoes had become an important element in the diet of Gallon's inhabitants, especially during the winter months.

Newtownstewart had an important brown linen market in the second half of the eighteenth century, £600 worth of linen being sold every week, so flax would probably have been grown extensively on the better land in Gallon during that period. John McEvoy[5] writing in 1802, found that many farmers sold their butter and some had taken up the weaving of linen in the evenings in order to provide cash for necessities such as salt, soap and candles.

McEvoy found that the standard of housing was very poor, with most people living in single storey thatched cottages built of stone and mud. He goes on to remark:

> one house answers for the family and the cow for more than one third of the peasantry.[6]

This arrangement, where the same house was occupied by the family and the cow, may have existed in Gallon in some instances up to the middle of the eighteenth century. However, increased prosperity and the availability of abandoned cottier houses by the middle of the nineteenth century eventually led to the provision of out-offices on most farms. The stones for these new·buildings were probably brought from two quarries on the slopes of Gallon mountain, well above the level of cultivation.

Sheep and pigs would have made an important contribution to the economy of Gallon's farmers during this period. Sheep were grazed on the common pasture of Gallon Mountain and in the dry parts of the pasture in Gallon Lower and Gallon Sessiagh. Every household would have kept pigs, which were fed on food scraps and potatoes. The money obtained from selling the pigs helped to pay the rent.

The use of animal manure to obtain better crops was well known, and the manure pile was often situated not far from the farmhouse. We have seen earlier how the landlords encouraged the use of lime to improve the fertility of the soil. Limestone was quarried on many local farms or brought from the landlord's quarry near Newtownstewart and fired in one of a number of lime kilns. Several quarries and kilns are marked on the earliest Ordnance Survey maps; some of the quarries were still discernible up to the 1960s.

During the early nineteenth century Ulster's farmers became more involved in selling their produce for ready cash to pay rents and tithes. The growing of flax and grain increased during these years, due to additional demands created by Britain's wars with France. Prices for livestock were also high. Quarterly fairs for the sale of farm produce and animals were held in Newtownstewart from 1810 until 1835; from 1836 onwards these fairs were held monthly. In those days there was also a ready market for turf to townsfolk and others who could not produce their own fuel. Nevertheless, there was little money to spare in Gallon during the 1830s.

ORDNANCE SURVEY MEMOIRS FOR THE EARLY NINETEENTH CENTURY

According to the Ordnance Survey Memoirs of Ireland for the parish of Ardstraw compiled by Lieutenant W Lancey in February 1834...

> potatoes and milk with herrings are their chief food. They seldom eat meat; loaf bread is more consumed than formerly, but meal is scarcer as the chief part of the oat crop is exported. The poor usually keep a cow.[7]

He goes on to describe the pattern of crop rotation.

> The usual method of cropping a lea field is first oats, then flax, potatoes, then wheat or oats or barley with clover, clover lea for two years, then again wheat or oats...
>
> Cows worth five to eight guineas are plentiful. The farmers rear the calves but there are no breeding or grazing farms to any extent. Butter and pigs abound; the immense number carried to Derry in winter from this and adjacent parishes is surprising. Good horses for country purposes are common, and some better description of cattle can always be purchased at Mr Colhown's near Newtownstewart. Sheep are scarce.[8]

He gives the prices for produce in Strabane market as follows:

> Prices for produce in Strabane market in 1833 are 7 pence a stone for oats, 15 shillings a barrel for barley, two pence a stone for potatoes, clover hay 35 shillings a ton, meadow hay 25 shillings a ton, wheat 23 shillings a barrel.[9]

There is some indication, however, that farm prices were unusually low in 1833.

Gallon farmers in the nineteenth century would have bought their spades at the foundry in Newtownstewart. Small quantities of corn were ground by hand on the farms, but when larger amounts were required, the corn was milled at the landlord's mill in Newtownstewart.

The establishment of the flax spinning mill at Sion Mills in the 1830s encouraged farmers to grow flax. The Ordnance Survey Memoirs describe the anticipated benefits of the new flax spinning mill:

> Weaving is general in the winter months when the people are not employed in husbandry. The females in the cabins were formerly much employed in spinning but since the flax spinning mills have been introduced, there is so little to be obtained by the wheel which is fast falling

> into disuse. There is at this moment a most extensive flax spinning mill being erected by a Belfast company. Much benefit is likely to be derived to the poor of the neighbourhood from this establishment in the increased means of employment it will offer and the flax grower will find a ready and convenient market for his produce at his door, which he is now obliged to carry to Derry for sale.[10]

Due to the increasing population, dependence on the potato for food became more apparent as the first half of the nineteenth century progressed. There were two serious difficulties arising from total dependence upon the potato for food. The first was the annual 'hungry time', normally the months of June and July, when the last season's crop of potatoes had been used and the new crop was not ready for digging. The people depended for sustenance on oats during these months, although this food was often scarce and expensive. The second difficulty arose from the frequent failure of the potato crop caused by bad weather or crop disease. When the potatoes failed many people had no option but to beg from their more fortunate countrymen.

> There is no county where the poor are worse off than they are in Tyrone. They evince the strongest anxiety to find work but cannot... The cabins of the cottiers are mere mud hovels, unfit for the residence of human beings... No Englishman could fail to be grievously shocked by the wretchedness exhibited in the streets of Omagh... Agriculture in this part of the country is far from being in a prosperous state, and the trade of begging is pursued with systematic regularity and perseverance.[11]

There were so many beggars and homeless people roaming through the countryside in the 1830s that the government enacted the Poor Law Act in 1838. The country was divided into Poor Law Unions, based on market towns.

Each Union was expected to erect a workhouse to accommodate the destitute poor. By 1842, workhouses had been completed at Strabane and Omagh, capable of accommodating 800 paupers each, with a smaller workhouse at Gortin, capable of holding 200 paupers. To obtain relief it was necessary for people to abandon their farms. No assistance was given outside the workhouse and anyone found begging was to be jailed as a vagrant.

The census figures for 1841 show that the three townlands of Gallon Lower, Gallon Upper and Gallon Sessiagh at that time supported a population of 522 people. Such population density, in an area where only one third of the land was arable, would not have been possible without the potato. Dependence upon the potato was not absolute, however, and when the potato failed during the Great Famine (1845-1850), the townlands did not for some years suffer the dramatic decline of population which was experienced in the west of Ireland (See Chapter 7).

North Tyrone was fortunate to escape the worst effects of the Great Famine but nevertheless there was considerable hardship. A partial failure of the potato crop occurred in 1845, but there were sufficient supplies of oats to prevent immediate catastrophe. The situation deteriorated further in 1846 and 1847 and the workhouses were soon overcrowded. Soup kitchens were set up at Baronscourt and a public meeting was held in the house of Mr Rogers at Glenock to demand the provision of public works for the destitute population. A number of public work schemes were later introduced, including the digging of the Canal Sheugh between Upper and Lower Gallon, in an effort to improve drainage in that area. The roads across Gallon Lower and Gallon Upper were also improved around this time, perhaps under one of these schemes.

AFTER THE GREAT FAMINE

Efforts to increase the productivity of Gallon's farms continued through the increased use of manure and lime. Potatoes and oats were still planted in ridges, but the more progressive farmers were moving towards flat tillage for corn crops and drills for potatoes.

In 1850, the acreage of crops in Gallon could be estimated as follows: 450 acres of oats, 70 acres of potatoes, 40 acres of turnips, 40 acres of flax and 30 acres of meadow clover. This was likely to be the high point for arable farming in Gallon. In the years that followed marginal land was set to grass, or in some cases abandoned to heather and wild mountain grasses.

The coming of the Great Northern Railway in 1851, together with the rise of urban population meant that new markets opened for Gallon's agricultural produce. Butter, eggs, fresh meat and dairy produce could now be delivered fresh to market in Omagh, Strabane and further afield. The use of imported guano, together with an increase in the number of livestock kept in the later nineteenth century helped to provide sufficient manure to ensure improved crops.

The market for butter and milk products led many farmers to change from the traditional longhorn cattle to the superior shorthorn cow:

> The shorthorn cow was a dual – purpose animal: in addition to its beef characteristics (improved performance in terms of live weight gain) it

also possessed good milking qualities. The latter was important not only in the context of the traditional butter-making industry, but also in relation to increasing urban demand for milk.[12]

Improved markets for their produce brought some prosperity to Gallon's farmers, and it was during this period that many of the single-roomed dwelling houses disappeared, to be replaced by the two-roomed dwelling, referred to in this book as the 'Traditional Gallon house'.

The prosperous days came to an end in the 1870s, when cheap food from America began to compete for the United Kingdom markets with goods produced in Ireland. The weather was also unkind: in August 1877 incessant rain rotted the potatoes in the ground, and flattened the oat crop, 1878 was not a particularly good harvest, and 1879 broke all records for rainfall. All crops suffered, but especially the potatoes, whose yield was reduced by 66% and the winter of 1879-80 was exceptionally harsh. In these circumstances, many tenants could not pay their rents: evictions in Ireland that year reached an estimated 1,098 people.

As the century progressed, the acreage under tillage decreased and hay, cut by scythe, became the predominant crop. Scythes were not widely used for harvesting corn until towards the end of the nineteenth century for fear that too much ripe grain would be shaken off during cutting. In any case, much corn was still grown on ridges not suited to the scythe. Reaping hooks and sickles were preferred, the reapers followed by binders who bound up the cut corn into sheaves.

Up until the middle of the nineteenth century, most cultivation on farms was still done by spade. This was because of the availability of cheap labour and the widespread belief that the deep digging, which could be done with the spade, produced better crops. Horse-ploughs only became common towards the end of the century, along with horse-drawn harrows and rollers.

Seed corn was usually broadcast by hand, from a bag of grain slung from the farmer's shoulders which was replenished occasionally by an assistant. Some farmers used a seed fiddle, especially when sowing grass-seed. Lazy-beds were gradually abandoned in favour of drills when planting potatoes, unless on newly broken-in ground.

In the early years of the twentieth century, a few farmers such as Robert Hill of Gallon Lower, bought one of the new threshing machines which was permanently installed in a barn and actuated through the action of cog-wheels by two horses walking around a close circle outside. Neighbouring farmers brought their corn to Hill's by cart for threshing. Albert Hill of Glenock was still using a barn thresher in the 1960s.

The steam-powered thresher made its first appearance in Gallon shortly after World War I. It was operated by W J Russell of Ballynamullan, Omagh. The machinery was so heavy that in wet weather it had to operate on the county road and the corn had to be carted out to it. Local people complained that it damaged the road, leaving deep ruts where it had travelled. Up to a dozen men were needed to operate the steam-driven thresher. The coal and water required for the machine had to be supplied by the farmer. The steam engine had an enormous appetite for water; local men and children hurried frantically to and from the nearest well or stream in order to keep up the supply.

Russell and his workman lodged in local houses during the threshing season, and neighbouring farmers co-operated to ensure that there were enough men available to keep the machinery working at optimum efficiency. Some of the oats were sold to Scott's mill in Newtownstewart, while the farmer may have kept some to feed the livestock on the farm.

Gallon's farmers had long appreciated the benefits of keeping farm produce indoors over the winter, but for many years they did not have sufficient outhouses to do so. During the late nineteenth century however, sheds and stables

Barn at Morris farm in Meenawiddy, constructed around 1900.

were built on to many farmhouses. In some cases, dwelling houses, which had been abandoned by cottiers, were taken over and used as outbuildings. More prosperous farmers built a two-storey barn, which housed horses and cows on the ground floor and grain, hay and straw upstairs.

The opening of the Model Creamery by Thomas Henderson at Newtownstewart in 1899 encouraged local farmers to produce more milk, in the knowledge that there would be a ready market. Taking the milk to the creamery by horse and cart became a daily ritual for Gallon's farmers; unfortunately there were often long delays at the creamery, wasting time which could otherwise be spent on farm work.

World War I brought an increase in the price of all farm produce, and the growing of flax increased. The flax was taken to be scutched at one of the three scutch mills in Milltown, near Ardstraw, belonging to the Smiths and the Clarkes. This period of high prices lasted for a few years after the war, encouraging farmers to invest in labour-saving machinery such as grass reapers and mechanical potato diggers.

In 1925, 26% of Northern Ireland's population were still employed in agriculture and the new Northern Ireland government took steps to improve the quality of farm produce in order to protect local farmers from foreign competition. These measures included the closer supervision of egg marketing, the development of pig farming and improvements to the quality of seed potatoes.

Occupations of the inhabitants of Gallon in 1901

Occupation	Gallon Upper	Gallon Lower	Gallon Sessiagh	Total
Farmer	22	10	5	37
Farmer's wife	1	4	2	7
Farmer's son	8	6	1	15
Farmer's daughter	10	5	1	16
Female / domestic servant	6	3	2	11
Agricultural labourer	19	4	6	29
Seamstress / dressmaker	28	5	9	42
Adult giving no occupation	8	1	0	9
Shoemaker	0	1	0	1
Wool weaver	1	0	0	1
Scholar	28	7	6	41
Children under five years	5	4	2	11
Totals	136	50	34	220

One hundred and five people, out of a total of 169 adults, were employed directly in agriculture. The number of individuals describing themselves as farmer's sons or daughters suggests that these people had never worked away from home. It is also likely that many of the 42 women who described themselves as seamstresses may not have been employed full time in that occupation, but they did bring in welcome cash through shirt-stitching and allied crafts in the home.

The *Tyrone Constitution* of 6 February 1891 gives an insight into the difficulties experienced by employers seeking cheap labour at the Strabane hiring fair, as well as disclosing some of the reporter's bias!

> STRABANE QUARTERLY FAIR
>
> This important hiring, cattle and horse fair was held on Monday, and was very largely attended by farm servants, farmers and dealers. Taking the fair as a whole the supply was large, and all the thoroughfares converging on Abercorn Square were thronged so completely that it was almost impossible to pass through...
>
> Farm servants attended in large numbers, but, judging by their exorbitant demands, it is evident that they have little fear of distress or want of employment. Ploughmen were seeking from £6 to £7 for the quarter, while boys with a very superficial knowledge of farm work declined to accept £4 10s or £ 5 10s. Girls were equally exacting. Useful looking domestics with some experience in milking and dairy work were engaged from £3 10s to £5 for the term, which is as much as they used to get for the half year. Others willing to work outdoors when required claim £3 to £4 10s.
>
> Very small girls and herd boys were getting from £2 10s to £3.[13]

According to the 1901 census, only six households in Gallon had living-in servants. These were probably prosperous households, such as Robert Hill of Gallon Lower or John McGarvey of Gallon Upper. It is difficult to determine from the census returns, however, whether additional servants were employed on a daily basis. Living-in servants from outside the area may have been hired at one of the quarterly hiring fairs held in Strabane in those years, but they do not feature to any extent in the census returns.

GROWING UP ON A FARM IN THE EARLY YEARS OF THE TWENTIETH CENTURY

During the early years of the century, boys and girls from the age of nine, especially the sons and daughters of cottiers, were hired out to local farmers. They lived with the farmer, often in dire conditions, overworked during the day, inadequately fed and expected to sleep on bags filled with straw placed upon the floor of the kitchen or even in an outhouse. Whether they were allowed to attend school during the summer depended upon the generosity of the farmer. When they were permitted to attend school they were expected to get up at six o'clock, bring in the cows for milking, and do other farmyard chores before going off to school. They had to hurry home from school and resume their farm chores without respite. In such circumstances, the children's education suffered and illiteracy among the poorer people was common. School inspectors frequently commented in the Report Book on the bad attendance of the pupils at Gallon School.

Eddie McLaughlin (1890-1960) and his brother Willie had been hired out to farmers from the age of nine. The farmers did not allow them to attend school on a regular basis. Eddie did not complain at the time, since he didn't like school much anyway. (His erratic attendance record can still be seen in the school's General Register.) Willie contracted frostbite while working at turnips in frosty weather and consequently many of his fingers were permanently damaged.

Eddie's sister Ellen had emigrated to the United States in the 1900s and had promised to send Eddie the ticket when he was ready to join her. When Eddie applied for admission some years later, he was rejected because he could not satisfy the newly introduced literacy requirements for immigrants.

By the 1930s, conditions for hired farm labourers on some farms were slightly better. Alice Donegan (born 1925) was the oldest of eight children of James Donegan, a packman (pedlar) who lived in Gallon Lower. According to Alice…

> I was still 13 when I went to the May hiring fair in Strabane. I was hired by Mr Stewart of Killydart until October for £8.00. I had to get up at 6.00am every morning. The first job was to clear out the kitchen range, light the fire, bring in the herd of cows and feed them nuts and help to milk them. Milking had to be finished by 7.00am. I then fed the fowl and washed enough potatoes to fill the farmyard boiler. I would then add

water and set the boiler's firebox going. The boiled potatoes would be used to feed the pigs in the evening.

I had breakfast at 8 o'clock, consisting of a cup of tea and porridge. I would then go out and do general farm work until 12.00 when I would come in for my dinner. There was only time to eat and wash the dishes, no time for relaxing.

After dinner I would do general farm work until 3.00pm when I would go in and bring out the tea to the three men working in the fields. I would bring in the cows for the milking which started at 4.00pm. I would milk five or six Friesian cows.

I would finish work at 6.00pm and get my tea, which would consist of plain bread and butter. After 6.00pm I would knit or stay around the farmyard, it was not the done thing for servant girls to go out walking. I was allowed home every other Sunday.'[14]

Right: Albert Hill of Glenock, one of the few dairy farmers in the area.

Below: Alice Donegan, (2000).

Jack McLaughlin, who grew up in Gallon, was hired by Charles McColgan of Gallon Upper in 1928, when he was just ten years of age.

> As a hired boy for the summer months, I got up at first light, as early as 4.00am, and let the cattle out of their byre. I drove them to the fields and herded them all day, keeping them out of the farmer's cornfield. I brought the cows in for milking just before 9.00am and went to school. After school, I returned to herding the cattle. I stayed out with the cows until dark (as late as 10.30pm) and then brought them in for milking.

The next year Jack worked with McGarveys of Gallon Upper under similar conditions and in the following years was hired on two different farms beyond Omagh. When he was fifteen he got a job as a ploughman on the Fyfe farm at Drumlegagh for a wage of £12 for six months.

From 1920 onwards, there was increased interest in milk production with the opening of the co-operative creamery at Newtownstewart. Up to this time most milk had been used in the cottage industry of butter-making, but the creamery ensured a sale for liquid milk. The opening of Nestle's milk factory at Omagh in 1945 led to the building of new byres and milk cooling houses on some farms. Milk production however, declined over the years, until by 1970 only one farm in Gallon was producing milk for sale. Similarly flax production reached its peak during World War I and World War II, but had disappeared entirely by the late 1950s.

Egg production was important from the 1930s until the 1960s; at its peak the McColgan farm in Meenawiddy was producing 2,500 eggs every week. Many farms had their own incubators and were able to hatch out a large number of chickens at the same time. However these days did not last; Gallon's farmers could not afford the high investment required to keep up with the intensive poultry farming which developed in other parts of Northern Ireland during the late 1960s, and commercial egg production in Gallon eventually disappeared.

Many farms reared turkeys and geese for the Christmas market. Some families also kept more exotic creatures, such as Muscovy ducks and guinea fowl, more as pets than for profit. The trapping of rabbits was a profitable sideline for farmers' sons in the 1940s and early 1950s, but the appearance of myxomatosis in the mid-1950s abruptly ended the trade.

World War II brought higher prices for farm produce and encouraged farmers to increase the productivity of their farms. Flax growing made a comeback,

The McColgan family (1990).

and almost every farm had at least one flax dam where the flax was soaked for several weeks. During the war, some families, such as Bradleys and Greggs of Gallon Lower made extra income by letting out rooms in their houses to evacuees from the cities.

Almost all farmers and even some cottiers had traditionally kept a pig or two, fed mainly on household waste. Some farmers, such as John McNamee and Eddie Bradley, increased their pig production significantly in the 1950s and 1960s. During the 1970s, however, most farmers found that the profits from this undertaking no longer justified the high outlay in feeding and caring for the animals, so pig production consequently decreased.

In the 1940s and 1950s, mixed farming was widely practised. Farmers planted seed potatoes and oats as cash crops and made hay to feed to the cattle over the winter. Cabbage and turnips were grown for home use and for sale. Some families kept goats, whose milk was thought to be free from diseases, which might be carried in untreated cow's milk. Sheep were not widely kept until

1957, when the McNamee brothers, John and Tommy, fenced in Gallon Mountain, allowing them to keep livestock on land which had not been fully utilised up to that time. All other farmers with traditional rights to grazing were allowed to keep a specified number of animals on the mountain.

Children, both boys and girls, were expected to help on the farm from an early age. In the spring, children would 'drop' the seed potatoes or fork manure in the drills. They would carry buckets of grain to the man sowing the oat crop. They planted vegetable seeds and kept the crop weeded. Hay was cut, put into lapps and later cocks before being built into stacks ('peaks') in the stack yard near the farmhouse.

Traditionally, the oldest son in a farming family was expected to leave school at 14 years and take on the duties of ploughman, opening and closing drills, digging potatoes, cutting grass and oats, etc.

The autumn was perhaps the busiest time, with the cutting, stooking and stacking of the corn crop and the gathering of potatoes. In winter, when some animals were kept indoors, they had to be brought hay and water twice each day. Apart from these duties, children also brought in the cows for milking each night, took food out to the men in the fields and sometimes 'herded' animals outdoors to prevent them straying into standing crops. The children of farmers who kept pigs often had to carry water to the pig houses every day and boil vast quantities of potatoes to feed the animals. Children seldom received, or expected, any recompense for their work: they accepted that these duties were a normal part of their lives.

CO-OPERATION BETWEEN NEIGHBOURS

Threshing was a farming activity which generated co-operation between neighbouring farmers, regardless of religion or politics. Apart from the owner of the machines, at least five other men were required to ensure that threshing day went smoothly:

> Two to fork the sheaves of oats from the stack to the top of the thresher,
> Two to cut the straps off the sheaves and feed them into the thresher,
> One to watch the grain as it came out of the back of the thresher, and make sure that the bags were changed and sewn up when they were filled.

Children from far and near were attracted to the noise and excitement of the threshing. Apart from watching the intricate operation of the machinery, they could join in the excitement as dogs chased rats and mice which were trying to escape as their homes in the corn stacks were destroyed. At the end of the day,

Mary Ann Bradley outside her son's house in Gallon Lower c 1930.

Henry and Rose Bradley, with children Tessie (in her father's arms) and Mary (hiding behind her mother). The boy in the background was a visitor. The photo was taken about 1930.

the workers would gather in the farmer's house for their supper, while outside the children played in the mounds of chaff. As darkness fell, poor people from the neighbourhood came and filled bags with chaff, which they used to stuff their home-made mattresses. When all the threshing had been done, the chaff was set on fire; neighbouring households would be treated to the sweet smell of burning chaff for the following two or three days.

Three men were required for turf-cutting, one to cut the turf with the turf-spade, one to reach for each pair of freshly cut turf and lift them out to the bank and a third man to shovel the turf a distance away in order to ensure that each individual turf had space to dry out.

Up to the 1940s, most farmers could afford to keep only one horse, which was sufficient for light farm work. When heavier work had to be done, such as ploughing or reaping oats, the farmer would borrow a horse from his neighbour and, later on he would loan his own horse to the neighbour in return.

The most frightening event of the year for farmers' children was the killing of the fatted pig. The pig butcher, either Willie Bradley or Albert McLaughlin, arrived on a Wednesday and laid out the gruesome tools of his trade at the pig house door. The door was lifted off the byre and placed on oil drums to make a table. Amid loud screams, the pig was stunned by a blow to its head with a cudgel. Its throat was then cut, and it was dragged out and placed on top of the table where the butcher and the farmer's helpers, using copious amounts of boiling water and sharp knives, shaved its entire body. The pig's innards were removed and the carcass was hung from the rafters of the scullery.

The next day the carcass was covered with a white cloth and sold at the pork market in Newtownstewart. The bladder was used by the local boys as a football and the liver was shared among the neighbours. Some families salted or smoked the pork and kept it for their own use, particularly at times when the price of pork was unacceptably low.

MECHANISATION

Mickey McAnena of Lower Gallon had owned a thresher and tractor before World War II and Charlie (Ginger) McNamee bought a tractor in 1936 which he used for contract work, but the first local farmer to buy a tractor solely for his own use was Tommy McNamee (senior) of Shannony East.

In the 1940s, Albert McIlwaine of Lislea cut most of the oats grown in Gallon with his binder, and Russell's steam thresher had been replaced by Willie Baxter's oil – powered machinery. After World War II, more and more local farmers bought their own binders and were able to cut their own crops.

In the years since World War II, Gallon's farmers have taken full advantage of government grants and subsidies in order to improve their land through draining, fencing, land reclamation and application of lime and fertiliser. Farmers' sons also attended night classes on agricultural skills held in Newtownstewart. Horsepower gave way to tractors in the late 1950s, and the more labour-intensive activities fell out of favour.

Up to the 1940s, most of Gallon's farmers produced milk for sale to the creamery in Newtownstewart or to Nestle's of Omagh. Over the years, government health regulations made greater demands upon farmers, who found that they had to build more modern byres and milk-cooling facilities in order to meet the new regulations.

The Dairy Shorthorn and the Aberdeen Angus were the most popular breeds of cattle on Gallon's farms until the 1960s, when newer breeds, such as the Limousin and Charolais began to appear, mainly through artificial insemination. Those farmers in milk production changed to Friesians around this time.

The most common breed of pig in the early part of the century was the Large White or York; the Landrace breed became popular in the 1960s. Similarly, the Texel has overtaken the Suffolk and Blackface breeds of sheep in popularity in the last thirty years.

Progressive mechanisation over the years gradually eliminated most of the backbreaking work from hay making. Since the 1960s the increasing popularity of silage harvesting on most farms has dramatically reduced the amount of the hay harvest.

The enjoyable activities associated with the oat harvest, such as cutting, stooking, stacking and threshing are no longer seen. Nowadays, the combine harvester deals with any corn crops in one dusty, noisy operation. Even turf cutting, which used to be a leisurely and companionable activity, is now carried on by very few farmers, and is done in a few hours by the turf-cutting machine.

The monthly fairs at Newtownstewart were replaced in the 1950s by marts for cattle, sheep and pigs organised by an auctioneer and held at purpose-built premises in the sale yard just across the old bridge from the town.

In the last three decades, arable cropping has declined drastically, and most land is now given over to sheep and cattle raising. The reduction in cropping combined with the rise in mechanisation in the last 40 years has led to a dramatic reduction in the number of people employed on the land. Almost all farm work nowadays is done by the farm families themselves, unless for specialised operations, such as silage making and sheep clipping, when contractors are often hired. Nowadays, farmers tend to employ specialist contractors to carry out work which formerly they did themselves, such as fencing, drainage and hedge-cutting.

KEEPING THE FARM IN THE FAMILY

Until the 1950s, very few Gallon people took the time to make a last will and testament. Usually, an older son had taken over the running of the farm long before his father's death and the other brothers and sisters did not dispute his

Next page: Statutory Declaration, prepared in order to assert Henry Bradley's ownership of his farm at Gallon Lower. This Declaration would refute the claims of his brothers and sisters, giving details of how they were all well established elsewhere.

Omagh
2/6

30/1/40

NORTHERN IRELAND
TWO SHILLINGS & SIX PENCE
31 1 40

STATUTORY DECLARATION.

I John Ross, of Glenock in the County of Tyrone, farmer aged 50 years and upwards hereby solemnly and sincerely declare

1. I was well acquainted with John Bradley of Gallon Lower who died on or about the 12th May, 1900 and I say that at the time of his death he left his widow and the following children him surviving:- William, Charles, John James, Henry, Maggie and Rose.

2. At the date of his death said John Bradley was tenant of a farm in Gallon Lower containing 24a. 1r. 38p. or thereabouts and deceased's widow and his son Henry still reside on the said farm. Deceased's son William emigrated to Australia on or about the 16th April, 1913 and returned about May, 1921 and shortly afterwards acquired a farm of his own where he has since resided. Deceased's son Charles emigrated to Australia in January, 1914 and returned when his brother William returned He has since acquired a farm of his own and resides thereon. Deceased's son John James left the farm and went to America about October, 1920 and has since remained there. Deceased's daughter, Maggie, was married in September, 1914 and since that date has ceased to reside on the farm and deceased's daughter Rose was married in November, 1918 and has since that date ceased to reside on the farm.

I make this Declaration conscientiously believing the same to be true and in pursuance of the Statutory Declarations act 1835.

John J. Ross

TAKEN and DECLARED this 29th day of January 1940 at Newtownstewart in the County of Tyrone before me a Justice of the Peace and I know the Declarant.

W Roche JP.
Newtownstewart

ownership. However, from time to time it was necessary to establish clearly the ownership of a farm, especially when a younger son had taken possession of the land. In such circumstances, a solicitor prepared a 'Statutory Declaration' which gave details of how the property came into the possession of the present occupier, and asserting that no other person had a valid claim on the land. Such declarations had to be signed by a responsible person who was acquainted with the all the relevant parties. Mr John Ross of Glenock was often called upon to sign these Statutory Declarations, and gained the reputation of being the guardian of the property rights of Gallon people.

CHAPTER 6: THE DEVELOPMENT OF COMMUNICATIONS

THE FIRST ROADS IN GALLON

Transport in prehistoric times had been along rivers, so the Newtownstewart area would have been an important route for individuals travelling north and south along the Foyle valley.

The earliest inhabitants of Gallon probably had to be content with tracks only wide enough for the passage of animals and pedestrians. The civil unrest of the early seventeenth century however, brought home to the government authorities the importance of good communications.

After the government's authority had been restored, disbanded soldiers from both sides of the conflict took to the hills and woods, robbing and harassing travellers and settled farmers alike. These robbers were known as "tories". Redmond O'Hanlan was one of the most infamous of these tories. One of his followers operated in the vicinity of Gallon in the middle of the seventeenth century:

> On Douglas Bridge I met a man, who lived adjacent to Strabane
> Before the English hung him high for riding with O'Hanlan.[1]

Sir William Stewart, (later Lord Blessington) boasted in 1683 that thirteen tories had recently been killed in County Tyrone.[2] Perhaps the Douglas Bridge tory was one of them!

Up until 1727, Gallon folk going into Newtownstewart had to cross the river by a ford just below Stewart's castle. In that year, the stone bridge was built across the Mourne to carry the main Dublin to Derry road, which at that time passed through Douglas Bridge.

Up to the middle of the eighteenth century, each landowner was expected to contribute to the county cess, which was intended to pay for the building and upkeep of county roads. Everyone was expected to work on the roads for six days each year without payment. However, this arrangement proved unsatisfactory. The Road Act passed by the Irish Parliament in 1765 permitted Ulster parishes to raise an extra parish cess to maintain minor public roads and towards the...

> making of narrow roads through the mountainous un-improved parts of this Kingdom.[3]

33. McCrea and Knox map showing roads through Gallon c 1813.

McCrea and Knox's map.

The map produced by William McCrea and George Knox in 1813 shows a road into Gallon from Glenock church and coming to an end at Meenawiddy. The first Ordnance Survey map of 1832/33 shows the Gallon Road complete from Glenock church to Koram hill on the Strabane-Plumbridge road. Magherabrack Road was also completed from Gallon Lower to Tullyherin.

The Gallonbridge Road across Gallon Lower, and the Crockatore Road, across Gallon Upper were completed later, perhaps as famine relief schemes. A road to connect Gallon Sessiagh with Gallon Upper near Gallon School was planned but was never built. There are, however, two private lanes with fords across the burn, which lead to Gallon Sessiagh: at Meenatumigan in Gallon Upper and at The Point in Gallon Lower. Pupils going to Gallon School crossed the Sessiagh Burn by a separate footbridge near the school.

CONTACTS WITH NEIGHBOURING TOWNS AND VILLAGES

Up to the beginning of the nineteenth century, anyone wishing to travel a distance had to walk, ride on horseback or hire a private jaunting car or coach. In 1805, a regular Mail Coach service was established between Derry and Dublin in both directions.

The Ordnance Survey Memoir by John Fleming Tait and J Hill Williams (c 1836) gives the following information about coaches which passed through Newtownstewart at that time:

> Royal Mail from Londonderry to Dublin, passes every day at 10.00am, from Dublin to Londonderry every day at 4.00pm.
> Shareholder (day coach) from Strabane to Dublin, passes on Monday, Wednesday and Friday at 6.40am and returns the other days except Sunday at 8.30pm.
> Wonder (day coach) from Omagh to Londonderry, passes every day (Sunday excepted) at 7.30am, returns same evening 7.30pm...
> Eclipse (day coach) from Omagh to Londonderry, passes every day (Sunday excepted) at 7.30am, returns same evening 7.30pm.[4]

Communications between Newtownstewart and the rest of Ireland were greatly improved with the opening of the Great Northern Railway in 1851, linking the town to Derry and Belfast.

Shirt stitching was an important home industry in Gallon in the last century, and Gallon girls within living memory have been known to walk with their completed work the six miles to Strabane once a week. Cattle would sometimes be walked to the fair at Strabane, in the hope of getting better prices than nearer home.

In more recent times, Plumbridge has been favoured by Gallon's farmers for the sale of sheep and cattle. Gallon men would meet at Dolly Ward's pub for a drink or two before starting the long walk home. In the years before motor transport became available to most people, the young people of Gallon would often cycle or even walk to dances held in the school at Legfordrum, or the parochial halls at Newtownstewart, Plumbridge, Gortin, Dregish, Drumquin or Knockmoyle. Older people would cycle to whist drives in the same places. During the summer months, young men and women from Gallon attended annual Sports Days held in Plumbridge, Cranagh, Gortin, Drumquin and Dregish.

Rows among neighbours all to often resulted in appearances at the County Court in Omagh. Children studying at grammar or technical schools in Omagh or Strabane caught the 7.55am train from Newtownstewart. In recent times many of Gallon's pupils have attended St Joseph's Secondary School in Plumbridge.

In the age of horse transport, genteel conveyance into Newtownstewart or to church on Sundays was by horse and trap. During the 1940s four families travelled down Gallon Road by horse and trap every Sunday: the Morris and

A fair day on the Main Street, Newtownstewart c 1900.

McColgan families from Gallon Upper, the Brogans from Tullyherin, and the McGillians from Legfordrum. The McGarveys of Gallon Upper had owned a trap in earlier years. Most of the congregation however walked to and from Mass every Sunday. In 1951 the McNamees of Shannony East became the first family in the Gallon area to own a motor car, but it was many more years before car ownership became widespread.

Henry Bradley's brother Charles and his family lived at Kingarrow, outside Omagh. During the 1950s, the Bradleys of Gallon Lower used to borrow Annie Morris' trap to visit their cousins every year on the 29 June, which was a church holiday. This outing required some preparation, because the horse had to be fitted with special horse shoes so that her feet would get a proper grip on the tarred road. However, those who took part in those outings have fond memories of them to this day.

The Gallon Road from Glenock Church to the crossroads above Gallon School was not tarred until 1951, and the remaining roads were tarred in 1956. In the 1970s, John Bradley of Lisnafin constructed a new road to connect his farm in Gallon Sessiagh with his other farm in Lisnafin. In more recent years, Mark McNamee build a road from Gallon Upper to Gallon Sessiagh, running close to Martin McGuigan's workshop.

CHAPTER 7: POPULATION GROWTH AND DECLINE

It appears likely that the population of Gallon remained static or even declined during the early and middle of the seventeenth century, due to the dislocation caused by the persistent wars of the period. However, there was a dramatic population increase throughout Ulster in the latter half of the eighteenth century, which no doubt was also reflected in Gallon.

The first census of population conducted in 1841 gives the population of the three townlands as 522 persons, the highest ever recorded. The highest recorded population of Gallon Upper was 300 persons in 1851, living in 55 houses. Lower Gallon had its highest recorded population in 1841, when it had 163 persons living in 28 houses. Gallon Sessiagh also had its highest recorded population in 1841, when it had 68 persons, living in 13 houses.

Gallon Upper and Gallon Lower both lost two thirds of their populations between 1841 and 1911. Gallon Upper lost 88 people between 1851 and 1871 and Gallon Lower lost 63 people between 1841 and 1851. Gallon Sessiagh's losses were more gradual. Perhaps Gallon Lower's cottiers were forced off the land earlier than those in Gallon Upper after the failure of the potato crops during the Great Famine.

Emigration was an important cause of the population decrease. In the early years of the present century, Gallon lost many of its young people to America and Australia. A few emigrants returned, having earned money abroad; Willie and Charles Bradley of Gallon Lower returned from Australia after eight years and purchased two farms, while Jack McConnell of Glenock spent many years in the United States, but returned to buy Robert Hill's farm at Gallon Lower. However, most of the emigrants never returned. Consequently, certain formerly extensive families, such as the Brogans and McGarveys, have entirely disappeared from Gallon.

The fate of the McGarvey families is worth noting. By 1901, the McGarveys had become the most extensive family grouping in Gallon. They owned a total of five houses and five farms between them as well as some other cottier houses. In 1935 the extended family still had five farms; yet by 1960 they had entirely disappeared from Gallon. Their disappearance was due to the younger members of the family emigrating and the reluctance of those who remained in Gallon to marry.

Opposite top: The Australian Bradleys. Back row, left to right, Barbera & Olive Frost, Ruth Dansie, Erica Harris. Front row, Theresa Munton, Harry Bradley (May 1991).

Opposite bottom: The Boston Bradleys. Their grandfather, John James Bradley left Gallon in the 1920s.

Right: Willie and Charles Bradley with a friend in Australia (1920s).

Below: Bradley family of Kingarrow, Omagh at the wedding of Annie to Michael McCullagh. The father of the family Charles Bradley had been brought up in Gallon Lower.

The fact that the populations of the three townlands did not experience a greater decline during the period 1911-1958 was probably due to the shortage of better quality housing elsewhere. The situation was most notable in the two decades after World War II, when the local authorities appeared unable or unwilling to provide new houses for those Gallon families who were living in severely sub-standard and generally overcrowded accommodation. The extent of overcrowding is discussed in greater detail in Chapter 8.

POPULATION OF GALLON 1841-2000[1]

UPPER GALLON

	INHABITANTS			HOUSES		
	Males	Females	Total	Inhab	Uninhab	Total
1841	147	144	291	50	10	60
1851	141	159	300	50	5	55
1861	129	121	250	48	4	52
1871	111	101	212	43	3	46
1881	101	92	193	42	2	44
1891	91	91	182	39	1	40
1901	67	69	136	28	6	34
1911	57	45	102	24	4	28
1935	52	37	89	20	1	21
1958	44	45	89	21	0	21
2000	25	17	42	16	1	17

GALLON LOWER

	INHABITANTS			HOUSES		
	Males	Females	Total	Inhab	Uninhab	Total
1841	65	98	163	28	4	32
1851	41	59	100	22	2	24
1861	52	57	109	23	6	29
1871	49	52	101	21	0	21
1881	36	41	77	15	1	16
1891	26	25	51	13	0	13
1901	22	28	50	12	0	12
1911	22	27	49	11	1	12
1935	22	27	49	11	1	12
1958	14	19	33	9	0	9
2000	7	6	13	3	2	5

GALLON SESSIAGH

	INHABITANTS			HOUSES		
	Males	Females	Total	Inhab	Uninhab	Total
1841	39	28	67	13	1	14
1851	30	19	49	9	0	9
1861	24	29	53	8	0	8
1871	21	22	43	8	0	8
1881	25	22	47	9	0	9
1891	16	16	32	7	0	7
1901	16	19	35	6	1	7
1911	17	15	32	5	2	7
1935	11	16	27	4	1	5
1958	4	8	12	4	1	5
2000	7	8	15	4	0	4

With the establishment of the Northern Ireland Housing Executive in late 1971, new houses were built in Newtownstewart, Omagh and Strabane and were allocated to many families from Gallon. It is estimated that the population of Newtownstewart rose from 1,129 in 1961 to 1,600 in 1986, partly as a result of the movement of people from the countryside. Proportional increases were experienced in Strabane and Omagh during the same period.

The table below shows the residence in 1994 of the cohort of Gallon's inhabitants who were enumerated in the unofficial 1958 census and were still alive.

Medal awarded to the family of Joseph Bradley who died in World War I.

RESIDENCE IN 1994 OF THOSE LISTED
IN THE 1958 UNOFFICIAL CENSUS.

	Residence (1994)		
	Males	Females	Total
Gallon	10	10	20
Newtownstewart	3	10	13
Omagh area	5	5	10
Strabane area	1	13	14
(inc Castlederg, Sion Mills)			
Coleraine, Limavady, Derry	1	2	3
Monaghan, Kildare, Cavan	2	1	3
England and Scotland	3	3	6
United States	1	3	4
Australia	1	0	1
Total size of the cohort	27	47	74

Twenty-four people who lived in Gallon in 1958 were still living there in 1994, but twice as many people were living elsewhere. The most significant destinations for those who left were Newtownstewart town and the Omagh and Strabane areas. Permanent emigration to Britain, Australia or the United States has not been such an important factor; a number of people actually lived for a time in Britain but did not settle permanently there.

In the forty odd years since 1958, the population of both Gallon Upper and Gallon Lower has been halved. Gallon Sessiagh has, however, shown a small increase. It is to be hoped that the population of the three townlands will stabalise at the present level, and there is some hope that this will be the case, given that there is a high proportion of young families living in the area.

Fortunately a number of young couples with family connections in the townland have renovated old farmhouses or built new houses and intend to bring up their families in the area.

CHAPTER 8: THE SEARCH FOR EMPLOYMENT IN THE LOCAL AREA AND ABROAD

Farming alone has never been able to keep all of Gallon's people in employment. Since the 1840s, numbers of Gallon people have left the area in search of work, many going as far as Australia and America, as has been described in Chapter 7. The majority of those who sought non-agricultural employment were without skills and took jobs as labourers or factory workers in Ireland or abroad, although a few were well educated and joined the professions or the religious life.

In the 1930s and 1940s, some Gallon farmers, such as the McColgans and McNamees, found additional employment during quiet periods of the year by working on road maintenance contracts for Tyrone County Council. They were contracted to maintain 20 miles of county road, filling potholes and cleaning outlets in the winter and cutting the grass in the summer. Additional non-farming employment was seen as a way of surviving the Depression of the 1930s, when the return from the sale of farm produce hardly met the cost of planting the crops. Many Gallon people emigrated to Britain and the United States during this period.

Since World War II, emigration from Gallon has continued, especially among non-farming families. Entire families have emigrated, establishing new homes in Britain or elsewhere. These emigrants often come 'home to Ireland' for their summer holidays.

Many young men and women worked in Scotland or England for a few years and returned home to settle. One of these was Pat McAnena of Gallon Lower. Pat had been living with his aunt and uncle, but when they died and the home was sold he decided to go to Scotland. He first found work with a farmer in Ayrshire and stayed there for eighteen months. In 1944, he then decided to accompany a friend to the hydro-electric scheme in the Highlands. He did not like his first job at the scheme where he was expected to scrub rocks twenty or thirty feet below ground level. He was glad when the general foreman asked him to move to the cement shed. This work was very well paid; he found himself earning £22 per week, good money for the time.

Minnie and Frances McLaughlin reared twelve children in a three roomed house in Gallon Lower. The 1935 census shows that all the children were still at home except Frances, the oldest son who had already emigrated. The 1958 census shows that Minnie was then living alone, her husband Francis (senior) had died and all the children had left home. The table below shows their place of residence in 1996 and their former occupations:

THE DISPERSAL OF THE MCLAUGHLIN FAMILY

Francis (junior)	Newcastle, England (labourer)
Jack	Newtownstewart (foreman)
Annie	Sydney (nurse)
Eileen	Duloy, Co Antrim (nurse)
Kathleen	died in Johnstone, Scotland (nurse)
Rosaleen	Coleraine (nurse)
Bridie	Huddersfield (nurse)
Jim	Newtownstewart (labourer)
Danny	Wales (foreman)
Monica	Canada (housewife)
Clare	Ballymena (secretary)
Philomena	Coleraine (secretary)

Sion Mill has provided employment for many of Gallon's young women since the 1950s. Maisie McCallion describes her career in the mill.

I left school in 1956 and got a job in Sion Mill on 11 December of that year. My father had died many years previously, and my mother worked for a few hours every week cleaning in Gallon school, but I was the first real wage earner in our family. I used to get up at 6.00am and have my breakfast. I would then walk to Newtownstewart; this would take me about an hour. I would catch the 7.30am bus for Sion and begin work at 8.00am. I had lunch from 12.30am until 1.15pm and finish at 5.45pm. The bus would leave me back in Newtownstewart at 6.15pm and I would walk home, arriving about 7.15pm.

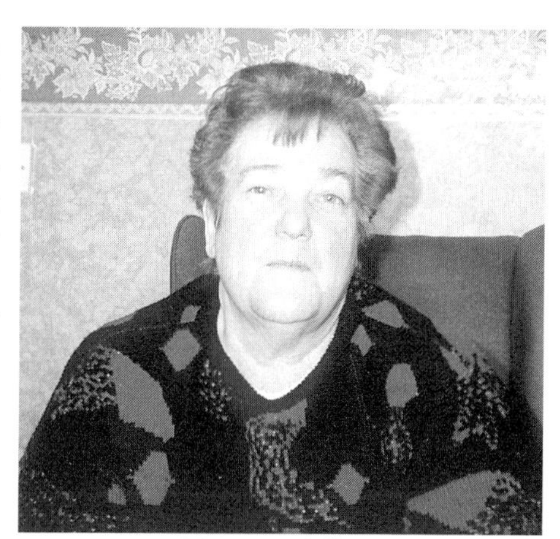

Maisie McCallion.

I was first trained to use the roving machine which made yarn for the spinning room but was transferred to the drawing machine which I have worked on ever since.

While I was training, I earned three pounds and ten shillings (£3.50) a week, rising to six pounds a week when I was fully qualified. I gave all my wages to my mother; she would give me enough money to go to the pictures on as Saturday night. I was working for two years before I had enough money to buy a bicycle. In later years, I was able to club up and hire a taxi with others who had to travel to Newtownstewart every day to catch buses.

Among those who worked in Sion Mills at that time were my sisters Maggie and Nora, Cassie and Kathleen O'Brien and Marian Browne. We had two weeks holiday in the year, in July. I got married in 1972 but I have worked in Sion Mills all my life. Some of my other friends worked in the Adria factory in Strabane.

The last fifty years have seen a dramatic reduction in the number of Gallon's inhabitants employed in agriculture. By 2000, no-one living in Gallon depends entirely upon farming for their livelihood.

Five farmers have been forced by economic necessity to take up other occupations, carrying out their farming chores in the evenings and at weekends. An example of one such farmer is Charles McColgan, who is a plumber during business hours but a farmer in the evenings. A number of full-time farmers who live outside Gallon own farms or rent out land for farming in Gallon. One such farmer, Brian Mullan, actually lives in the town of Strabane.

The 2000 census shows the occupations of Gallon's inhabitants, and provides a stark contrast with the figures for 1901 (See Chapter 5).

OCCUPATIONS OF INHABITANTS OF GALLON IN 2000

	Gallon Upper	Gallon Lower	Gallon Sessiagh	Total
Professionals (nurse, accountant, etc)	4	1	0	5
Tradespeople (plumber, carpenter, etc)	2	0	1	3
Farmers and unskilled workers	19	4	6	29
Retired farmers	5	1	0	6
Scholars and infants	12	7	8	27

The table above does not attempt to measure the levels of unemployment among Gallon's inhabitants. Many of those who are officially unemployed may, however, undertake casual employment as it arises. A valuable new source of employment in Gallon is Martin McGuigan's workshop in Gallon Upper, which manufactures items for the construction industry.

In 2000, twenty three individuals own farms in Gallon, compared to fifty-seven in 1859. Only eleven of these landowners actually live in Gallon: this helps to explain why there are no full-time farmers in the table above.

CHAPTER 9: THE COMMUNITY AND ITS TRADITIONS

A PLACE APART

Gallon has always had a distinct character. The fact that Gallon had its own school from 1831 until 1969 and its own shop for many years, together with the lack of transport, meant that the children of the area had little contact with Newtownstewart children. Gallon people did not even have to go into town to attend Mass on Sundays, since the church was almost a mile outside the town in the same direction as Gallon. Being allowed into Newtownstewart unaccompanied was a special event for Gallon children and occurred only on special events, such as St Patrick's Day.

The three townlands, Gallon Upper, Gallon Lower and Gallon Sessiagh were seen as an entity, and the inhabitants thought of themselves as Gallon people rather than Newtownstewart people. In fact anyone who turned up the Gallon Road at Glenock Church was taken to be from Gallon, even if they lived in Glenock, or even further afield in Shannony East, Legfordrum or Beaghs.

Three public houses in Newtownstewart, the Castle Bar, the Castle Hotel and McBride's Bar were favoured by Gallon men, especially on Saturday nights and on fair days. Gallon men invariably gathered in a group outside Glenock Church each Sunday morning, discussing crops and farm prices, and they tended to occupy adjoining pews in the gallery of the church during Mass.

In the early years of the present century, Gallon had its own football team, which was a match for any team that Newtownstewart could produce, if not in footballing skill, at least in pugilistic ability. Gallon School also had a tug-of-war team, which gained considerable success at the parish sports during the 1950s.

ORANGE AND GREEN POLITICS

The vast majority of Gallon's inhabitants have always been predominantly nationalist / republican in politics. Around the beginning of the twentieth century there was a renewed interest in the Irish language and Gaelic culture. Irish language lessons conducted in Gallon school were well supported, and for a time, Gallon could field a Gaelic football team. A number of Gallon's young men joined the Irish Volunteers and were involved on the republican side during the Troubles of 1919–1921. They drilled with wooden rifles on a flat field on the northern edge of Gallon Lower known as "the Island".

Republican courts had been set up in the Gortin area, but their influence did not extend to the main river valleys and they failed to win the respect of the wider nationalist community. Attacks were carried out on police barracks and roads were trenched sporadically, but poor discipline, a shortage of weapons and ammunition and the lack of initiative shown by the leadership meant that Irish Volunteer activity was not extensive.[1]

The Duke of Abercorn at that time was a prominent supporter of the Ulster Volunteer Force, and the local unit of the Irish Volunteers believed that UVF weapons were stored in a coach house at Baronscourt Castle. A lieutenant in the Irish Volunteers who lived in Gallon described many years later how a raid had been carried out on the castle in May 1920:

> In the middle of the month of May 1920, I remember going to a house in Mill Street, Newtownstewart that was used as the Sinn Fein Club Rooms and for Irish Volunteer meetings. Most of the men had left before I got there. I still remember two or three cardboard boxes that held revolver cartridges. I went with a few of the others to the Wood Hills and joined the main party of Volunteers and remained there till darkness. I can still see the bluebells in the spaces between the trees. Arms were distributed; the one I got was, I think, a blunderbuss, a muzzleloader with a long barrel and a heavy brass butt. There was no ammunition for it and I was told that if it came to be required I was to hold the barrel and use the butt. I saw that a few of our men had revolvers, but there were no rifles or shotguns.
>
> When it got dark, we set off in single file and I got a glimpse of our captain wearing a volunteer uniform with pleats in the back. He had some boot polish on his face. I heard orders to two men to watch Crow's cottage. There was some talk of poisoning the guard dogs at the castle and whiskey for a man called Young who it appears, was the only watchman at the castle that night. I think that the Duke was not in residence at the time. The men with me had a revolver and we were posted at the main entrance. We had to look out for volunteers from Douglas Bridge and Strabane. Others were sent to meet the men from Carrickmore on the road near where Envagh school is now.
>
> Towards midnight the cars came in and work started. I was not up near the doors but there was a great noise of timber and glass being smashed. The horses in the stables became frightened and kept up a great deal of stamping. In due course the all-clear was passed along and each company fell in and started for home.

> We were a bit disappointed as there were no arms to be got; of course there were some old swords and some of them were taken as souvenirs.
>
> The exercise was valuable to the morale of the Volunteers and it showed that men could be brought together at short notice without the knowledge of the Crown Forces. I remember the next day going into the RIC barracks in Mill Street to enquire about a Sugar Card. The door of the barracks was chained so that it could only open about nine inches.
>
> Soon after that (the policemen) went in twos or threes on their patrols.
>
> For security reasons, no names are mentioned but no ex-British soldiers were involved. There are still about a dozen survivors of the raid alive today. (Written in 1970).[2]

The acceptance by the Irish Free State government that Tyrone should become part of the new Northern Ireland state was seen by many nationalists and republicans as a betrayal, resulting in a general disillusionment with constitutional politics, which persisted for the next fifty years.

The fact that Gallon was within the predominantly Protestant Moyle ward of Omagh Rural District Council meant that local representation was always in unionist hands from 1921 until the 1970s. The local Member of Parliament for North Tyrone in the Northern Ireland Parliament was invariably a unionist. There was a perception that Catholics were disadvantaged by their religion in applying for employment and local authority housing.

Meanwhile, young men whose sympathies lay with the Northern Ireland Government found part-time employment in a new police reserve force, known as the 'B Specials', which were set up in 1920 to counter republican insurgency. Leading members of the 'B Specials' in those early days were Sam Monteith of Gallon Upper, Eddie Hunter and Bobby Gordon of Tullyherin and Joe and David John McConnell of Grange. Their patrols on bicycle along the roads and lanes of Gallon were viewed with a mixture of amusement and resentment.

For many years there has been a well supported Orange Lodge in Strawletterdallan (Strawhill). The Strawletterdallan Pipe Band is also based at the lodge. In the summer evenings, those who were working in the fields of Gallon Lower used to enjoy listening to the band as it marched along the roads of Crosh practising for the forthcoming marching season. Many of the band's tunes, such as 'The Green Glens of Antrim' and 'Scotland the Brave' were well known to the Gallon listeners. St Eugene's AOH Accordion Band from Newtownstewart sometimes practised along the Gallon Road, but their music did not carry as far as the Strawletterdallan Pipe Band.

A group of 'B Specials' photographed at Newtownstewart c 1923. The 'B Specials' were set up in 1920 to counter the activities of the Irish Volunteers.

Strawletterdallan Orange Hall

Membership of the Orange Order seldom effected the good relationships between Catholics and Protestants in the Gallon area. A notable (but not unusual) example of friendship between neighbours of differing religious and political views was that between Henry Bradley of Gallon Lower and Andy John Graham of Strawletterdallan. Andy John was an elder of the Presbyterian church, a member of Strawletterdallan Orange Lodge and a long serving 'B Special'. Henry was a staunch Catholic and an ardent republican, yet two or three nights every week Andy John and his son Johnny ceilidhed[3] in Bradley's house.

On one of his visits to Bradley's house, Andy John surveyed the Bradley girls who were all sitting around in the warm kitchen, doing their homework or sewing. After some thought, he turned to his friend Henry and said, very seriously and rather regretfully:

> It's a fine lot of daughters you have here, Henry. Indeed I tell you, any one of them would do our Johnny rightly. Isn't it a pity that they're all the wrong sort! (i.e. the wrong religion)

When Henry Bradley was incapacitated in the spring of 1944, following an accident, it was Andy John who completed the planting of the spring crops on the Bradley farm. Andy John and Johnny Graham helped every year at the corn threshing on the Bradley farm, and Henry and Eddie Bradley helped the Grahams when their threshing day came around.

Andy John's daughters, Sarah, Ethel and Dorothy sustained their friendship with the Bradley sisters over many years, even though they had moved away from the area.

All neighbouring farming families co-operated closely in the activities which required additional manpower, such as ploughing, turf-cutting, harvesting and threshing, irrrespective of religious differences. Catholic and Protestant neighbours joined to console each other at wakes and funerals, although until the 1960s Catholics were not encouraged to enter Protestant churches, even for funerals.

Ethel and Sarah Graham, Annie Black, Cissie Monteith and John Black take a tea break from gathering potatoes. (c 1950).

Protestant children living in Gallon or its vicinity attended Gallon Primary School, although their numbers were always quite small. Their numbers were boosted for a short time during World War II, when three families which had been evacuated from Belfast came to live locally. Protestant pupils were allowed to start school half an hour later than the Catholics; this allowed time for the teacher to take religious education with the Catholics.

Andy John Graham and his wife Annie on their wedding day, 1916.

According to the 1901 census, there were eight Protestants living in Gallon and five farms were owned by Protestants. By 1958 there were only two Protestants still living in Gallon and both were tenants, without any property in the townland. Three non-residential farms still belong to Protestants up to the present but all three farmers live on their main farms some distance from Gallon. The fact that there are no Protestants living in Gallon at present should not be seen as a mark of sectarian sentiments; relations between Protestants and Catholics in the Newtownstewart area have been consistently good, even during the past thirty years which saw sectarianism emerge in other areas.

The wedding of Sarah Graham and Sam Hill, with best man Henry Palmer and bridesmaid Dorothy Graham (1959).

Dorothy Parke (Graham) and Johnny Graham (2000).

CEILIDHING, BIG NIGHTS, WAKES AND STATIONS

One of the strongest traditions, which existed very strongly in Gallon up to the television age, was that of ceilidhing. Some houses, such as Peggy Morris' in Meenawiddy, were well known for card-playing and players would travel considerable distances to play 'Twenty Five' and Poker in her house every Monday night during the 1950s and 1960s.

Dances were sometimes held in barns bringing the neighbours together for a special reason. A number of dances were held in Annie Morris' barn in the 1940s, and a special dance was held in Bradley's barn in Gallon Lower in 1948, a few days before Mary Quinn emigrated to the United States.

Any house with daughters of marriageable age was seen as a place where eligible young men with good prospects were always welcome. 'Big nights', with music and singing, were arranged without undue formality, often arising spontaneously because one or two musicians happened to arrive on the same night. Notable traditional fiddlers who played in Gallon during those years included Seamus Morris and Eddie Bradley. Freddie Young, who worked on Neil McAnena's farm at that time, was a notable singer. During 1960, 'big nights' to celebrate weddings were held in Caldwell's and McClure's houses in Gallon Upper.

The last old-style barn dance in Gallon was held in Neil McNamee's new hayshed in 1968. Music was provided by Hugh Morris, and Robbie McClure was one of the singers. The seating consisted of straw bales, timber planks and long forms from Gallon School. Everyone had a good time, and the dance continued until dawn, but it was several days before the most enthusiastic dancers recovered from the effects of dancing all night on the concrete floor!

In nearby Strawletterdallan, parties were held in Ross' house to celebrate the end of the corn harvest in early September, and the potato harvest at Hallowe'en. The young men and women who had worked on the neighbouring farms were welcome to attend these parties, where the music for dancing was provided by Johnny Ross on his accordion. Alex Sproule of Glenock and Billy McNicholl of Ballynasollus sang on these occasions.

McColgan's of Meenawiddy were the first family to own a wireless in the 1930s. McAleer's of Meenaheap soon acquired a set, and the house used to be crowded on Sundays to listen to Gaelic football matches broadcast from Athlone (Radio Eireann).

Some houses, such as Bradley's of Gallon Lower or McLaughlin's of Glenock bought 'wind-up' gramophones in the 1940s and could have music for dancing and entertainment even when no fiddler was available. Another outlet for musical ability was St Eugene's AOH Accordion Band, based in Newtownstewart. Paddy Maguire of Gallon Lower was for a time the leader of this band.

A death in Gallon was marked by a wake, usually lasting two nights, when neighbours visited the house to sympathise with the bereaved family. During the day, the neighbours helped the people of the house to get everything ready for the wake. The menfolk made sure that the farmyard was tidy and that the animals were looked after.

Maggie Quinn (O'Brien) and Mary Patton (1939).

All those who attend the wake were given a cup of tea and perhaps a sandwich. Wakes were not always sad affairs. Once the visitor has paid his respects to the bereaved, he usually engaged in conversation with the other visitors to the wake. In former times, clay pipes, tobacco and snuff were distributed. Clay pipes gradually gave way to cigarettes in the mid 1940s and nowadays, with the awareness of the health dangers of smoking, the provision of cigarettes is on the decline.

A small group of neighbours or relations usually sits up with the deceased and members of the immediate family during the two nights of the wake. The funeral is held after 11.00am Mass in Glenock church.

Before the age of mass entertainment, wakes were considered as potentially enjoyable social occasions, especially by the younger generation. In former times, games were sometimes played at wakes in Gallon. These were most likely to be played at wakes of old people, where the death was not unexpected. The last known occasion when games were played at a wake in Gallon was in 1946, at the wake of John James Quinn of Gallon Sessiagh. Bernard McColgan took part in the games:

> The leader of the games was Paddy McAnally. Others who took part included my brother Gerald McColgan and myself, Hugh Morris, Pat

Photo of AOH band, Newtownstewart.

McAnena, Mickey McNamee, Denis Devenney, Eddie McConnell, Cecil O'Neill and Dan McLaughlin.

Many of the games played at wakes in Gallon up to the 1950s were similar to games described by William Carleton, who was writing about customs in Tyrone in the early years of the nineteenth century.

> The next play they went to was the Sitting Brogue. This is played by a ring of them, sitting down upon the bare ground, keeping their knees up. A shoemaker's leather apron is then got, or a good stout brogue, and sent round under their knees. In the mane (sic) time, one stands in the middle; and after the brogue is sent round, he is to catch it as soon as he can. While he stands there, of course, his back must be to some one, and accordingly those that are behind him thump him right and left with the brogue, while he, all the time, is striving to catch it. Whoever he catches this brogue with must stand in his place, while he sits down where the other had been and then the play goes on as before.[4]

Bernard McColgan recalls that this game was known in Gallon as 'Hunt the Brogue'. The person caught with the brogue was smeared with soot before taking his place in the middle to allow the game to continue.

Many of the games followed similar lines; the leader asked the players to undertake a variety of tasks or to give correct responses. If the players failed to do so in the allotted time, they were punished; their faces would be smeared with soot from the open chimney or even cow dung from the byre.

Carleton describes another game, called 'Horns'.

> A droll fellow takes a lump of soot or lamp-black, and after fixing a ring of the boys and girls about him, he lays his two fore-fingers on his knees and says, 'Horns, horns, cow horns!' and then raises his fingers by a jerk above his head; the boys and girls in the ring then do the same thing, for the meaning of the play is this: the man with the black'ning always raises his fingers every time he names an animal; but if he names any that has no horns, and that the others jerk up their fingers, then they must get a stroke over the face with the soot... 'Horns, horns, goat horns!' – then he ups with his fingers like lightening; they must all do the same, bekase a goat has horns. 'Horns, horns, horse horns' he ups them again, but the boys and girls ought not bekase a horse has not horns; however, any one that raises them then, gets a slake. So that it all comes to this;– Anyone who lifts his fingers when an animal is named that has no horns – or anyone that does not raise them when a baste is mentioned that has horns, will get a mark.

In another game, the participants were expected to imitate the deliberately complicated actions of the leader. In the game 'Shoe the Donkey' the leader called out: 'Cock in the corner is selling oats. How much money have you got?' Everyone had to call out a price immediately when asked, eg 10 pence, 18 pence, etc. In yet another game, the players were given parts of an animal's body, the less fortunate individuals being given embarrassing parts. When their turns came, the players had to call out the parts immediately or risk punishment.

Mock religious ceremonies were also carried out as part of the games at wakes in Gallon, where someone dressed up as a priest and pretended to marry young couples. These activities were also described by William Carleton.

Another interesting custom, general throughout the Derry Diocese, was the collecting of 'offerings' at funerals. The closest relations of the deceased were expected to contribute most, typically £1 in the 1950s, while neighbours gave amounts ranging from five to ten shillings. The money collected was kept by the priest and used to help to run the parish. The number of people attending the wake and the amount of money collected at the funeral could measure a dead person's standing in the community. The collection of 'offerings' at funerals was abolished in the 1960s.

The 'Stations' is a tradition which is very much alive in the Gallon area, when the Parish Priest arranges to say Mass in private houses during the spring and autumn and all the neighbours are welcome to attend. The custom may have originated in the seventeenth and eighteenth centuries, when there were very few Catholic churches. It had died out in the Ardstraw East parish, but was reintroduced by the parish priest Fr Campbell in the 1920s.

Each house would have the Stations every third or fourth year, according to rota. Preparations were often elaborate in a community which normally had neither the resources nor the inclination to be house-proud. The dwelling house would be whitewashed or painted both outside and inside, and re-thatched if necessary. The farmyard was tidied up and all timber and ironwork would be given a fresh coat of paint. Although they might complain of the extra work involved, most housewives were secretly proud to be chosen for the Stations, and glad that their husbands would be forced to devote some time and money to the appearance of the house and the farmyard.

After Mass had been said, the priest collected the stipend. Every household represented at the Stations was expected to give a contribution. A few of the neighbours would remain in the Station house to share the traditional breakfast of bacon, eggs and sausages with the priest. Sometimes the Stations were held at night, especially where members of the family were out at work during the day. Neighbours tended to stay longer at evening Stations and sometimes there was singing and dancing.

SEASONAL CUSTOMS

Eggs were saved up for weeks before Easter to make sure that there was an ample supply for every member of the family on the big day. 'Easter houses' were built by erecting low stone walls to shelter a temporary fireplace. If the weather was fine the eggs would be boiled and eaten outside. There would often be keen rivalry to see which of the childlren could eat the most eggs. Chocolate eggs had been available earlier, but did not become popular until the 1960s.

In the last few Sundays in October, the local children would go 'down the burn' to gather nuts in the hazel woods along the Glenock Burn. Apples and nuts would also be bought in the Newtownstewart shops. The usual Hallowe'en games were played, including tying an apple up by a string and seeing who could take the biggest bite, and floating apples in a basin of water. In houses that still had an open fire, two large hazel nuts would be set up beside the fire. These two nuts represented two people who were rumoured to 'have a notion of each other'. If the nuts stayed close together, that was a sign that the relationship would flourish. If, however, as sometimes, happened, the two nuts sprang apart, that was a sign that nothing lasting would come out of the relationship.

In early December, groups of mummers visited houses in Gallon. These were groups of young men dressed in very tall straw hats which hid their faces, and coats tied around the waist with straw ropes. They were so well disguised that, to the present day, those who watched them perform can only guess at their true identities. The Ross brothers of Strawletterdallan and their friends were among the most dedicated mummers in the 1950s, with Johnny Ross playing his accordion. There was also a group of mummers from Legfordrum. Younger children would be frightened because of the mummers' appearance and the antics which they performed as part of their play. Usually there would be six or seven in the full company, Jack Straw Striddle, Devil Doubt, Brian Boru, Beelzie Bub, a Doctor and a few others who were not named.

Their words and actions were usually as follows:

THE MUMMER'S PLAY

Jack Straw Striddle was the first to come in.
'Here comes I, Jack Straw Striddle,
Kissed the devil through a riddle, through a reel, through an old spinning wheel, through a barrel of pepper, through a mill hopper, through a bag of salt. If you don't believe what I say here comes Devil Doubt.'

Devil Doubt comes in.
'Here comes I, Devil Doubt, the biggest wee devil was ever let out. If you don't believe what I say, enter in Brian Boru and he'll soon clear the way.'

Brian Boru comes in.
'Here comes I, Brian Boru, from Ireland I have sprung. I have conquered many nations since this world first begun. I fought the jolly Normans, I chased the Danes away'...

Beelzie Bub comes back in and interrupts Brian Boru, saying:
'You're a liar, sir. Here comes I Beelzie Bub and under my arm I carry my club. And in my hand I carry my pan and I think I am a jolly good fighting man.'

'Take out your sword, and fight' says Brian Boru.
Proceed to battle with swords, Belzibum and Brian Boru.

Beelzie Bub and Brian Boru fight. Brian kills Belzie Bub..
'Murder, murder what have I done? I have killed my sister's only son! Five pounds for a doctor, ten pounds for a doctor. Is there a doctor to be had?

The doctor comes in carrying a small case. He gives Beelzie Bub snuff from a snuff box. Beelzie Bub recovers... An un-named character comes in, carrying a tin for collecting money.

I'm the man that collects the money. All silver, no brass, bad money won't pass. Money I want, money I crave. If you don't give me money I'll sweep you all to your grave'.

The accordion player plays a few tunes, the actors sing a few songs together and leave. They might, surreptitiously take away a freshly baked loaf of bread or something eatable from the kitchen with them on the way out.

Preparations for Christmas on the farms of Gallon in the 1950s and 1960s were often frantic. Turkeys, geese had to be slaughtered and plucked for sale to

Pat McAnena's former home, Gallon Lower.

the butchers in the town, and special provisions had to be purchased for the festival. Christmas Day itself was one of the few days in the year when the fire in the sitting room was lit, and games of cards were played all day. Broth would be eaten at midday, with the main meal at 'delfal' (nightfall). Up to the 1950s, many families ate goose for the Christmas dinner, but this was gradually replaced by turkey in later years.

THE TRADITIONAL GALLON HOUSE

During the second half of the nineteenth century, the 'traditional Gallon house' gradually became the norm, replacing earlier single roomed houses or byre dwellings. In his book 'Rural Houses of the North of Ireland', Alan Gailey points out that byre dwellings had been in widespread use throughout rural west Ulster in the early nineteenth century.

> The mildness of the climate over most of Ireland permits keeping sheep and dry cattle outdoors at most times, but milk cattle need housing in winter and during the night in spring and autumn. On the relatively small peasant farms in much of Ulster in the past, many farmers had only four or five milk cows at most which could easily be accommodated in one end of a byre dwelling.[5]

It is likely that the extension or abandonment of the single-roomed houses and byre dwellings and their replacement by two-roomed houses (with bed outshot) occurred in the latter half of the nineteenth century. Sometimes two attached houses were converted into one house, as happened with the Morris house in Meenawiddy.

The earliest systematic record of the quality of housing in Gallon appears in the 1901 census, which shows that all but two of the dwelling houses occupied at that time had only two rooms and two windows to the front. These, one may assume, were 'traditional Gallon' houses.

The two rooms were referred to as the 'kitchen' and the 'room'. Every traditional house had an 'outshot'. This was an outward extension of the back wall of the kitchen. The outshot contained a bed, which was often used by the parents of the family.

The outshot bed was concealed from the remainder of the kitchen by a curtain. The remaining furniture in the kitchen consisted of a large table, located under the window, three or four home-made chairs, and a number of home-made stools. These stools would be taken out to the byre at milking time. The room contained one or more beds, depending on the number of people living in the house. The mattress (tick) consisted of flour bags sewed together and stuffed with chaff collected during the autumn threshing season. The male and female portions of the room were sometimes separated by a curtain.

Almost all traditional houses were thatched. On top of the roof timbers there was a layer of sods ('scraws') which provided insulation and anchorage for the final part of the roof. The outer covering of the roof consisted of barley or flax straw, held in position by bent wooden pins ('scollops') driven into the scraws.

Most houses had two windows to the front of the house and two windows in the back with no back door. Because of the small windows, the interiors were never really bright. If she wanted more daylight, the housewife would have to leave the front door open, depending on the closed half door to keep out the farmyard livestock, hens, turkeys or piglets. This meant that the kitchen could not be really warm in cold weather.

At night the kitchen was lit by candles or by lamps which burned paraffin oil. The lamps would not be lit until the house was well and truly dark. Anyone wishing to have a light in the 'room' would use a candle. On bright evenings, during the summer months, lamps would often not be lit at all.

Some houses still had clay floors until the 1930s, when they were replaced by paved or concrete floors which were swept several times each day with a heather broom. The centrepiece of the kitchen was the dresser, the top part of which contained particularly valuable crockery, such as large willow pattern plates. Bowls

The dresser in the kitchen of Pat McAnena's house.

and soup plates for everyday use were placed on lower shelves. Cups were only used for special occasions. The bottom part of the dresser was used for storing foodstuffs such as bread, flour and eggs.

Beside the dresser stood the churn, which was used for making butter. There was also a tea chest or a bin for storing meal. Above the fire was a shelf, on which were placed items which would suffer from dampness, such as tea and sugar. There was often a special box for storing salt hanging from its own nail beside the fire.

HOUSING AND LIVING CONDITIONS IN THE FIRST HALF OF THE TWENTIETH CENTURY

According to the Census of 1901, the largest house in Gallon had six rooms and five windows to the front. This house belonged to Robert Hill of Gallon Lower. The smallest house was also in Gallon Lower, and belonged to Alice (Allie) McAnena. She only had one room, with one window. Only two houses were slated at that time, Robert Hill's and John James Bradley's; the latter had built a new two-roomed house in 1894. He was one of the last householders in Gallon to 'better himself' by moving into a new house in the nineteenth century. He substituted slates for thatch, but apart from that his house was built in the traditional style including a small outshot.

Pat McAnena sitting at the fire (1996).

Most of the traditional houses listed in the 1901 census continued in use with minor modifications, until the 1970s. In many cases, however, corrugated iron or asbestos sheeting replaced the thatch. Normally the thatch was removed, but in one house at least, the thatch was retained and the iron roof was fixed on top of it. Apart from the inevitable fire hazard, which is associated with a thatched roof, an iron roof on top of thatch gave the advantages of heat insulation and noise proofing. In a number of instances, porches were built on to the front of the two-roomed houses to reduce heat loss, and sometimes a water tap was installed.

From 1910 onwards, the local authorities were encouraged to build labourer's cottages in rural parts of Ireland. In return for a nominal rent, the fortunate tenant had a comfortable three or four-roomed house with a slated roof and a large garden, intended to be large enough to provide sufficient potatoes and vegetables to feed the family. Only one of these cottages was ever built in Gallon, at Crockatore in 1924, although there had been plans to build further cottages near the same location.

ANALYSIS OF FAMILY AND HOUSE SIZES, 1935 AND 1958

	1935 House size			
Family size	One room	Two rooms	Three rooms	4/5 rooms
1	1	3	0	0
2	1	5	0	0
3	0	5	0	0
4	0	2	0	0
5	0	1	1	0
6	0	1	1	1
7	0	2	1	0
8	0	0	1	2
9	0	2	0	0
10	0	1	0	1
11	0	0	0	1

	1958 House size			
Family size	One room	Two rooms	Three rooms	4/5 rooms
1	2	7	1	0
2	0	2	1	0
3	0	1	1	0
4	0	3	0	3
5	0	3	0	1
6	0	1	1	0
7	0	2	0	0
8	0	0	0	0
9	0	1	1	1
10	0	0	1	0

Very few new houses were built in Gallon in the first half of the twentieth century. Henry Bradley of Gallon Lower build a 'two up, two down' house on his marriage in 1926 and doubled its size in 1931. Another two-up two down house was built in Magherabrack in the 1930s but there were no further dwelling houses built in Gallon until the 1970s.

Large families and small houses led to many instances of overcrowding in Gallon as the 'census' of 1935 illustrates: one two-roomed house was home to nine people, eight people lived in another two-roomed house and five further houses with only three rooms held eight or more people in each. In 1958 a two roomed house in Gallon Lower was home to a family of nine, and three house houses with only two rooms held six or more people in each.

Living conditions for the inhabitants of Gallon were still outdated by the standards of townsfolk up to the 1970s. Mains water, electricity and modern sanitation were relatively unknown, even in the houses of the more prosperous farmers. Work on the farm and in the home was often tedious, backbreaking and time-consuming, leaving little time for leisure. After a hard day's work, Gallon folk sat on kitchen chairs around the fire. The everyday use of armchairs at that time was almost unknown.

Drinking water for many houses had to be carried in buckets from local spring wells, sometimes a considerable distance away. The well was shared by several families, and going to the well could be a social occasion, (akin to going to the corner shop for townsfolk) when one could expect to meet a neighbour and hear some of the local gossip. The drinking water was carried home in special buckets and kept in a cool, clean place along with the cow's milk. The spring well was treated with great respect and was cleaned out and limed regularly to ensure the purity of the water. A neighbour, who was lucky enough to have a cure, would lead children suffering from ailments such as chicken pox or mumps in a horse's halter to the well. The most reliable well in Gallon was Crockatore well, which has never been known to dry up, even during the most prolonged drought.

'Rough water', for domestic animals or for washing, was collected in barrels under downpipes from slated or corrugated iron roofs or from streams. In dry weather, the streams and rough water wells often dried up, and the inhabitants would find themselves drawing water from the nearest burn. In those days, therefore, water was always used with care and the same basin of water would be used by several members of a family to wash their hands at the end of a day's work.

Bathrooms were unknown and children were often washed in a tin bath in front of the kitchen fire. In hot weather, adventurous children bathed in the Glenock burn, which had a firm pebble bed and clean, unpolluted water. Lavatories were not normally built; the stable or the byre was often used as a substitute. A visitor from the United States in 1952 caused consternation when he asked Joe McAnena if he could use his lavatory. Joe, who was hard of hearing, thought he said 'library' and he wondered where, in his two-roomed house, he was expected to have a library!

John Devine's house. Pat McAnena built the one roomed house for John in Gallon Lower in the 1960s.

Unless a range was installed, all cooking was done on the open fire in the kitchen, using large pots. These were hung from iron links, which were suspended from a crane swinging above the fire. Pots were lowered or raised, according to the stage at which the cooking was proceeding. Soda bread, farls and indian and bran bread were baked on the griddle. 'Purdy pudding' was made from mashed potatoes, spices, milk and occasionally raisins and was cooked for hours in a pot oven over the open fire.

The family often had boiled eggs and bread for breakfast, or sometimes porridge. The mid-day meal during the week was often bacon and cabbage, followed by rice or semolina for dessert on special occasions. There was bread and tea at teatime and sometimes "ponade" was made for supper by boiling crusts of bread with milk and sugar. Chickens which had ceased to produce eggs were culled by thrifty housewives and cooked for Sunday lunch; but, on other occasions, cheap cuts of beef was bought from the butcher in Newtownstewart.

From the 1960s onward, a few householders installed bottled gas as a replacement for tilley lamps or oil lamps. The gas lamp was not quite as bright as the tilley lamp, but was much easier to light and brighter than the older style of oil lamp. However, the old hurricane lamp was still required for going out to look at sick animals at night!

Joe McAnena (1955).

Once installed, gas could be used for cooking and ironing. The gas iron displaced the box iron which had to have its inner metal block heated until red hot in the coals of the fire and then placed inside its metal box; a laborious task for a busy housewife.

Up until the 1950s, some women made extra money by working at crochet and embroidery in the evenings. This was known as 'white work' and was very demanding on eyesight, especially when the light in the house was inadequate. The cloth then had to be washed, starched and ironed with a box iron. The women of the house were also expected to knit sufficient socks and pullovers to keep the family warm throughout the year, as well as making running repairs to everyday clothes.

Some of the older women still used tobacco snuff, which they believed was an antidote to eyestrain. The women and children were also expected to make butter from the cow's milk...

> Some of the milk was sent to the creamery, but there was always some milk kept for the house. This milk was churned, again no easy method. The churn staff consisted of a circular base with criss cross pieces of board attached and fitted with a long handle. This staff had to be plunged down and up in the churn until the butter appeared. Sometimes it seemed to take a very long time and your arms became very sore. A little hot water could be added to speed up the process, but you needed to

> be careful not to add too much in case the butter would be scalded, which meant it would be pale in colour. The butter was then taken from the churn and put in a bowl. The liquid was all drained off and salt added. It was much tastier than the butter we get nowadays. I always loved it...[6]

Animals and fowl were well cared for, especially when sick, when giving birth or during inclement weather. Delicate piglets and lambs were often bottle-fed and kept in the kitchen overnight, where their well being could be easily monitored. 'Clucking' hens were sometimes to be found under the kitchen table, where they would be safe from the attentions of marauding foxes or the family dog.

Members of the farming families sat up with expectant sows, to prevent the mother accidentally lying down on the newborn babies, or even, as sometimes happened, eating them. During really cold weather, it was not unknown for the sow and her litter to be brought into the kitchen where they had pride of place in front of the fire for a week or ten days. This arrangement did not amuse the family dog, which found his temporary exile from the kitchen difficult to bear. Sometimes, the mother pig would become so alarmed at all the activity going on around her in the kitchen that in her concern for the welfare of her piglets, she would attempt to drive any unfamiliar humans out!

In the summer months many Gallon children discarded their footwear and went almost everywhere, even to school, on their bare feet. Walking through soft, mossy ground was blissful, and even the untarred county roads were pleasant, because they often had grass growing in the middle. Toes were occasionally 'napped' (hit) against stones, nettles had to be avoided at all costs and walking through a field of stubble at harvest time required a special technique, but by the end of the summer, children's feet had usually grown so tough that they no longer noticed occasional pricks.

Minnie McLaughlin of Gallon Lower and Matilda Hill of Shannony were the local 'midwives' during the middle years of the present century, when home confinements were the norm. Although lacking in any formal training, the presence at the bedside of one of these ladies was a source of great confidence for many expectant mothers.

Gallon did not escape the various illnesses and medical problems which were prevalent in Ireland in the early years of the century. Diseases such as tuberculosis and fevers of various kinds took their toll, and clinical depression, the bane of country living, was always a threat. Medical attention was available in the hospitals in Omagh and Strabane. Thankfully many of these diseases had been brought under control by the middle of the century. The introduction of the National Health Service in 1948 at last removed the last vestiges of the Workhouse system, so that everyone could at last enjoy the benefits of free medical care.

John McNamee had electric lighting in his house at Blackdyke a full decade before any other farm, thanks to a generator which he installed in the 1950s. Many other farmers eventually followed his example but mains electricity did not arrive in Upper Gallon until the early 1970s.

Minnie McLaughlin (1960).

From the early 1970s onwards, housing in Gallon was revolutionised by the introduction of improvement grants. Within the following fifteen years, several traditional houses were renovated up to modern standards with mains water, sanitation and mains electricity. Many other sub-standard houses have been abandoned while the occupants either built new houses nearby or left for new local authority housing in the towns.

Catherine Bradley feeds the hens (1950).

Bradley children of Gallon Sessiagh (1940s).

John and Mary McNamee (c 1955).

Bradley children of Gallon Lower (1940s).

Pat McAnena, who lived in the last remaining traditional house in Gallon, moved to a new pensioner's house in Newtownstewart in May 1999. In his new house he has all the modern conveniences, which he did not have in his former home. He is also much closer to shops and services and has the benefits of central heating, electricity and water with minimal effort.

MODERN AND RENOVATED HOUSES IN GALLON

Pat's new house in Newtownstewart.

Donna, Ronnie and the McNulty family.

Geraldine and Martin McGuigan.

Vincent McNamee outside his home.

Tess Patton and friends outside her home.

Sadie McNamee outside her home.

The Cottage, home of Angela Gormley.

Pat McAnena, Upper Gallon, outside his home.

Mary and Charlie McColgan's new home (left) and the old home.

The Hood Family in their new home.

McClures house (abandoned).

McGurks farmhouse.

Tina McConnelly, Glenock (1930).

Hegarty's abandoned farmhouse. Also in the photo are Dr Bill Crawford (left) and Tommy McNamee.

REPORT ON THE CONTITION OF HOUSES IN GALLON 1958 AND 2000

Map no	Householder in 1958 No of occupants in brackets	Description in 1958	Householder in 2000 No of occupants in brackets	Description in 2000
Meehawiddy and Meehaheap				
1	Seamus Morris	Raised, slated	Hugh McElwee	Renovated
2	Bernard McColgan Sen	Raised, slated	Bernard McColgan Jr	Re-built
3	David Devine	Trad, iron roof	vacant, derelict	
4	James Gilchrist	Trad, iron roof	down	
5	Vacant house	Trad, thatched	down	
Aghnahassan and Meenatumigan				
6	John McAneny	Trad, iron roof	Pat McAnena	Trad, iron roof
7	Charles McColgan	Trad, iron roof	vacant	
			Charles McColgan	New house
8	Charles Quinn	Trad, thatched	Sean Devine	Re-built
9	Gallon School	Slated	vacant	New roof
10	Vacant house	Raised, slated	down	
			Martin McGuigan	New house
11	Neil McNamee	Trad, iron roof	John McNamee	Re-built
			Mary McNamee	New house
Aghnaglarig, Blackdyke and Crockatore				
12	Willie Ashenhurst	Trad, asbest roof	down	
13	Neil Kelly	Trad, improved	Willie Patton	Re-built
14	Bessie McLaughlin	1 room, iron roof	derelict	
15	Willie McClure	Raised, slated	vacant	
16	Lila McCallion	Trad, asbest roof	down	
			Damien McNamee	New house
			Tommy McNamee	New house
			Robin Stewart	New house
			Anthony Hood	New house
17	Michael O'Brien	Trad, thatched	Sadie McNamee	Re-built
18	John McNamee (Jr)	Trad, improved	down	
19	John McNamee (Sr)	Labour cottage	Angela Gormley	Re-built
20	Willie McGillian	Trad, asbestos rf	derelict	
21	Paddy Tracey	Trad, asbestos rf	derelict	
Magherabrack				
22	Vincent McNamee	Slated	derelict	
23	Charles McNamee	Trad, thatched	down	
24	Charles McAnena	Trad, iron	down	
			Vincent McNamee	New house

GALLON LOWER

1	Jack McConnell	Two storey farmhse	derelict	
2	Vacant (Ducks)	Two storey farmhse	holiday home	Renovated
3	Neil McAnena	Slates, improved	John McNamee	Re-built
4	Vacant (Donegan's)	Trad, thatched	down	
5	John McAnena	Trad, thatched	vacant	Trad, thatched

6	John Devine	One room, iron roof	derelict	
7	Paddy Maguire	Two room, slated	vacant	New roof
8	Henry Bradley	Two storey farmhse	Helen Nicholas	Re-built
9	Mickey McAnena	Trad, thatched	down	
10	Minnie McLaughlin	Slates, improved	derelict	
11	Bella McGurk	Trad, thatched	down	
12			Kevin McNamee	New house

GALLON SESSIAGH

1	Alice Morris	Two storey, slated	derelict	
2	Maggie Quinn	Trad, iron roof	Ronnie McNulty	Re-built
3	Mary Bradley	Improved, iron roof	Noel O'Brien	Re-built

TRAVELLERS, ITINERANT LABOURERS AND BEGGARS

Members of the travelling community ('tinkers') called occasionally at the houses in Gallon. In the early years of the century, they sold and repaired tin mugs, buckets and cans, but later, when these items became more affordable in the shops, many of the men turned to scrap iron collection, while the women turned to selling trinklets and small household items as well as begging. Travellers were not always welcome; over time they learned to call only at the houses where they would be tolerated.

During the 'hungry thirties' and into the 1940s, certain kindly homes in Gallon became stops on a circuit traversed by inerant labourers and beggars. These individuals did not necessarily belong to the 'traveller community' but were often settled people who had lost their permanent homes and had taken to the road as tramps, hawkers and beggars. Jimmy Smith was one of the best known itinerant labourers, who would work for two days on a farm, collect his wages and then disappear for several weeks or months. When working for Bradleys of Gallon Lower, he knew that he would be well cared for, but he preferred to sleep in the barn. Jimmy ('the Gander') O'Neill was another itinerant labourer who used to work occasionally for the McGarveys of Upper Gallon. His speciality was pulling heather to provide bedding for the horses. Sam Mullan and Kitty McNulty occasionally visited Gallon to labour with local farmers or to beg.

LOCAL SHOPS AND SERVICES

The local shoemaker was Charlie Brogan of Lisnafin, who had been invalided out of the British army after World War I. His house was also a well-known ceilidhing house. The saddler in Newtownstewart was Mr McMaster and there were two blacksmiths: Harkin's in Methody Lane and Wilkinson's in Mill Street.

As well as making shoes for horses, the blacksmith made all the iron or steel objects used in farm or home, including gates, harrows and links for hanging pots over the kitchen fire. Pots and pans were sold and repaired by itinerant tinsmiths, known colloquially as tinkers.

Katie Anne Kelly had a shop at Aghnaglarig up to the 1930s and Henry Bradley opened a shop in his house at Gallon Lower in 1932. The heyday of Bradley's shop was during World War II, when Henry administered the rationing as fairly as possible in those days of scarcity. The shop survived until the mid 1960s selling a wide variety of merchandise, as the following extract from the shop book shows:

EXTRACTS FROM HENRY BRADLEY'S SHOP BOOK 1950-1951

> 12 Dec 1950: Eddie McConnell:
> Large loaf 1sh 11d, jam 2sh 4d, socks 3/6, tea 1/6, sugar 1/1, warhorse tobacco 7sh 2d, total 17 shillings and 5 pence.
>
> 13 Dec 1950: Barney McNamee:
> One pound of butter, leaving one and a half pounds of sugar to get in the 8th period.[7]
> 29 Jan 1951 John McAnena: frost nails 1sh 1d, wire nails 3d.
> 7 Feb 1951 Bessy McLaughlin: cigarettes 2sh 7d, salt 3d, jam 2sh 3d, aspro 3sh.

Another person who provided a "home shopping service" before the term had been invented was the local packman, Jamie Donegan...

> He had a pack made up of some kind of waterproof material lined with a piece of sheeting. Opposite corners were tied together, and there was a space left where he could put his arm through and hoist the pack on his shoulder. He seemed to pack a wide variety of goods, laces, polish, combs, and ladies' aprons of the crossover style, outdated items of underwear and occasionally a pair of very old-fashioned shoes. He also had whangs, which were fine strips of leather used to fasten men's working boots.[8]

Poverty was widespread in Gallon in the 1940s and 1950s and an understanding shopkeeper often stood in the way of hunger for some families. When these families could not pay their accounts, Henry Bradley would allow them to pay off the debts by working for a few days on his farm.

During and immediately after World War II, many foods and everyday items such as sugar, tea, tobacco and cigarettes were severely rationed. Customers who had used up their allocated quota were a constant headache for Henry, and he sometimes accommodated these customers in the hope of replenishing his stocks by unofficial means.

These means included occasional forays to Lifford, in the Irish Free State, where tobacco and cigarettes could be bought without restriction. However, such enterprises were not without risk, as the customs authorities did not approve of such activities. There is no memory of Gallon ever having an alehouse, but poteen was made in Gallon Sessiagh and Legfordrum at various times up the 1930s. In more recent years it could still be obtained easily for wakes, weddings or 'big nights'.

Gallagher's of Newtownstewart and Doherty's of Mountjoy East (Omagh) called weekly to buy eggs from the local egg producers. Beattie's lorry from Corrick called at many houses in Gallon Upper, selling the full range of groceries, apart from bread. Doherty's and Beattie's lorries were most welcome to Gallon's younger folk, because they sold sweets, mineral drinks and other treats.

At one time Gallon was served by different bread vans on four days per week. The most popular bread man in the 1950s and 1960s was Jackie Blackburn of Newtownstewart who had inherited the bread run from his father.

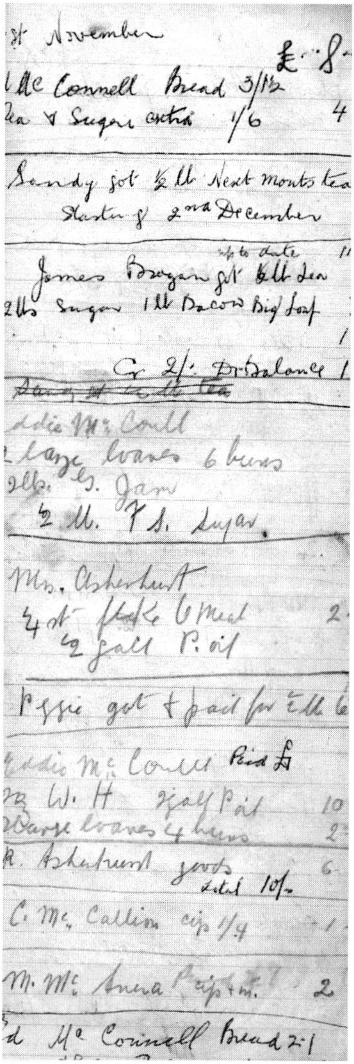
November
McConnell Bread 3/1½
Tea & Sugar extra 1/6 4
Sandy got ½ lb Next Months tea
Starting 2nd December
James Brogan got ½ lb Tea up to date
2 lbs Sugar 1 lb Bacon Big Loaf
Cr 2/- Dr Balance
Mrs. Ashurst
Peggie got & paid for
C. McCallion
McConnell Bread

An extract from Henry Bradley's shop book.

Another bread man, Gerry McCrory of Omagh, delivered the two local weekly papers every Thursday, the *Ulster Herald* and the *Tyrone Constitution*. The *Herald* was nationalist in outlook, while the *Constitution* was unionist, but many households took both papers.

The weekly shopping was usually done in Newtownstewart.

Henry Bradley returns from Newtownstewart with supplies for his shop (1939).

BUSINESSES OF NEWTOWNSTEWART IN THE EARLY 1960S

Garages: John McGlinchey, Castle Brae and George Wilson, Douglas Road.
Petrol Stations: Alfie Hone, Castle Brae and Bernard McNamee, Main Street.
Newspapers and fancy goods: Brendan McDevitt, Jack O'Neill and Frank Kirk, Main Street.
Drapery: Frank Hood, John Kemps and Samuel Carson, Main Street.
Grocery shops: New Reform Stores (Beattie and Quinn) and W J Millar, Main Street; Lawrence McNamee, Mill Street.
Hardware: Frank Hood, Main Street.
Chemists: John McBride and Albert Hassard, Main Street.
Public houses: Castle Hotel, Avre Arms, Central Bar, Abercorn Arms Hotel, Fonnie Gallagher's, Paddy McGarvey's, Alfie Hone's Hotel.
Butcher shops: Bob Kinloch and W J Gallagher, Main Street; Houston's, Mill Street.
Hairdressers: Mickey McGuigan (gents) and Mrs McNamee (ladies), Main Street.
Taxis: Jack O'Neill, James Roche, Michael Crudden and Phil Harkin.
Corn mill: Scott's, Mill Street.
Doctors: Dr Lyle, and Dr Cochrane.

For many years, Bertie and his brother Mervyn ran the family grocery business of W J Millar on the Main Street. Mervyn and his wife still work there.

At Bertie's funeral, Rev Mervyn Crooks reminded the congregation that Bertie had always thought of himself as a 'real Gallon man'.

GALLON REMEMBERED IN SONG AND STORY

Gallon is commemorated in a number of songs, such as 'Green Tyrone' which was composed by Michael McGarvey, who emigrated to the United States in the 1923 and died there.

GREEN TYRONE by Michael McGarvey 1897-1979[9]
(Sung to a tune similar to Patsy Fagan)

My thoughts go back to Gallon's braes, not far from Omagh town
Near that country schoolhouse long ruled by Master Brown;
The happy days I spent with him come back when I'm alone,
As I live beneath the stars and stripes, far, far from green Tyrone.

I loved to look at Bessy Bell while running off to school
And watch the train come beating round the winding banks of Strule;
Our teacher sleeps his long last sleep, his soul to heaven has flown,
While his body rests so peacefully in his native green Tyrone.

Where are those loving school boys who went to school with me
And played along sweet Gallon braes beneath the green palm trees;
Some no doubt are still at home while many more have flown
To far off, foreign distant lands far, far from green Tyrone.

The Brogans, Quinns and Devlins keep coming to my mind
Brave Kellys and McConnells are never far behind
In fancy I see all the boys with whom I used to roam
In the days we oft played football, when we lived in green Tyrone.

I'd love to stand just once more on old Cloghogle rock
And view O'Neill's great castle from the banks of sweet Glenock;
In that isle so sweet and fair, no sweeter spot is known
From Rooskey's top to old Strabane away in green Tyrone.

Tyrone has long been Ireland's boast, for at Blackwater's side
O'Neill with his great army held back the Saxon tide;
The same blood runs in our veins as in our hero Owen
When he was lord and master and ruled over green Tyrone.

Farewell once more to Gallon's braes and winding banks of Mourne,
Those native scenes and boyhood days in memory I have borne;
My childhood days I oft recall while wandering here alone,
Through California's distant land, far far from green Tyrone.

The Millar family of Glenock. Back row: Raymond, Terence, Ross and Malcolm.
Front row: Bertie and Jane.

Mary Joe and Margaret Maguire with Philomena Bradley (1960).

Emigration to Britain and the United States, as well as migration to the towns has had a dramatic effect on Gallon's population. Not one of the five family names mentioned in the song survives in the area at present, although some families can claim descent from them.

Another notable poet, Robert Kerr of Newtownstewart, who died at the battle of Jutland (1916) wrote a poem which he called "Gallon and the Plum" (Plumbridge).[10]

One verse is as follows:

I wonder if I'll watch a summer day fade once again,
The peaceful twilight settling down o'er hill and dale and plain
See the cottage lights a twinkling as they peep out one by one
On the heather slopes of Gallon and the mountains of the Plum.

Patrick Kelly, of Gallon Upper, who left Ireland in the 1920s describes in his autobiography *One Lifetime is not Enough* his frustration with life on a Gallon farm in a bad harvest...

> I was cutting oats with a scythe; it was so flattened by storms that the mechanical reaper mower could not handle it. I had to pick it up and lay it out in unbound sheaves. The water oozed from it and I was cold and sodden. I seized the scythe, hurled it into the middle of the crop and walked home. I got a pen and wrote an urgent plea to Aunt Nell in America asking if she could sponsor me into the States.[11]

Eventually Patrick emigrated to Australia where he died in 1996.

Left: Patrick Kelly
Opposite top: Neil Kelly, Kathleen Caldwell, Mary Caldwell, Andy Caldwell c 1960
Opposite bottom: Cassie Ellen (Kelly) McNamee, Gallon's oldest resident in 1994

Contisoft

THE GALLON DIALECT

The Ordnance Survey Memoirs for the parish of Ardstraw reported in 1835:

> English is spoken by all but the vernacular tongue of the highlands is Irish, but is on the decrease.[12]

This would indicate that Irish language probably died out of general usage in Gallon during the early years of the nineteenth century, although the 1901 census shows two elderly women who could still speak Irish.

Relics of the language survive in many place names, especially in Gallon Upper and also in words and turns of speech in common usage. The dialect is a mixture of Mid-Ulster English and Ulster Scots and is similar to that which can be heard spoken by country people in other parts of West Tyrone, East Donegal and Inishowen.

THE GALLON DIALECT

Abeen = above
agin = against
clabbar = wet, slimy mud
drolie = the runt of the litter
delfal = the edge of darkness, twilight
erick = a young hen
A glam = an embrace
a stour = a cloud of steam
girn = to complain
poreen = a small potato
nacket = a brat
stiggened = to be very cold
a nadger = a small child
to goul = to shout. a shannagh = a talk
to join = to start
juke = to bend or hide
to deave = to deafen
to jundy = to push past someone
scunnered = disgusted, bored
gra = a liking for someone
Pishymullogs = ants
That skitter would taver a saint!
= what an obnoxious child!

A union = a group gathered to bring in a neighbour's crop in an emergency, especially on a Sunday.

whommel = to cover something, especially fowl, so that it cannot escape. "Whommel that clocking hen!"

NICKNAMES USED IN GALLON IN YEARS GONE BY

The use of nicknames was once common in Gallon. In some cases these names served a useful purpose, distinguishing two or more individuals who shared the same official names.

Examples of these nicknames are:

Delop: James Brogan (Tullyherin)
Corbett: John J. Devlin
The Snake: Paddy McLaughlin
The Moon: Dan McLaughlin
Mickey Duck: Mickey Brogan
The Rockman: J.J. Quinn
Jumping Jack: John McGillian
Rab: Henry McAleer
The Daddler: James Brogan
Maginn: Mick Devlin
Poundies: Denis Devenney
The Point Man: Robert Hill
The Duke: Charlie Brogan
Jarvis: Charlie Quinn
Gratton: Henry Bradley
Bella Paul: Bella McGurk

Top and left: the Maguire family of Gallon Lower.

Bottom: Charles, Mary and Sarah McColgan (1996).

Kevin McNamee.

Rory McGuigan.

Left: Gary, Patrick and Bridgeen Drum.

Below: Lila McCallion.

Top: Nicholas family, Gallon Lower.

Left: Rosemary and Sean Devine.

Bottom left: Shane McNamee.

Bottom right: Jim McCallion.

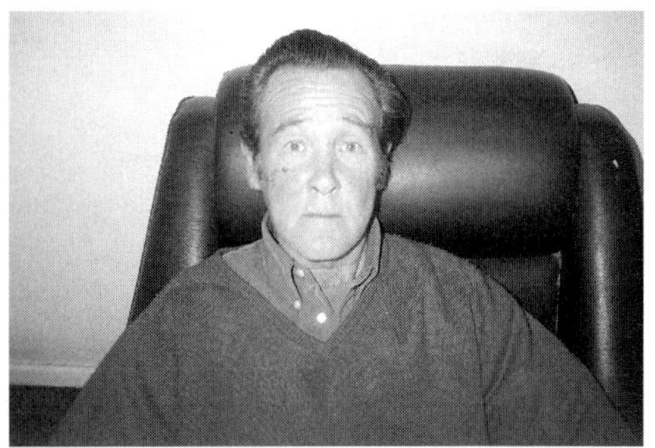

Glenock Church.

CHAPTER 10: GLENOCK CHURCH

Confirmation Day at Glenock 1953.

Following the dissolution of the monasteries at Pubble and Corrick around 1600, there is no record of a permanent Catholic church until 1785. There are two fields in Gallon, one in Gallon Upper and the other in Gallon Sessiagh, both known as the Mass Fields. According to local tradition Mass was said outdoors at these locations at the height of the Penal Laws.

In 1785 a new church was opened at Glenock. The original church was a small rectangular building with a thatched roof. It was enlarged in 1823. The Ordnance Survey Memoirs for the parish of Ardstraw (1831) provide further information:

> The Roman Catholic chapel, situated in the townland of Glenknock is a rectangular building in the form of the letter T, 72 feet in length and 57 feet in extreme breadth, containing 3 galleries and lighted by 12 windows. It accommodates 1,500 persons and the average attendance is 1,000. It was built by private subscription about the year 1785 and repaired with additions in the year 1823 at an expense of £150 raised by private subscription. In the year 1834 a temporary wooden steeple and belfry... was erected at the side of the chapel. Its total height is 53 feet and it contains a bell weighing 330 pounds.[1]

Glenock church is reputed to be the first Catholic church in the diocese of Derry to have a bell in its belfry. This bell, which is still rung each evening at 6.00pm can be heard clearly in most of Gallon. In former times workers in the fields or the farmyards stopped work to say the Angelus when the bell rang out. Children loved to hear the bell, because it was a sign that the end of another day's work in the fields was near.

Sheila Donegan on her Confirmation Day 1946.

Up to the 1980s, attendance at Saturday evening or Sunday morning Mass was almost universal among Gallon's inhabitants. If some-one was not seen at the particular Mass, which he normally attended, there was genuine con-cern for his welfare.

Over the years, Gallon men and women have risen to prominence in the Catholic Church, including Fr Denis Morris of Meenawiddy (1860-1944) who served in Canada. Fr Denis's sisters, Mary Jane and Alice, became nuns and worked in South Africa and England. A cousin, also called Fr Denis Morris (1866-1903) worked in the Derry Diocese. Patricia McNulty of Aghnaglarig worked as a nun in New York and died there in 1982.

Guests at the wedding of Rose Bradley to George Mullan.

The first half of the nineteenth century saw a revival in the Catholic Church, with determined efforts made by the parish priests to improve church attendance and to eliminate dubious practices, such as the 'pilgrimage' to the cairn on the top of Bessy Bell on St John's Eve (23 June).

One of Glenock's most notable parish priests was Fr John K O'Doherty, who served from 1865 to 1890 and who later became bishop of Derry. Fr John McGowan, who was parish priest at Glenock from 1942 until 1971 had a special friendship for the Gallon people. Two curates who took a special interest in Gallon were Fr B Blee (1949-1954) and Fr B Bryson (1964-1972).

During the 1970s, the new Bishop of Derry, Dr Edward Daly, introduced a new devotion, the blessing of the graves, on an agreed Sunday each year. This devotion has proved to be very popular.

A family group at the blessing of the graves in the parish graveyard (1985).

Presbyterian Church, Newtownstewart.

LIST OF PRIESTS WHO SERVED IN GLENOCK CHURCH[2]

Parish Priests	Curates
1785 Fr C McBride	1910 Fr H Smith
1799 Fr Higgins	1913 Fr W Murphy
1806 Fr P Morgan	1918 Fr P J Geary
1813 Fr J O'Kane	1921 Fr E McNamee
1821 Fr P Porter	1923 Fr J McGowan
1839 Fr A O'Doherty	1926 Fr T Bradley
1860 Fr W Hagarty	1934 Fr HC Browne
1865 Fr J K O'Doherty	1937 Fr J McRory
1890 Fr W T O'Doherty	1940 Fr A Gillespie
1892 Fr Denis Morris	1942 Fr J McKee
1905 Fr J J McGlade	1949 Fr B Blee
1908 Fr W McLaughlin	1954 Fr E Boyle
1924 Fr A Campbell	1956 Fr P McGuigan
1942 Fr J McGowan	1963 Fr J J Chesney
1971 Fr B Feeney	1964 Fr B Bryson
1976 Fr D Mullan	1972 Fr L Keavney
1978 Fr D McNicholl	
1986 Fr M Mullan	
1995 Fr S Kearney	

Fr J K O'Doherty later became bishop of Derry.
Fr J J McGlade later became parish priest of Omagh. He toured America to raise funds to pay for the Sacred Heart Church and published an illustrated book of his travels.

In the past few years, Glenock church has suffered from periodic flooding. Car parking has also become a problem, along with the distance of the church from the town. However, the present parish priest, Fr Kearney and his parish council have maintained Glenock church to a very high standard.

In recent years, discussions were held with a view to building a new church in Newtownstewart to replace Glenock as the parish church. About twenty years ago, the former school building in Main Street was converted to an oratory, where weekday Masses were said; at present, the oratory is being re-built. It is hoped that Glenock church will continue to be well maintained and that it will retain its status as the main church of the parish.

Left to right: Damien (father), Ciara, Bishop Hegarty, Caolan, Siobhan, Cahir, Edna and Gavin at Ciara's confirmation, 1998.

Left to right: Noel O'Brien, Christopher Tibbs, Marie O'Brien, Caoimhe O'Brien and Cathy Tibbs.

Left to right: Anne, Paul, Robin and Emmet Stewart (1991).

Molly Malanophy, Peggy Morris, Susan McNamee and Alice McElwee.

CHAPTER 11: GALLON SCHOOL

THE FIRST GALLON SCHOOL

For almost one hundred and fifty years, the school in Gallon was an important focus of identity for the whole community. A local man, Master Maguire, had operated a hedge school in Gallon during the early years of the nineteenth century. In 1831 he moved to a purpose-built school in Gallon Upper at Aghnahassan. In his submission to the Commissioners of National Education for grant aid, the parish priest, Fr Porter, estimated that there would be 60 male pupils and 40 female pupils attending the school during the summer months.

The schoolhouse was to be 20 feet by 16 feet. Rev Porter asked for £20 to pay the master's wages for a year and to equip the school and buy books. He applied for a further £15 to buy desks, seats, slates and paper. Charles McColgan and James McNally were named as two respectable neighbours who would act as guarantors for the school.

APPLICATION TO THE COMMISSIONERS OF NATIONAL EDUCATION BY REV PORTER, PARISH PRIEST, FOR A SCHOOL AT GALLON UPPER, NEWTOWNSTEWART, DECEMER 1831

Will the school be in connection with any society?
No.
When open for teaching?
Open six days from 9.00am until 4.00pm.
Enrolment.
Summer: 60 males, 40 females – Winter: 40 males, 20 females.
Dimensions
20 feet X 20 feet. Two windows in the front and one in the back
Assistance so far obtained
Funds from the parish. There are 100 small children in the area needing schooling.
Income
From poor parents £7 per year. There are no funds and the parents of the children, being nearly mendicants.
Teachers
There is no mistress, the master is one Maguire, educated in the parish, a married man of good character. The school will be under the direction of the Parish Priest and respectable neighbours, Charles McColgan, James McNally and Chas... (surname illegible)

Books
The Universal Spelling Book, Masons Spelling book, primers and a few testaments supplied by the parents.
State of the building
In a bad state of repair, being lately built.
Seating
There are no seats, but sods upon stones around the room.
Aid required
£10 to put the schoolhouse in order. £10 for the master for a year, Books for the children and £15 for desks, seats, slates and paper.[1]

The school was closed by the Commissioners of National Education in 1845 because the building had become so dilapidated. When it re-opened in 1856, it still had an earthen floor and a thatched roof. Scholars were expected to pay one shilling per term. The new teacher, Mr John Kelly, was to be paid £6 per year.

Application of 1856.
2 desks, 10 forms, six foot long each, accommodation 50 children.
No teacher's desk, no press, no blackboard, no clock, no boards for tables.
Present teacher: John Kelly aged 31.
Scholars pay one shilling per term, school fees £2 per quarter.
School hours: Saturday from 10 to 1 for Religious Education.
Secular instruction: 5 days for 5 hours, 10.00am to 3.00pm.[2]

In 1870 a new school with a slated roof, wooden floors and large windows was opened about 200 yards from the old building. By this time, schooling had become compulsory and the new school began to play a vital role in the life of the area. In the early years of the present century, night classes for older pupils and adults were provided in English, Irish and Arithmetic. Concerts and dances were also held in the school in those years.

Scholars travelled for many miles to attend Gallon school, from as far away as the Corrick in one direction and Douglas Bridge in the other. The school's enrolment fluctuated around 50 pupils, who were mostly Catholic, but sometimes included a few Protestants. Until the early 1920s, the school consisted of one room only with one teacher.

In earlier times, the pupils were expected to bring a turf to school every day, but this practice died out in the 1930s, when Master O'Donnell arranged that those families who cut turf should deliver a load to the school on a rota basis.

Gallon School never had running water or electricity installed, so thirsty pupils had to drink from a bucket of water in the infant classroom and wash their hands in a communal basin after using the dry toilets in the playground. On special occasions, such as night classes or examinations, the teacher brought in paraffin lamps to the school.

The children sat on long benches in front of long desks which extended the width of the classroom. These were not particularly comfortable, and there was always the danger of falling backwards. The pupils' benches were often used as seating for 'big nights' in local houses and barns.

THE TEACHERS

John Kelly was the first principal of the new Gallon school, having been appointed to the original school in 1856. He served in the new school until 1875. The next five principals were Patrick Tracey (1875-1881), Patrick Logue (1881-1882), James Logue (1882-1884), Joseph McBride (1884-1885) and Charles Browne (1885-1904).

James Crampsie, a native of Clonmany, Co Donegal, was principal of the school during the politically turbulent years from 1904 until 1925, when he moved back to his home town. Although his relationship with inspectors was often strained, he was well thought of by his former pupils who maintained contact with him and visited him regularly until his death in the 1960s.

From 1856 until 1907 the principal had been the only teacher in the school. In that year, Mary McAnena of Gallon Lower was appointed Junior Assistant Mistress.

Con O'Donnell was principal from 1925 until 1941. He is remembered as an effective teacher who expected all the pupils to work hard. He achieved high academic standards for those pupils who had ability.

From 1941 to 1946 there were three principals, John L O'Donnell, (1941-43), Leo O'Neill (1943-44) and John Ward (1944-46).

John (Sean) O'Doherty was appointed principal in 1946. He is remembered as an excellent teacher, who provided his pupils with a wide range of educational experiences in a humane and caring atmosphere. He moved to Liscrevaghan School in 1957.

James Grant served as principal from 1957 until 1959, and was succeeded by John Bradley, of Gallon Sessiagh. John Bradley moved to Drumnabey Primary School in 1967. The last principal of Gallon School was William John Bradley, who served from 1967 until the school closed in 1969.

When Mary McAnena retired as Junior Assistant Mistress in 1940, she was succeeded by Annie Doherty of Newtownstewart. Annie Doherty moved to

Liscrevaghan School in 1948 and was replaced by Mary Bradley, a sister of John Bradley of Gallon Sessiagh. Annie Doherty and Mary Bradley provided their infant pupils with an excellent foundation for their studies in the upper classes.

In June 1969, Gallon Primary School closed down and the teachers and pupils moved to the newly erected St Patrick's Primary School in Newtownstewart.

THE PUPILS

The earliest surviving Registers for Gallon School cover the period 1896-1934 and have been deposited at the Public Record office in Belfast (PRONI). There are separate registers for girls and boys, and together with more modern registers, it has been possible to reproduce a complete list of all the children who attended the school from 1896 until the school's closure. (See Appendix E). The Registers give each child's date of birth, address and parent's occupation. The dates of birth have been reproduced for the older registers only, in order to respect the privacy of the former pupils.

The principal was expected to complete details of each child's attendance, his / her progress from one standard to the next, the date when he / she left Gallon School and his / her destination. These details were not always completed, but those which are available, provide valuable insights into the educational standards of the school. It is interesting, for example, to note the number of children who reached Sixth, Seventh and Eighth Standards. (See the School Registers which are reproduced in Appendix D.) Those children who did not make good progress were often impeded by bad attendance at school.

Fragments of Inspectors Reports from 1856 are also on deposit at PRONI, providing information on pupil numbers and insights into the running of the school in the early years.[3]

The numbers of pupils present for the inspectors' visits in 1876/77 were as follows:

October 1856	Boys	Girls	July 1857	Boys	Girls
Infants	3	2		2	2
First class	7	5		3	1
Second class	9	5		3	1
Third class	4	3		3	0
Fourth class	1	1		4	0
Fifth class	1	2		0	0
	Total 43			Total 19	

The small attendance in July is notable, perhaps explained by the tendency of farmers to keep their children at home during the summer and autumn to help with farm chores.

When Mr Wm Nicholl inspected the school on 18 Feb 1881, he found 49 pupils present, but when he returned on 19 Oct 1881, there were only 29 pupils present, (17 boys and 12 girls).

Sporadic school attendance was most widespread before the introduction of compulsory school attendance for children in the Irish Education Act of 1892. Poor attendance was frustrating for the teacher, because his salary was calculated on the pupil attendance and academic progress as measured by the inspectors on their visits.

Mr Charles Browne had been principal for just over a year when Mr Henry Cox inspected the school. He reported:

> Answering is only very middling. It seems to me that more attention to detail is wanting. Work in books and on the slates today is wanting in care. But I must add that the attendance during the year is far from satisfactory. Better work cannot be expected from better attendance only. No sale stock on hand worth speaking of. Pupils talk and copy.[4]

The reference to sale stock is a reminder that in those days pupils were expected to pay for their text books and exercise books. It is not surprising that there was "no sale stock on hand worth talking about", given the poverty of the pupils and the fact that the principal was expected to pay the book supplier on delivery.

The provision for compulsory attendance seemed to improve attendance during the summer months from 1895 onward; perhaps a fall in the population of the area can explain the drop in attendance towards the end of the century:

Date	Year	Number of pupils present
18 July	1895	54 (27 boys, 27 girls)
15 July	1896	57
26 July	1897	45
18 Jul	1898	46
18 Jul	1899	36
11 Jul	1900	39
10 Jul	1901	32

The attendance on 11 Jul 1902 was as follows:

	Boys	Girls
Infants	8	7
First	5	0
Second	6	4
Third	0	0
Fourth	1	0
Fixth	0	3
Total	15	14

Roll books survive from the 1917-1918 school year. A selection of these have been reproduced in Appendix E.

Another examiner whose visits were treated with apprehension by pupils and teachers alike was the Diocesan Religious Inspector. The children were expected to know the Derry Catechism by heart, as well as several prayers. Many of the concepts in the Catechism were too complex for even adults to understand, but the Religious Inspector would take a careful note of the standards attained by the pupils. Each school was awarded one of five grades in the Religious Examination: 'excellent', 'very good', 'good', 'fair' or 'not satisfactory'. The grades were read out by the Parish Priest at all the Sunday Masses and every school was expected to reach the 'excellent' grade.

Former pupils have generally fond memories of Gallon school, and academic levels were also very good for the times. In the years before free secondary education, some parents were prepared to make sacrifices in order to make sure that their children would proceed to further education.

In the closing years of the last century, some of the Morris children of Meenawiddy were sent to the Convent Grammar school in Strabane. Later, Seamus Morris was sent as a boarder for some years to St Columb's College in Derry.

In the 1940s, Mary and Kathleen Bradley of Gallon Sessiagh became boarders at Loreto Convent Grammar School in Omagh, while Mary Bradley of Gallon Lower attended as a day pupil. A few years later John Bradley of Gallon Sessiagh left to attend the Christian Brothers' Grammar School in Omagh.

The Education Act of 1948 introduced free Grammar school education to those pupils who passed a qualifying examination at the age of eleven. Among the first pupils from Gallon School to take advantage of the new provisions were Catherine Bradley of Gallon Lower and Maureen McNamee of Gallon Upper.

Children remaining at primary school could take an examination for admission to the Technical School in Strabane at 13 years of age, where they could take courses in Office Practice or Domestic Studies. The remaining children could leave Gallon School at 14 years. Girls would hope to find employment in the linen factory at Sion Mills, while boys worked at home or sought employment with local farmers until they were old enough to emigrate to England or Scotland. Some former pupils also found success in the various professions in Ireland or further afield.

Three former pupils of Gallon school returned in later years to teach there; Mary and John Bradley of Gallon Sessiagh and their cousin William John Bradley of Gallon Lower.

Up to the late 1940s, children usually had unbuttered bread for lunch, washed down by a drink of water which they drank at O'Brien's well. Tyrone Education Committee began to provide milk for the pupils of Gallon School around 1948. At first the milk came in large creamery cans and each child was expected to bring in his own mug. Later the familiar small milk bottles were introduced, with their circular cardboard tops which the teachers taught the pupils to use in craft activities.

In 1952 Gallon school was used by Fr Blee and the Gallon Players to rehearse for the play "The Whiteheaded Boy" which was performed to packed audiences in Newtownstewart and Donemana and Aghybrack.

20

LESSON 13. OF THE FIRST COMMANDMENT

Repeat the First Commandment.
I am the Lord thy God, thou shalt have no other Gods but Me.
What does the First Commandment oblige us to do ?
It obliges us to believe in God, to place our hope in Him, to adore Him, and to love Him entirely from our hearts.
Make an Act of Adoration.
Great God! I adore and honour Thee. I acknowledge Thee to be my Creator and Sovereign Lord; I submit myself entirely to Thy divine will.
Is it lawful to adore the Blessed Virgin Mary or the saints ?
No; for by adoration is here meant the honour due to God alone.
Does this Commandment forbid us to honour the saints ?
No; for the honour we give them is different from that which we give to God. We honour the saints as friends and faithful servants of God.

LESSON 14. OF THE SECOND COMMANDMENT

Repeat the Second Commandment.
Thou shalt not take the name of God in vain.
What does the Second Commandment oblige us to do ?
To speake with reverence of God, of His saints, and of all holy things.
What else are we obliged to do ?
To keep our lawful oaths and vows.
What does the Second Commandment forbid ?
It forbids not only all manner of false oaths, but also true ones when unnecessary.
What else ?
It forbids us to curse ourselves, or anything else.
If one swears to do an unlawful thing, is he obliged to perform his oath ?
No; he is obliged to repent for having taken such an oath.
How must we then express ourselves in order to avoid sinning ?
By yes and no, as Christ has taught us.

LESSON 15. OF THE THIRD COMMANDMENT

Repeat the Third Commandment.
Remember thou keep holy the Sabbath Day.
What obligation does this Commandment lay on us ?
It obliges us to keep holy the Lord's day.

Extract from the Derry Cathechism.

CAST OF THE WHITEHEADED BOY[5]

Mrs Geoghagan	Mary Bradley
Kate	Rosaleen Bradley
George	Pat McAnena
Jane	Claire McLaughlin
Peter	Tommy McNamee
Hannah	Annie McClure
Baby	Phyllis McLaughlin
Donough	Gerald McColgan
John Duffy	Bernard McColgan
Delia	Josephine McAnena
Aunt Ellen	Tessie Bradley
Denis	Eddie Bradley

Even by the standards of the 1960s, the facilities at Gallon School were totally inadequate. There was no mains water, electricity and the nearest telephone was a mile away in John McNamee's farm. Drinking water had to be carried in buckets over a hundred metres from the well in Harry O'Brien's farmyard. The dry toilets were flushed once or twice each week by senior boys who carried several bucketfuls of water from a ditch in a nearby field. The excrement was washed out of the toilets into an open ditch by the force of the water where it lay until it disintegrated.

The absence of electric lighting in the school did not strike the pupils as inconvenient, since only one home had electricity in those days. Artificial light was not normally required, but on the days when the Qualifying Examination was held the principal brought a tilley lamp from home.

In spite of these deficiencies, Inspectors' Reports repeatedly praised the teachers for broad and balanced curriculum offered to the children. Former pupils who progressed to secondary school often found that they had learned more at Gallon School than their classmates who had attended large town schools.

From the 1960s onwards, school inspectors and parents realised that the school would have to be modernised or replaced. Enrolment had fallen to 32 pupils by 1968 and it was decided the three Catholic primary schools in the parish, Gallon, Magheracolton and Newtownstewart, should be amalgamated into a new primary school in Newtownstewart. The school eventually closed in 1969, just one year short of its centenary.

Pupils from Gallon in St Patricks Primary School, Newtownstewart with the principal, Neil McGuigan. Back row: Lindsay Nicholas, Dean Nicholas, Edna McNamee, Dean McNamee, Kieran McNulty. Front row: Michaela McNulty, Leon McNamee, Neil McGuigan (principal), Patrick Drum, Jack Hood. Absent: James McNulty, Caolan McNamee, Cahir McNamee, Daryl McNamee, Caolan McNamee.

Master James Crampsie (left) and Mary McAnena, Junior Assistant Mistress with pupils, c 1920.

PUPILS AND TEACHERS OF GALLON SCHOOL 1926

Teachers: Con O Donnell and Mary McAnena. Back row: Barney McAnena, Tom Brogan, ----------, ----------, Jack McLaughlin, Hugh Morris, Maggie Quinn (O'Brien), Cissie McAnena, Lisnafin, Susan McAnena, Cassie Maguire(McIvor), Mary Maguire (Parkinson). Second row from back: ----------, Eileen McLaughlin, (O'Donnell), Mary Kelly (Caldwell), ----------, Jim McAnena, James McNamee, Hughie Maguire, ----------, David Devine, ----------, ----------. Third row from the back: Arthur McAnena, Annie McColgan, Mary McAnena, Kathleen Maguire (Conway), Rosie Brogan, Ballynasolus, Bella McColgan, Rosie McColgan, (Gallagher) ---------- McNamee, Peggy Morris, Alice Morris (McElwee), ----------, 12 Paddy McNamee Magherabrack. Front row: Barney McColgan, Frank Maguire, Joe Devine, Charles (Ginger) McNamee, Jim McColgan, ----------, Seamus Morris, Pat McAnena Gallon Lower, ----------, ---------- McColgan.

PUPILS AND TEACHERS OF GALLON SCHOOL 1939

Back row: Mr Con O'Donnell (teacher), Cecil O'Neill, Jim McLaughlin, Michael McGone, Tom McNamee, John Coyle, Mich McNamee, Jim Brogan, Pat McAnena, Billy Maguire. Second row from the back: Susan Quinn, Annie Quinn, Eileen Coyle, Bridget McCone, Mary Bradley, Mary Quinn, Kathleen Bradley, Sarah Devenney, Kath Brogan, Rose Bradley, Alice McNamee, Bernadette Brogan, Mona McLaughlin, Eliz Smith, Jane McAnena, Josephine McAnena. Third row from the back: Dan McLaughlin, Barney Maguire, Jim Morris, Patsy Devenney, Kathleen McConnell, Teresa Bradley, Kathleen Bradley, Annie McClure, Agnes McNamee, Bridie McNamee, Clare McLaughlin, Phylis McLaughlin, May McClure, Josephine Bradley, Teresa Bradley, Lena Maguire, Billy Morris, Gerld McClogan, Denis Devenney. Front row: John J McGillian, ---------- Tracey, ---------- O'Hagan, Joe Gallagher, Tony Maguire, Patrick McConnell, ----------, Patsy Coyle, Vincent McNamee, George Maguire, Chas McNamee, Tom McConnell, Wm McGillian, Jim Coyle, George Maguire, Charles Coyle, Barney McNamee, Neil McNamee.

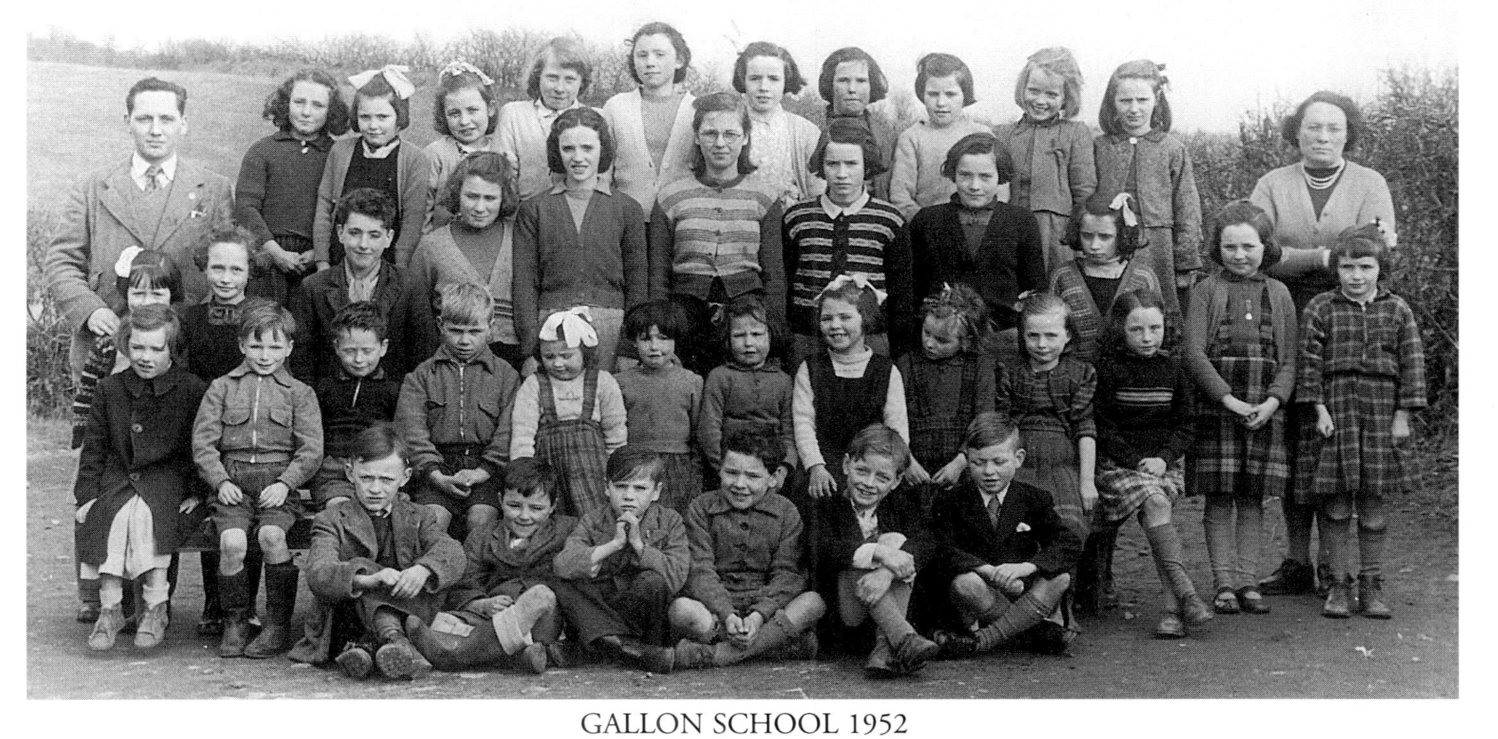

GALLON SCHOOL 1952

Mr Sean Doherty and Miss Mary Bradley with the pupils of Gallon School (1952).
Teachers: Mr Sean O'Doherty and Miss Mary Bradley. Back row: Rose Tracey, Mary Jo Maguire, Patricia Bradley, Serena McClure, Kay Maguire, Anna Patton, Maisie McCallion, Nora Caldwell, Maureen McSorley, Rose McNamee. Second row from back: Bernadette Patton, Brenda Coyle, John McLaughlin, Tess Caldwell, Josephine McNamee, Bridie McConnell, Ruby Ashenhurst, Frances Patton, Gracie Ashenhurst, Kathleen Parkinson, Rose McNamee. Front row standing: Pam McLaughlin, Tommy McNamee, Jack Tracey, Phillip Caldwell, Ann Maguire, Lila McCallion, Margaret McCallion, Margaret Maguire, Elizabeth Morris, Kathleen McMenamin, Jo Tracey. Front row sitting: James Morris, Luke Caldwell, Joe McMenamin, Hugh McLaughlin, Willie John Morris, John Bradley.

PUPILS AND TEACHERS OF GALLON SCHOOL 1969

Mr John Bradley and Miss Mary Bradley with the pupils of Gallon School (1969).

Teachers: Mr W John Bradley and Miss Mary Bradley. Top row: Martin Devine, Brenda Doherty, Jennifer Devine, Liam McLaughlin, Noel McLaughlin, Raymond McNamee, Eugene Brown, Martin McNamee, Rosemary McColgan, Teresa McLaughlin, Dermot McNamee, Daniel McNamee, Fidelma Devine, Brian McColgan, Siobhan McNamee, Bridget McAnena, Regina McNamee. Middle row: Kieran McNamee, Patrick Maguire, Tony Maguire, Tony Doherty, John McNamee, Michael Devine, Tony Conway, Christopher Patton, Declan McNamee, Damien McNamee, Tony McLaughlin, Jacqueline Devine, Agnes Browne, Rose McNamee. Front row: Sean McAnena, Geraldine McLaughlin, Don McClure, Martina Conway, Geraldine McNamee, Madge McNamee, Billy McClure, Liam McNamee, Rosemary McClure, Patricia Doherty, Angela Devine, Carmel McNamee, Geraldine Browne.

CHAPTER 12: PROSPECTS

When Strabane District Council drew up its Area Plan 1986-2000[1], it designated various settlements as towns, villages or hamlets. Development areas were set aside within these locations, where housing and industry would be permitted or encouraged. Development outside these "development areas" would be unwelcome, unless in special circumstances. Gallon was not recognised as a settlement, and has no development area under the Plan. Furthermore, Gallon's position within the Sperrin Area of Outstanding Natural Beauty means that all buildings have to satisfy additional criteria concerning their effect upon the landscape.

Given these constraints therefore, it is encouraging that a number of new houses have been erected in all three townlands over the past decade. Gallon has also been fortunate in that many of its children have chosen to stay in the townland after marriage, commuting to work in Omagh, Strabane and elsewhere.

Gallon Lower has fared less well in the last number of years, and there are now (2000) only thirteen residents in the townland. There is little prospect of an increase in population, because of planning constraints and the fact that most of the land is now owned by farmers who live outside the area.

All the old rented dwellings have been abandoned, and the tenants have moved to new public authority built houses in surrounding towns. One may regret the loss of inhabitants, but at least the workers, who cannot always afford cars, are spared the hardship, endured by generations of Gallon's youth in the past, of cycling or walking into Newtownstewart to catch buses or trains to work in Sion Mills, Strabane or Omagh.

In January 2000, Martin McGuigan re-opened his workshop at Gallon Upper. The enterprise at present employs four local men full-time and another man part-time and has orders well into the future. This is a very encouraging development.

Gallon's rich archaeological heritage, combined with its scenic character, suggests potential for the development of tourism. The ancient field system of Meenawiddy, the portal tombs of Glenock and Crosh and other lesser monuments in Gallon could compliment the imaginatively re-created copies of monuments at the Ulster Folk Park outside Gortin, and the few remaining traditional Gallon houses could be restored, in situ, to add validity to the restored buildings at the Ulster American Folk Park in Camphill.

Close to Gallon is Newtownstewart, with its old stone bridge and winding river, still one of the best salmon rivers in Europe. Even closer on the Glenock Burn is a little known, mysterious place called the "Rumbling Rocks", where the burn falls in a series of rapids and waterfalls, making a noise which can be heard from half a mile away. In autumn, this was also a favoured spot for collecting hazelnuts.

The future of the countryside lies in its children. It is pleasing to know that so many families have chosen to bring up their children in the country so that, hopefully, there will always be a vibrant living community in Gallon.

Martin McGuigan in his workshop.

Australian visitors at the old bridge in Newtownstewart.

GALLON'S CHILDREN

Liam McDermot and his cousin Stephen McNamee, visiting their cousins in Gallon.

Left-right: Kevin, Roisin, Aileen and Shareen Devine.

Stephen Bradley and friends from Derry enjoying a holiday in Gallon.

NOTES

Preface

1. Crawford, W.H. and Foy R.H. *Townlands in Ulster.* Belfast, 1998. The book includes an general introduction to the study of townlands by Dr Crawford and accounts of eight townlands by local historians.

Chapter 1: Location

1. The meanings of these places are given in Appendix A. The clusters are marked on the map on page 38.

Chapter 2: Gallon's Early History up to the Plantation of Ulster

1. Archaeologists classify these magalithic tombs into four different types: Court graves, passage graves, portal graves (sometimes called dolmens) and wedge graves.
2. Weir A., *Early Ireland, a Field Guide,* Belfast 1980. The best known examples of neolithic field systems are those at Ceide Fields, Co Mayo. The field system and hearth found in Gallon were verified by Ms Clare Foley, Ancient Monuments Division, Department of the Environment in 1991.
3. Davies O and Henderson W R, 'Finds near Newtownstewart, Cist at Shannony East' in *Ulster Journal of Archaeoloy, Vol 4. Part 1. Jan 1941.* Belfast: Queens University.
4. Jeffries Henry and Devlin, Ciaran (eds) *History of the Diocese of Derry from Earliest Times.* Dublin, 2000.
5. Tir Owen. The spelling Tir Owen is used to denote the Gaelic kingdom ruled over by the O'Neill clan and comprising the modern counties of Tyrone, Armagh and Derry. The O'Cahan's were minor kings who had some authority in County Derry, but who were normally subservient to the O'Neills.
6. Quotation by Dowcra from H G Gebbie in *Ardstraw: Historical Survey Parish.* Omagh, 1970.
7. Kennedy M., *By the Banks of the Mourne.* Strabane 1996.
8. Gallowglasses were mercenary soldiers, usually from Gaelic speaking western Scotland and the Western Isles.

Chapter 3: The Establishment of the Newtown and Lislap Estate and the Creation of Farms in Gallon

1. Inquisitions of Ulster, Tyrone (5) Car I. quoted in Hill, George. *The Plantation of Ulster.* London 1877.
2. Hill, George. *The Plantation of Ulster.* London 1877.
3. Pynnar's Survey, quoted in Hill, George. *The Plantation of Ulster.* London 1877.
4. Cox, Michael et al: *The Strabane Barony during the Ulster Plantation (1607-1641).* Privately published.
5. Registry of Deeds, Dublin: Book 56, Page 136, No 37,300.
6. Registry of Deeds, Dublin: Book 95, Page 57, No 65669 (1 May 1724).

7. Registry of Deeds, Dublin: Book 77, page 150 No 53138.
8. Preference in the granting of 31 year leases were generally given to Protestant tenants in the eighteenth century. Protestant tenants were often given leases for three lives, whereas Catholics could not hold these long leases until 1783.
9. Tithe Applotment Records PRONI.
10. Tithe Applotment Records PRONI.
11. Ordnance Survey Memoirs for Co Tyrone.
12. ibid.
13. Valuation Reports for 1885-1905. PRONI.

Chapter 4: The Landlords of Newtown and Lislap (1610-1932)
1. Gardiner's Relief Act 1782.
2. McEvoy, John. *Statistical Survey of Tyrone (1803).* Belfast 1991.
3. Charles John Gardiner, Earl of Blessington had inherited his father's commitment to improving the lot of Catholics in Ireland. His early death may have been hastened by his insistence on travelling from Paris to London while in bad health in order to vote in the House of Lords in support of the Duke of Wellington's Bill for Catholic Emancipation.
4. Sadleir, Michael. *Blessington D'Orsay, a Masquerade.* London, 1933.

Chapter 5: The Development of Farming in Gallon
1. Department of Agriculture for NI: Soil Profiles 1994.
2. Bell J and Watson M *Irish Farming 1750-1900.* Edinburgh, 1986.
3. Dooher, J *A Strabane Famine in the 1740s* in Concordia No 4. Strabane, 1987.
4. Mitchell and Ryan *A history of farming in Ireland.* Edinburgh, 1984.
5. McEvoy, John. *A statistical Survey of Co Tyrone (1802)* Belfast, 1991.
6. ibid.
7. Day, Angelique and Patrick Williams (eds) *The Ordnance Survey Memoirs of Ireland, Vol 5. The Parishes of Co Tyrone 1.* Belfast; QUB (1990).
8. ibid.
9. ibid.
10. ibid.
11. Binns, Jonathan, *The Miseries and Beauties of Ireland* London, 1937.
12. Bell J and Watson M, ibid.
13. *Tyrone Constitution.* Omagh. 1891.
14. Alice Donegan in conversation with the author.

Chapter 6: The Development of Communications
1. The Ballad of Douglas Bridge, a ballad, author unknown.
2. Bardon, Jonathan, *A History of Ulster.* Belfast 1992.
3. Crawford W H (1982) "Economy and Society in eighteenth century Ulster" PhD Thesis QUB Belfast.
4. Day, Angelique and Patrick Williams (eds) *The Ordnance Survey Memoirs of Ireland, Vol 5. The Parishes of Co Tyrone 1.* Belfast; 1990.

Chapter 7: Population Growth and Decline

1. Census material 1841-1911 from official census, PRONI.
The populations for the other years are as follows:
1935: Retrospective census from memory compiled by Tommy McNamee.
1958: Census carried out in 1958 by the author.
2000: Census carried out by Mary McColgan and Tommy McNamee.

Chapter 9: The Community and its Traditions

1. Dooher, John. *Tyrone Nationalism and the Question of Partition (1910-1925)* MA Thesis: University of Ulster 1986.
2. Personal account written in 1970 by a former Irish National Volunteer from Gallon.
3. 'Ceilidhing: a friendly visit to a neighbour's house, especially in the evening' from McAfee, C. I., *A Concise Ulster Dictionary*, Oxford 1996.
4. Carleton, William. *Traits and Stories of the Irish Peasantry*, Gerrards Cross 1965.
5. Gailey, Alan. *Rural Houses of the North of Ireland*, Edinburgh 1984.
6. McCrossan, Josephine. Unpublished autobiography.
7. "leaving... to get this period" rationing was still in operation, and Barney had already got some of his ration for the 8th quarter.
8. McCrossan J. ibid.
9. The song was composed by Michael McGarvey who emigrated to the United States in the 1930s and died there in the 1970s.
10. Kerr, Robert, *Tyrone Constitution, Souvenir Edition,* Omagh: 1950.
11. Kelly Patrick. *One lifetime is not enough,* unpublished autobiography.
12. Ordnance Survey Memoirs, ibid.

Chapter 10: Glenock Church

1. Day, Angelique and Patrick Williams (eds) *The Ordnance Survey Memoirs of Ireland, Vol 5. The Parishes of Co Tyrone 1.* Belfast; (1990).
2. For further information about the history of Glenock Church, refer to Mr Bride, Brian (ed) *The Parish of Ardstraw East 1785-1985.* Newtownstewart 1985.

Chapter 11: Gallon School

1, 2. Public Record Office for Northern Ireland: Application for Grant aid ED1/28 (1835-41) and ED1/30 (1848-62).
3. Inspectors' comments in Report Books for Gallon School, PRONI.
4. Inspectors' comments in Report Books for Gallon School, PRONI.
5. Robinson, Lenox, (1982) *Selected Plays;* Gerrards Cross (1982).
Notes on Chapter 12; Prospects.

Chapter 12: Prospects

1. Strabane District Council (1998) Strabane Area Plan.

APPENDIX A: LIST OF MAPS AND PICTURES

COVER

CHAPTER 1

CHAPTER 2

CHAPTER 3

CHAPTER 4

CHAPTER 5

CHAPTER 6

CHAPTER 7

CHAPTER 8

CHAPTER 9

CHAPTER 10

CHAPTER 11

CHAPTER 12

APPENDIX B: NAMES OF CLUSTERS AND FIELD NAMES

NAMES OF CLUSTERS OF HOUSES IN GALLON WITH THEIR SUGGESTED MEANINGS

Aghnahassan (Irish, Achadh na h-easa): the field of the waterfall.
Aghnaglarig (Irish, achadh na gclarach): the field of the bridge of planks.
Bartymore (Irish, barr (an) ti moir): The summit of the big house.
Clochgare (Irish, cloch garbh): The rough stone
Crockatore (Irish, cnoc a'toir): The hill of pursuit or (cnoc an tobhair): the hill of the well.
Loughnakeery (Irish, loch na caorach): the lake of the sheep.
Magherabrack (Irish, machaire breac): speckled or cultivated field.
Meehaheap (Irish, min na cipe): the meadow of the (coarse) grass
Meenatumigan (Irish, min na dtumachan): the meadow of the dippings, or (min a' tumachain), the meadow of the sheep dipping place.
Meenawiddy (Irish, min an mheidigh): the meadow of the stallion.
Meenavig (Irish, min bheag) small meadow.
Sessiagh (Irish, seiseadh): Gallon's sixth part or division.

EXAMPLES OF FIELD NAMES WITH THEIR SUGGESTED MEANINGS

Gallon Upper

1. The Park (Irish, pairc), the field
2. The Three Acres.
3. The School Field
4. Mor's Field
5. Grainne (Irish, greannach), gravelly site.
6. The Hill
7. The Scrogg(Irish, scroig): long thin neck.
8. Newlands
9. Burn Field
10. The Rap (Irish: rapach): Land or field abounding with rabbits.
11. Mass Field: A place where Mass was said during Penal Times.
12. Brae Field
13. Kilnbrae: A kiln was marked nearby in the earliest O S map.
14. Park; as no 1.
15. The Big Garden
16. The Black Hill.
17. Mary Ann's Dandies: a good field
18. Kiln Hill: location of another kiln in the last century.
19. Spout Field; This field had a drain channelled into a pipe for collecting water.
20. Well Field.
21. Spa Field: The water flowing into this field is discoloured by iron oxide, a reddish colour.
22. Clochglare (Irish, cnoc glarach): a muddy hill.
23. Crockraffers (Irish, cnoc rathmhar): a prosperous hill
24. Parkure (Irish, parc ur): fresh field, not cultivated.
25. Strawduch (Irish, srathduch) = wet holm.

26. Banshiks (Irish, ban sicfhear): hayfield
27. Meadow Brae
28. Forthkeen (Irish, foirceann): boundary.
29. Hollow Field
30. Craggers (Irish, creig ur): fresh, stony or barren, not yet broken in.
31. Kelly's garden.
32. Orchard.
33. Old Hills
34. Big Brae
35. Kiln Hills
36. Pane o' Glass
37. Barley Field
38. Smalle'en
39. Garrowglass (Irish, garradh glas): green garden
40. Crockban (Irish, cnoc ban): white hill
41. Crockfada (Irish, cnoc fada): long hill
42. Turnaflochan (Irish, tor na bhfliuchan): hill of the water pools (or tor na flocan: the hill of the bog cotton).
43. Sally's Big Field.
44. Dogholes: Perhaps a place where dogs were drowned.
45. Meenavig (see above).
46. Kiln Hill
47. Meadowland
48. Peggy's Field
49. The Plantings
50. Outside Newland
51. Torr Hill (Irish, tor): a bush
52. The Park
53. McGarvey's Flough (Irish, fliuch): wet (place)
54. Monteith's Flough.
55. Newland
56. Crockard (Irish, cnoc ard): high hill
57. Lees (Irish, liath mhuine): grey shrubbery (mhuine no longer said.)
58. Back o'McAnena'
59. Brae Field
60. Monteith's Field
61. Vincent's White Holes.
62. Drumoleary (Irish, druim a' laoi reidh), ridge of the quiet calf.

Names of fields in Gallon Lower:
Cregan's hole, The Park, The Loop, Hugh's Garden, Ann's Field, Brook Park, Sarah's Pipe, Downtown.

Names of fields in Gallon Sessiagh:
Crocknagarney, Padandaddy, Nag hill, Logue's field, Mullan, Dundoon, The Ket, Rocks, Sheelin Hill.

APPENDIX C: CENSUS MATERIAL

CENSUS OF IRELAND 1901 GALLON LOWER

Note: Abbreviations used – R/W: can read & write – Cannot R: cannot read (illiterate) – R: can read only – Agr: agricultural – Dm: domestic – CoI: Church of Ireland – RC: Roman Catholic – Presb: Presbyterian. Also note that the occupation of the wife of the head of the house is seldom given.

	Names	Relation	Relig	Education	Age	Occupation	Married?
1	Patrick McAnena	head	RC	R/W	62	farmer	married
	Anne	wife	RC	cannot R	58		married
	John	son	RC	R	34	farmer son	not
	Patrick	son	RC	RW	25	farmer son	not
	Neal	son	RC	R/W	21	farmer son	not
	Cath Anne	daughter	RC		30	farmer daughter	not
	Susan	daughter	RC	R/W	27	farmer daughter	not
	Mary	daughter	RC	R/W	23	farmer daughter	not
	Bridget	daughter	RC	R/W	18	farmer daughter	not
	Letitia	daughter	RC	R/W	15	scholar	not
2	Robert Hill	head	Presb	R/W	44	farmer	married
	Sarah Hill	wife	Presb	R/W	40		married
	Margaret	daughter	Presb	cannot R	4	farmer daughter	not
	Maria	daughter	Presb	cannot R	8mth	farmer daughter	not
	Matilda Scott	servant	CoI	R/W	30	general servant	not
	John Conway	servant	RC	R/W	18	farm servant	not
3	Michael Brogan	head	RC	cannot R	34	farmer	not
	Patrick Brogan	brother	RC	cannot R	28	agr labourer	not
4	Catherine McAnena*	head	RC	cannot R	70	farmer	widow
	Patrick	son	RC	R/W	36	farmer son	not
	James	son	RC	R/W	34	farmer son	not
	Jane Watson	servant	RC	cannot R	16	dm servant	not
5	Patrick Donnelly	head	RC	R/W	54	shoemaker	married
	Catherine	wife	RC	cannot R	48		married
	Matilda	daughter	RC	R/W	13	scholar	not
	Margaret	daughter	RC	R/W	11	scholar	not
6	Mary McAneney	head	RC	cannot R	65	seamstress	widow
	Alice	daughter	RC	R	25	seamstress	not
	John	son	RC	cannot R	22	agr labourer	not
7	Michael McAneney	head	RC	cannot R	36	farmer	not
	Rose Anne McAneney	sister	RC	R/W	29	seamstress	not
8	Mary Anne Bradley	head	RC	R/W	34	farmer	widow
	Charles	son	RC	R/W	12	scholar	not
	William	son	RC	R/W	10	scholar	not
	Maggie	daughter	RC	R/W	8	scholar	not
	John James	son	RC	cannot R	5	scholar	not
	Rose Ann	daughter	RC	cannot R	3	infant	not
	Henry Edward	son	RC	cannot R	1	infant	not
9	John James Bradley	head	RC	cannot R	60	farmer	married
	Mary Bradley	wife	RC	cannot R	60		married
	Sarah	daughter	RC	R	23	farmer daughter	not

* Note: Can speak Irish

10	Bridget McAnena	head	RC	R	66	farmer	widow
	Joseph	son	RC	R/W	26	farm son	not
	Bridget	daughter	RC	R/W	20	seamstress	not
11	John McLaughlin	head	RC	R/W	45	farmer	not
	Kate Carlin	niece	RC	R/W	20	seamstress	not
	Patrick McLaughlin	servant	RC	cannot R	30	farm servant	not
12	Patrick McGurk	head	RC	cannot W	40	farmer	married
	Margaret McGurk	wife	RC	R/W	42		married
	Mary Watson	servant	RC	cannot R	15	servant	not

CENSUS OF IRELAND 1901 GALLON UPPER

	Names	**Relation**	**Relig**	**Education**	**Age**	**Occupation**	**Married?**
1	Charley McAneny	Head	RC	cannot R	60	Farmer	married
	Susanna	wife	RC	cannot R	55		married
	James	son	RC	R only	27	agr labourer	not
	Annie	daughter	RC	R/W	23	seamstress	not
	Susan	daughter	RC	R/W	16	seamstress	not
	John	son	RC	R/W	15	agr labourer	not
	Maggie	daughter	RC	R/W	10	scholar	not
2	Patrick Kelly#	head	RC	R/W	70	agr labourer	married
	Rose#	wife	RC	Read	48	seamstress	married
	Hugh#	son	RC	R/W	30	agr labourer	not
	Ann#	daughter	RC	R/W	23	seamstress	not
	Eileen	daughter	RC	R/W	18	seamstress	not
	Margaret	daughter	RC	R/W	16	seamstress	not
	James	son	RC	R/W	12	scholar	not
3	Bernard McNamee	head	RC	cannot R	63	farmer	married
	Margery	wife	RC	R/W	52		married
	Susan	daughter	RC	R/W	21	seamstress	not
	Mary Ann	daughter	RC	do	18	seamstress	not
	Teresa	daughter	RC	do	15	seamstress	not
	Bridget	daughter	RC	do	1	scholar	not
4	John Barton	head	CoI	R/W	69	farmer	married
	Eliza	wife	CoI	R/W	63	farmer wife	married
	James	son	CoI	R/W	30	farmer son	not
	Jennie	daughter	CoI	R/W	22	farmer daughter	not
5	John McNamee	head	RC	R	50	farmer	not
	Bridget	sister	RC	cannot R	40	seamstress	not
6	Vacant house belonging to John McGarvey						
7	John McNamee	head	RC	R/W	45	farmer	married
	Bridget	wife	RC	Read	44	seamstress	married
	Charles	son	RC	R/W	17	farmer son	not
	Susan	daughter	RC	R/W	15	farmer daughter	not
	Michael	son	RC	R/W	12	scholar	not
	Bernard	son	RC	R	8	scholar	not
	Thomas	son	RC	R	5	scholar	not
	Charles McTaggart	nephew	RC	R/W	18	labourer	not
	Mary A' McTaggart	neice	RC	R/W	16	seamstress	not
	Fanny McTaggart	neice	RC	R/W	14	seamstress	not

Born in County Donegal.

8	Patrick Kelly	head	RC	R/W	30	labourer	married
	Jane*	wife	RC	Read	38	seamstress	married
	John Jas	son	RC	Read	9	scholar	not
	Catherine A McNamee	step-daug	RC	R/W	18	seamstress	not
9	James Martin	Head	RC	cannot R	48	agr labourer	married
	Margaret	wife	RC	R/W	40	seamstress	married
	Sarah Ann Martin	daughter	RC	R/W	23	seamstress	not
	Margaret Jane	daughter	RC	R/W	15	scholar	not
10	John McGarvey	head	RC	R/W	44	farmer	not
	James	brother	RC	R/W	47	farmer	not
	Catherine McTaggart	servant	RC	cannot R	70	servant / housek	not
	James Collins	labourer	RC	R/W	50	labourer	married
11	Vacant house belonging to Michael McGarvey						
12	Vacant house belonging to Michael McGarvey						
13	Edward McLaughlin	head	RC	cannot R	47	agr labourer	widower
	William	son	RC	cannot R	17	agr labourer	not
	Catherine	daughter	RC	R/W	15	scholar	not
14	Michael McGarvey	head	RC	R/W	59	farmer	married
	Catherine	wife	RC	cannot R	56	seamstress	married
15	Vacant house belonging to Michael McGarvey						
16	Tom McGarvey	head	RC	RW	50	farmer	married
	Sarah	wife	RC	R/W	37		married
	Rose	daughter	RC	R/W	17	seamstress	not
	Thomas	son	RC	R/W	15	scholar	not
	Michael	son	RC	R/W	12	scholar	not
	Maggie	daughter	RC	R/W	11	scholar	not
	Mary	daughter	RC	cannot R	6	scholar	not
	Sarah	daughter	RC	cannot R	3		not
	Cassie	daughter	RC	R	1		not
	Margaret O'Kane	visitor	RC	R	76	nurse, dm servant	widow
	William McClintock	servant	CoE	cannot R	37	farm servant	married
17	Vacant house belonging to John McGarvey						
18	Ellen McLaughlin	head	RC	cannot R	32	seamstress	widow
	Ellen McLaughlin	daughter	RC	R/W	17	scholar	not
	Frances	son	RC	R/W	15	farm servant	not
	Daniel	son	RC	R/W	13	scholar	not
	William	son	RC	R	10	scholar	not
	Edward	son	RC	R	8	scholar	not
19	Jane Cochrane	head	RC	cannot R	40	farmer	widow
	Joseph	son	RC	cannot R	21	farm son	not
	Lizzie	daughere	RC	R/W	16	farmer daughter	not
	Catherine Ann	daughter	RC	R/W	12	farmer daughter	not
20	Eliza O'Hagan	head	RC	cannot R	65	seamstress	widow
	James Dolan	son	RC	cannot R	32	agr labourer	not
21	Sarah McKinney	head	RC	cannot R	64	seamstess	widow
	John McKinney	son	RC	R/W	45	agr Labourer	not
22	Bernard McGarvey	head	RC	R/W	60	farmer	married
	Jane	wife	RC	R/W	50		married
	Bridget A	daughter	RC	R/W	20	farmer daughter	not
	Sarah Jane	daughter	RC	R/W	18	farmer daughter	not
	Patrick	son	RC	R/W	16	farm son	not
	William Toland	servant	RC	R/W	25	servant	not

* Note: Can speak Irish.

23 Thomas Brogan	head	RC	R/W	32	farmer	not
Catherine	mother	RC	cannot R	70	farmer	widow
Bridget	sister	RC	R/W	30	seamstress	not
24 Edward McAnally	head	RC	cannot R	50	farmer	not
Mary	sister	RC	cannot R	60	cook, servant	not
John	brother	RC	Read	40	agr labourer	not
25 Bridget McColgan#	head	RC	Read	35	seamstress	widow
Michael	son	RC	R/W	12	scholar	not
Daniel	son	RC	R/W	10	scholar	not
Bella	daughter	RC	R/W	8	scholar	not
26 Margaret McNally	head	RC		56	farmer	widow
James	son	RC	R/W	17	farm son	not
Patrick	son	RC	R/W	17	scholar	not
William	son	RC	R/W	13	scholar	not
Maggie	daughter	RC	R/W	12	scholar	not
Dan	son	RC	R/W	6	scholar	not
27 Vacant house belonging to Charles McColgan						
28 Rose Quinn	head	RC	Read	57	housekeeper	widow
Mary	daughter	RC	R/W	25	seamstress	not
Henry E	son	RC	R/W	17	farmer	not
Charles J Bradley##	nephew	RC	R/W	9	scholar	not
29 John McCrory	head	RC	R/W	60	farmer	not
Susan	sister	RC	R/W	65		not
Mary	sister	RC	Read	68		not
30 Daniel Quinn	head	RC	R/W	35	farmer	not
Maggie Ann	sister	RC	R/W	30	housekeeper	not
31 National school						
32 John Devlin	head	RC	R/W	60	farmer	married
Mary	wife	RC	R/W	42		married
Rose	daughter	RC	R/W	26	seamstress	not
James	son	RC	R/W	24	labourer	not
Patrick	son	RC	R/W	20	labourer	not
Dan	son	RC	R/W	17	labourer	not
Michael	son	RC	R/W	14	scholar	not
Mary Ann	daughter		R/W	11	scholar	not
Maggie	daughter	RC	cannot R	6	scholar	not
Frances	son	RC	cannot R	3		not
33 Henry McAleer	head	RC	R/W	30	farmer	not
Hugh	brother	RC	R/W	28	labourer	not
Margaret Kelly	aunt	RC	R/W	70	servant	widow
34 Peter Morris	head	RC	R/W	60	farmer	widower
Mary	daughter	RC	R/W	40	farmer daughter	not
James	son	RC	R/W	38	farmer son	not
Peter	son	RC	R/W	36	farmer son	not
Bridget	daughter	RC	R/W	34	farmer daughter	not
35 Denis Morris	head	RC	R/W	60	farmer	widower
James	son	RC	R/W	35	farmer son	not
Maggie	daughter		R/W	32	dressmaker	not
Bridget	daughter	RC	R/W	30	farmer daughter	not
Anne	daughter	RC	R/W	24	dressmaker	not
Cassie	daughter	RC	R/W	22	farmer daughter	not

Born in County Donegal. ## Born in County Derry.

CENSUS OF IRELAND 1901 SESSIAGH OF GALLON

	Names	Relation	Relig	Education	Age	Occupation	Married?
1	Charles McColgan	head	RC	R/W	38	farmer	not
	James	brother	RC	R/W	34	farmer	not
	Mary	sister	RC	R/W	45	cook, servant	not
	James McColgan	uncle	RC	cannot R	65	agr labourer	not
2	James Quinn	head	RC	R/W	72	wool weaver	not
3	Hugh Devlin	head	RC	cannot R	60	farmer	married
	Catherine	wife	RC	R/W	50		married
	Mary	daughter	RC	R/W	19	seamstress	not
	Sarah	daughter	RC	R/W	17	seamstress	not
	John James	son	RC	R/W	15	farmer son	not
	Catherine	daugher	RC	R/W	13	farmer daughter	not
	Maggie Jame	daughter	RC	R/W	12	scholar	not
	Patrick	son	RC	R/W	10	scholar	not
	Rose Ellen	daughter	RC	R/W	5	scholar	not
4	William Morris	head	RC	R/W	30	farmer	married
	Eliza	wife	RC	R/W	25		married
	John	son	RC	R/W	7	scholar	not
	William	son	RC	R/W	5	scholar	not
	Maggie	daughter	RC	cannot R	3		not
	Aggie	daughter	RC	cannot R	1		not
	Mary McDevitt	sister-in-law	RC	R/W	20	cook, servant	not
	Neal Kelly	servant	RC	R/W	21	farm servant	not
5	John Quinn	father	RC	R	60	farmer	widow
	John J	son	RC	R/W	25	labourer	not
	Mary Ann	daughter	RC	R/W	27	seamstress	not
	Catherine	daughter	RC	R/W	22	seamstress	not
	Mary Morris	aunt	RC	R/W	53	seamstress	not
6	Vacant house belonging to Hugh McAleer						
7	Rose Conway	head	RC	R/W	48	seamstress	widow
	Mary	daughter	RC	Read	23	seamstress	not
	James	son	RC	R/W	21	agr labourer	not
	Sophia	daughter	RC	Read	19	seamstress	not
	John	son	RC	R/W	18	agr labourer	not
	Rose Anne	daughter	RC	R/W	15	seamstress	not
	William	son	RC	R/W	13	agr labourer	not
	Cassie	daughter	RC	R/W	10	scholar	not

RETROSPECTIVE CENSUS FOR 1935

Prepared by Mr Tommy McNamee

Note: This census was compilied in 1999 from memory. Details may not therefore be totally accurate. Ages are particulary liable to error.

GALLON UPPER – Total pop: 83 (49 males, 34 females) 20 houses

	Occupier	Relation to head	Age	Married?	Occupation
1	Annie Morris	aunt (5)	65	not	housekeeper
	Denis	head	18	not	labourer
	Seamus	brother	14	not	farmer
	Alice	sister	16	not	farm daugh
	Peggy	sister	17	not	housekeeper
2	Bernard McColgan	head (8)	55	married	farmer
	Bridget	wife	50	married	farmer's wife
	Patrick	son	20	not	farmer's son
	Annie	daughter	18	not	farm daugh
	Bella	daughter	15	not	farm daugh
	Rose	daughter	17	not	farm daugh
	Bernard	son	12	not	farmer's son
	Gerard	son	9	not	farmer's son
3	Henry McAleer	head (2)	65	not	farmer
	Hugh	brother	63	not	farm labourer
4	James Brogan	head (2)	70	married	ret farmer
	Katie	wife	68	married	ret farm wife
5	Michael Devlin	head (1)	50	not	farmer
6	Mary A Mc Namee	head (1)	53	not	ret farmer
7	John McAnena	head (9)	50	married	farmer
	Bella	wife	41	married	farmer's wife
	Mary	daughter	18	not	farm daugh
	John	son	16	not	farmer's son
	Arthur	son	12	not	scholar
	Bridget	daughter	10	not	scholar
	Patrick	son	9	not	scholar
	Jane	daughter	5	not	scholar
	Josephine	daughter	2	not	infant
8	Charles McColgan	head (7)	31	not	farmer
	Maggie	sister	33	not	farm worker
	James	brother	29	not	farm worker
	Rosie	sister	22	not	nurse
	Owen	brother	24	not	farm worker
	Mary Ellen	sister	28	not	farm worker
	Johnny	brother	18	not	farm worker
9	Charles Quinn	head (2)	60	not	farmer
	Maggie	niece	30	not	housewife
10	James Gilchrist	head (2)	40	married	farm labourer
	Lizzie	wife	40	married	housewife
11	Paddy McNally	head (3)	40	not	farmer
	James	brother	40	not	farm worker
	Willie	brother	38	not	farm worker
12	Neil Kelly	head (6)	60	married	farm worker
	John McNamee	son-in-law	30	married	labourer

	Cassie	daughter	27	married	wife
	Charlie	son	7	not	scholar
	Neil	son	5	not	scholar
	Barney	son	>1	not	infant
13	Vacant house (McGarvey's)				
14	Andy Caldwell	head (2)	25	married	labourer
	Mary	wife	24	married	housewife
15	William McClure	head (9)	38	married	farm worker
	Alice	wife	38	married	housewife
	George Morris	step-son	14	not	scholar
	Billy Morris	step-son	12	not	scholar
	Jim Morris	step-son	8	not	scholar
	May McClure	daughter	4	not	scholar
	Annie McClure	daughter	1	not	scholar
	Robbie	son	1	not	infant
15	Pat O'Brien	head (5)	60	married	farmer
	Rose	wife	60	married	farm wife
	Michael	son	35	not	farm worker
	Harry	son	30	not	farm worker
	John McGillian	friend		not	labourer
17	Charles McNamee	head (8)	50	married	farmer
	Maggie	wife	48	married	housewife
	James	son	21	not	labourer
	Charlie	son	18	not	labourer
	Paddy	son	17	not	labourer
	Mickey	son	15	not	labourer
	Vincent	son	11	not	scholar
	Annie	daughter	11	not	scholar
18	Willie McGillian	head (4)	40	not	farm worker
	Biddie	mother	65	married	housewife
	Minnie	gr-child	14	not	scholar
	Lily	gr-ch	12	not	scholar
19	John Flynn	head (3)		married	labourer
	Sara Flynn	wife		married	housewife
	.....Flynn	son		not	infant
	.....Flynn	daughter		not	infant
20	Paddy McLaughlin	head (3)	45	married	labourer
	Bessie	daughter	20	not	labourer
	Nellie	daughter	18	not	labourer

GALLON LOWER – Total pop: 50 (22 male, 27 female) 12 houses

	Occupier	**Relation to head**	**Age**	**Married?**	**Occupation**
1	Vacant house (the late Michael Brogan)				
2	Neil McAnena	head (5)	55	not	farmer
	Biddy	sister	52	not	farm worker
	Katy Ann	sister	64	not	farm worker
	Susan	sister	61	not	farm worker
	Johnny	brother	68	not	farm worker
3	Jamie Donegan	head (9)	40	married	pack-man
	Martha	wife	39	married	housewife
	Alice	daught	11	not	mill worker
	John James	son	9	not	scholar

	Anthony	son	7	not	scholar
	Kevin	son	8	not	scholar
	Mickey	son	6	not	scholar
	Sheila	daughter	4	not	infant
	Sam Donegan	brother	42	not	pack-man
4	James McAnena	head (6)	50	married	farmer
	Mickey	son	26	not	shop assist
	Hanna	daughter	22	not	housekeeper
	Jim	son	20	not	labourer
	Hugh	son	24	not	labourer
	John	son	14	not	scholar
6	Alice McAnena	head (1)	70	not	housewife
7	Sarah Maguire	head (3)	53	married	farmer
	Cassie	daughter	23	not	farm daughter
	Mary	daughter	21	not	farm daughter
8	Henry Bradley	head (8)	35	married	farmer & shop
	Rose Bradley	wife	34	married	housewife
	Mary A Bradley	mother	68	widow	ret farm wife
	Rose Bradley	mother-in-law	68	widow	ret farmer
	Mary	daughter	7	not	scholar
	Tessie	daughter	5	not	scholar
	Eddie	son	4	not	infant
	Rose	daughter	1	not	infant
9	Mickey McAnena	head (3)	70	not	farmer
	Rose Ann	sister	68	not	housewife
	Pat McAnena	nephew	18	not	farm worker
10	Joe McAnena	head (1)	58	not	farmer
11	Frank McLaughlin	head (11)	43	married	labourer
	Minnie	wife	41	not	housewife
	Jack	son	22	not	labourer
	Annie	daughter	20	not	nurse
	Eileen	daughter	18	not	nurse
	Bridget	daughter	12	not	scholar
	Jim	son	10	not	scholar
	Daniel	son	7	not	scholar
	Mona	daughter	5	not	scholar
	Claire	daughter	3	not	infant
	Philomena	daughter	1	not	infant
12	Bella McGurk	head (2)	50	widow	farmer
	Bella McCullagh	cousin	30	not	housekeeper

GALLON SESSIAGH – Total pop: 27, (11 males, 16 females) 4 houses

	Occupier	**Relation to head**	**Age**	**Married?**	**Occupation**
1	William Bradley	head (7)	36	married	farmer
	Margaret Bradley	wife	35	married	housewife
	Mary	daughter	10	not	scholar
	Kathleen	daughter	9	not	scholar
	Rosaleen	daughter	7	not	scholar
	Josephine	daughter	5	not	scholar
	Teresa	daughter	4	not	infant
2	John James Quinn	head (7)	30	married	farmer
	Maggie Quinn	wife	30	married	housewife

	Katie	sister	28	not	farm worker
	Mary	daughter	7	not	scholar
	Annie	daughter	5	not	scholar
	Susan	daughter	4	not	scholar
	Pat	son	8	not	infant
3	John J Devlin	head (3)	50	not	farmer
	Margt Jane Devlin	sister	53	not	housewife
	John Devine	nephew	23	not	farm worker
4	Lizzie Morris	head (10)	60	not	farmer
	John	son	44	not	farm worker
	William	son	41	not	farm worker
	James	son	38	not	farm worker
	Dan	son	35	not	farm worker
	Maggie	daughter	37	not	farm worker
	Alice	daughter	40	not	farm worker
	Lily	daughter	33	not	farm worker
	Agnes	daughter	31	not	farm worker
	Hugh	son	25	not	farmer' son
5	Vacant house (McColgan's)				

UNOFFICIAL CENSUS OF GALLON CARRIED OUT IN MAY 1958
by Mr W J Bradley

Note: This unofficial census was carried out in 1958 by the author as a boy aged 15. It therefore lacks the rigour of an official census. Ages are not given.

GALLON UPPER Total pop: 89 (43 males, 46 females) 21 houses

	Occupier	**Relation**	**Married?**	**Occupation**
1	Seamus Morris	head	not	farmer
	Peggy Morris	sister	not	housekeeper
2	Bernard McColganSen	head	married	farmer
	Bridget McColgan	wife	married	farm wife
	Bernard McColgan Jr	son	not	farmer's son
	Gerald McColgan	son	not	farmer's son
3	David Devine	head	married	labourer
	Gertrude Devine	wife	married	housewife
	Brendan	son	not	scholar
	Mary	son	not	scholar
	Thomas	son	not	infant
	Martin	son	not	infant
4	Michael Devlin	head	not	ret farmer
5	James Gilchrist	head	married	labourer
	Lizzie Gilchrist	wife	married	housewife
6	Charlie McColgan	head	not	farmer
	Mary Ellen McColgan	sister	not	farmer
	Maggie McColgan	sister	not	housewife
7	Charlie Quinn	head	not	retd farmer
	Harry O'Brien	nephew in law	married	farmer
	Maggie O'Brien	neice	married	housewife
	Rosemary	grand niece	not	scholar
	Kathleen	grand niece	not	scholar
	Cissie	grand niece	not	infant
	Patricia	grand niece	not	infant
8	Neil McNamee	head	married	farmer
	Mary McNamee	wife	married	housewife
	Geraldine	daughter	not	infant
	Bridget Connolly	niece	not	infant
9	John McAneny	head	married	farmer
	Bella McAneny	wife	married	housewife
	(Pat McAneny	son	not	farmer's son
	Josephine McAneny	daughter	not	farm daughter
10	John McNamee Jr	head	married	farmer
	Mary	wife	married	housewife
	Philip	son	not	scholar
	Sean	son	not	scholar
	Brendan	son	not	scholar
	Terence	son	not	scholar
	Kevin	son	not	infant
	Mary	daughter	not	infant
	Eugene	son	not	infant
11	William McClure	head	married	labourer
	Serena	daughter	not	mill worker

	Pauline	daughter	not	mill worker
12	Lila McCallion Sr	head	widow	housewife
	Jim	son	not	labourer
	Maisie	daughter	not	mill worker
	Nora	daughter	not	scholar
	Margaret	daughter	not	scholar
13	Bessie McLaughlin	head	not	farmworker
14	Neil Kelly	head	widower	labourer
	Andy Caldwell	son-in-law	married	labourer
	Mary Caldwell	daughter	married	housewife
	Dannie	son	not	labourer
	Tess	daughter	not	factory work
	Vera	daughter	not	scholar
	Rose	daughter	not	scholar
	Philip	son	not	scholar
	Clare	daughter	not	scholar
	Anne	daughter	not	scholar
15	Willie Ashenhurst	head	not	labourer
	Annie Ashenhurst	wife	not	housewife
	Frances	daughter	not	factory work
	Ruby	daughter	not	factory work
	Gracie	daughter	not	scholar
16	Michael O'Brien	head	not	farmer
17	Paddy Tracey	head	married	labourer
	Jeannie Tracey	wife	married	housewife
	Rose	daughter	not	factory work
	Josephine	daughter	not	factory work
	Jack	son	not	scholar
	Tony	son	not	scholar
18	Willie McGillian	head	not	labourer
19	John McNamee (sen)	head	married	farmer
	Cassie E McNamee	wife	married	housewife
	Barney	son	not	labourer
	Kathleen	daughter	not	factory work
	Maureen	daughter	not	factory work
	Rose	daughter	not	scholar
20	Charlie McNamee (jun)	head	married	farmer
	Betty McNamee	wife	married	housewife
	Leo McNamee	son	not	labourer
21	Charlie McNamee (sen)	head	married	farmer
	Maggie McNamee	wife	married	housewife
	Vincent McNamee	son	not	farmer's son
	Michael McNamee	son	not	labourer
	Charlie (C) McNamee	son	not	contractor

GALLON LOWER Total pop: 31 (14 males, 17 females) 9 houses

	Occupier	**Relation**	**Married?**	**Occupation**
1	Bella McGurk	head	widow	farmer
	Bella McCullagh	cousin	not	housewife
2	Minnie McLaughlin	head	widow	housewife
3	Mickey McAnena	head	not	thatcher
4	Henry Bradley	head	married	farmer

	Rose Bradley	wife	married	housewife
	Tessie	daughter	not	dress designer
	Eddie	son	not	farmer's son
	Rose Bradley	daughter	not	shop assistant
	Catherine	daughter	not	nurse
	Patricia	daughter	not	student
	Philomena	daughter	not	student
	John	son	not	student
5	Paddy Maguire	head	married	labourer
	Eileen Maguire	wife	married	housewife
	Kay	daughter	not	scholar
	Margaret	daughter	not	scholar
	Ann	daughter	not	scholar
	Patrick	son	not	scholar
	Anthony	son	not	scholar
	John	son	not	infant.
	Bernadette	daughter	not	infant.
6	Jack McConnell	head	not	farmer
	Eddie McConnell	brother	not	housekeeper
7	John McAnena	head	not	farmer
	Pat McAnena	brother	not	labourer
8	John Devine	head	married	labourer
9	Neil McAnena	head	not	farmer
	Susan	sister	not	housekeeper
	Biddy	sister	not	retired
	Katie Ann	sister	not	retired

GALLON SESSIAGH. Total pop: 12 (4 males, 8 females) 4 houses

	Occupier	**Relation**	**Married?**	**Occupation**
1	Alice Morris	head	not	farmer
	Willie John Morris	nephew	not	scholar
2	Maggie Quinn	head	widow	retired farmer
	Tommy McNamee	son-in-law	married	farmer
	Susan McNamee	daughter	married	housewife
	Ann Patricia	grand-dau	not	infant
	Kieran	grand-son	not	infant
3	Mary Bradley	head	not	teacher
	Rosaleen Bradley	sister	not	housewife
	John Bradley	brother	not	teacher
	Vera Bradley	sister	not	scholar
4	Maggie Jane Devlin	head	not	farmer

PRIVATE CENSUS OF GALLON HELD ON 7 APRIL 2000

Note: This is an unofficial census and lacks the rigour of an official census. Ages are not given.

GALLON UPPER. Total pop: 42 (25m, 17f) 16 occ houses

	Occupier	Relation to head	Married	Occupation
1	Vacant house belonging to Hugh McElwee			
2	Bernard McColgan	head	yes	retd farmer
	Mary McColgan	wife	yes	retd nurse
3	Charles McColgan	head	yes	plumber / farmer
	Mary McColgan	wife	yes	nurse
	Sarah McColgan	daughter	not	scholar
4	Sean Devine	head	yes	farmer / labourer
	Rosemary Devine	wife	yes	housewife
	Seanin	daughter	not	catering
	Kevin	son	not	student
	Aileen	daughter	not	student
	Patricia O'Brien	sis-in-law	not	unemployed
5	Martin McGuigan	head	yes	steel fitter
	Geraldine McGuigan	wife	yes	accountant
	Rory	son	not	student
6	John McNamee	head	yes	labourer
	Shane McNamee	son	not	labourer
7	Mary McNamee	head	widow	housekeeper
	Mark McNamee	son	yes	farmer
	Majella McNamee	daught-in-law	yes	factory work
8	Patrick McAneny	head	not	retired farmer
9	William J Patton	head	yes	lorry driver
	Tess Patton	wife	yes	housewife
	Mary Patton	daughter	not	factory worker
10	Damien McNamee	head	yes	labourer
	Siobhan McNamee	wife	yes	housekeeper
	Gavan	son	no	scholar
	Ciara	daughter	not	scholar
	Caolin	son	not	scholar
	Cahir	son	not	scholar
11	Thomas McNamee	head	widower	retired farmer
	Kieran McNamee	son	not	farmer / labourer
	Dermot McNamee	son	not	labourer
12	Sadie McNamee	head	widow	farmer
	Bernard McNamee	son	not	labourer
13	Vacant house belonging to Anthony Hood			
14	Robin Stewart	head	yes	lorry driver
	Anne P Stewart	wife	yes	nurse
	Paul	son	not	scholar
	Emmet	son	not	scholar
	Anne P Stewart	wife	yes	nurse
15	Angela Gormley	head	not	factory worker
16	Vincent McNamee	head	yes	retired farmer
	Eamon McNamee	son	not	farmer / labourer

17 Apr 2000: 2000

GALLON LOWER – Tot pop: 13 (7m, 6f) 3 occ houses

	Occupier	**Relation to head**	**Married**	**Occupation**	
1	Vacant house belonging to Pat McAnena				
2	John McNamee	head	yes	retired farmer	
	Eugene McNamee	son	not	farmer / labourer	
	Declan McNamee	son	not	labourer	
3	Kevin McNamee	head	yes	yes	nurse / farmer
	Teresa McNamee	wife	yes	yes	housewife
	Emma	daughter	no	not	infant
	Niamh	daughter	no	not	infant
4	Helen Nicholas	head		yes	p/t waitress
	Charlene	daughter	no	not	scholar
	Darren	son	no	not	scholar
	Stephen	son	no	not	scholar
	Deane	son	no	not	scholar
	Lindsay	daughter	no	not	scholar

GALLON SESSIAGH – Tot pop: 15 (7m, 8f) 4 houses

	Occupier	**Relation to head**	**Married**	**Occupation**	
1	Noel O'Brien	head		yes	labourer
	Maria	wife		yes	housewife
	Cathy	daughter		no	scholar
	Christopher	son		no	scholar
	Caoimhe	daughter		no	scholar
2	Ronny McNulty	head		yes	labourer
	Donna	wife		yes	housewife
	James	son		no	scholar
	Michela	daughter		no	scholar
	Conor	son		no	infant
3	Anne McNulty*	head		widow	housewife
4	Gary Drum*	head		yes	butcher
	Helen Drum*	wife		yes	factory work
	Patrick *	son		no	scholar
	Brigeen *	daughter		no	scholar

* Note: Two families live on Sessiagh Road, but in the townland of Glenock.

SUMMARY	Gallon Upper	Gallon Lower	Gallon Sessiagh	Total
Professionals	4	1	0	5
Tradespeople	2	0	0	2
Unskilled	19	4	4	27
Retd farmers	5	1	0	6
Scholars / infants	12	7	6	25
	42	13	10	65

APPENDIX D: GENERAL REGISTER OF GALLON SCHOOL FROM 1896 TO 1969

REGISTER OF GALLON PUBLIC ELEMENTARY SCHOOL 1896-1934 (BOYS)

Copied from old register

Entry date	Name	Date of birth	Address	Parent's occupation	Previous school	Struck off	Highest class
1896	Patrick Brogan	25.3.86	Gallon Upper	Cottier	Gallon NS	1900	–
	John J Devlin	30.8.85	Gallon Sessiagh	Farmer	Gallon NS	1900	–
	Tom McGarvey	13.12.85	Gallon Upper	Farmer	Gallon NS	1900	–
	James McNally	12.8.83	Gallon Upper	Farmer	Gallon NS	1898	–
	William Conway	19.12.86	Gallon Sessiagh	Widow	Gallon NS	1900	–
	Neil McAnena	7.4.78	Gallon Lower	Farmer	Gallon NS	1897	–
	Henry E Quinn	24.10.82	Gallon Upper	Farmer	Gallon NS	1900	–
	James Brogan	2.12.82	Gallon Upper	Cottier	Gallon NS	1898	–
	Patrick McCullagh	9.9.83	Gallon Lower	Shopkeeper	Gallon NS	1901	–
	Frank Boyle	1.1.85	Glenock	Navvy	Gallon NS	1897	–
	Patrick McAnena	–	Gallon Lower	Publican	Gallon NS	–	–
	Michael McGarvey	22.4.88	Gallon Upper	Farmer	Gallon NS	1901	–
	Charles Brogan (John)	3.87	Ballynasolus	Farmer	Gallon NS	1898	–
	Francis McLaughlin	7.10.85	Gallon Upper	Tradesman	Gallon NS	1900	–
	Charles Kelly (Pat senior)	11.9.87	Tullyherin	Cottier	Gallon NS	1901	–
	Patrick McNally	12.8.83	Gallon Upper	Farmer	Gallon NS	1900	–
	William Cochrane	4.10.86	Gallon Upper	Widow	Gallon NS	–	–
	Dan McLaughlin	19.2.88	Gallon Upper	Thatcher	Gallon NS	–	–
	Michael McNamee	11.11.88	Gallon Upper	Farmer	Gallon NS	–	–
	Michael Devlin	3.6.86	Gallon Sessiagh	Farmer	Gallon NS	–	–
	Patrick McLaughlin	10.2.90	Gallon Upper	Cottier	Gallon NS	1901	–
	Francis Brogan	5.90	Tullyherin	Farmer	Gallon NS	1901	–
	Charles Bradley	18.11.88	Gallon Lower	Farmer	Gallon NS	1905	–
	James Kelly	21.7.89	Tullyherin	Cottier	Gallon NS	1901	–
	Patrick Smith	30.10.88	Strawletterdallan	Baker	Gallon NS	1903	–
	William Bradley	15.6.90	Gallon Lower	Farmer	Gallon NS	1904	–
	Micheal Brogan	8.12.89	Glenock	Farmer	Gallon NS	1901	–
	James Brogan	16.4.91	Glenock	Farmer	Gallon NS	1905	–
	Wm John McColgan	27.3.87	Gallon Upper	Widow	Gallon NS	1901	–
	Michael McColgan	25.11.88	Gallon Upper	Widow	Gallon NS	1903	–
	William McLaughlin	19.3.90	Gallon Upper	Cottier	Gallon NS	1900	–
	Daniel McColgan	21.9.90	Gallon Upper	Widow	Gallon NS	1901	3
	Daniel McGillian	6.1.88	Gallon Upper	Cottier	Gallon NS	1905	–
	Patrick McGillian	3.1.90	Gallon Upper	Cottier	Gallon NS	–	–
	John J Kelly	25.5.90.	Gallon Upper	Shopkeeper	Gallon NS	–	4
	Chales Kelly (Pat jr)	17.1.92	Gallon Upper	Shopkeeper	Gallon NS	1904	4
	Patrick Devlin	24.1.92	Gallon Sessiagh	Farmer	Gallon NS	1907	6
	Edward McLaughlin	19.6.92	Gallon Upper	Cottier	Gallon NS	1905	–
	Michael Brogan	5.92	Tullyherin	Farmer	Gallon NS	1907	4
	Patrick McAnena	6.82	Tullyherin	Farmer	Corrick NS	1896	3
	Bernard McNamee	27.12.92	Gallon Upper	Farmer	Gallon NS	1908	6
	John McAnena	9.85	Gallon Upper	Farmer	Corrick NS	1900	3
	Charles Brogan (Patk)	7.86	Tullyherin	Farmer	Gallon NS	1901	5
	Charles McNamee	3.84	Gallon Upper	Farmer	Gallon NS	1902	5
	Dan Devlin	2.83	Gallon Upper	Farmer	Gallon NS	1901	5
1897	Wm McGillian	12.93	Gallon Upper	Cottier	First school	1907	3
1897	Wm McNally	3.87	Gallon Upper	Widow	First school	1902	–
1897	James McClintock	6.91	Gallon Upper	Cottier	First school	1899	–

1897	Robert Morris	7.87	Gallon Sessiagh	Cottier	First school	1903	–
1897	Wm James Morris	6.91	Gallon Sessiagh	Cottier	First school	1903	–
1898	Edward Morris	6..93	Beaghs	Cottier	First school	1905	–
1898	William Brogan	9.93	Tullyherin	Farmer	First school	1906	5
1898	Joseph Bradley	7.91	Gallon Upper	Farmer	Cliffony, Sligo	1907	4
1898	Charles Brogan	4.95	Corrick	Farmer	First school	–	–
1899	John Morris	7.94	Gallon Sessiagh	Farmer	First school	1907	–
1899	William Morris	7.95	Gallon Sessiagh	Farmer	First school	–	–
1899	Patrick J McGarvey	6.83	Gallon Upper	Farmer	First school	1899	–
1899	Daniel McNally	5.94	Gallon Upper	Widow	First school	1907	4
1899	John Jas McGillian	9.96	Gallon Upper	Cottier	First school	1908	–
1899	John Jas Bradley	3.94	Gallon Lower	Farmer	First school	1909	4
1900	Thomas McNamee	5.96	Gallon Upper	Farmer	First school	1910	4
1901	John James McConnell	3.97	Glenock	Farmer	First school	1910	5
1901	Bernard Brogan	1.98	Glenock	Widow	First school	1911	6
1902	Charles Brogan	9.93	Tullyherin	Cottier	Corrick NS	1906	–
1902	Edward Brogan	8.96	Tullyherin	Cottier	Corrick NS	1907	3
1903	Owen Morris	7.98	Gallon Upper	Cottier	First school	1911	–
1903	Con McGillian	8.98	Glenock	Navvy	First school	1913	4
1903	Henry Bradley	7.99	Gallon Lower	Widow	First school	1913	7
1903	Patrick Brogan	12.91	Tullyherin	Cottier	First school	1916	2
1904	James McElrea	12.93	Tullyherin	Farmer	Corrick NS	1906	5
	There may be entries missing between 1904 and 1907						
1907	Pat Harkin	10.5.00.	Lisnafin	Rail worker	First school	1913	6
1907	Edward McConnell	11.8.03	Glenock	Farmer	First school	1915	3
1907	James Dolan	22.8.03	Ballynasolus	Mason	First school	1908	–
1907	Patrick Brogan	27.5.02	Gallon Upper	Farmer	First school	1915	5
1907	Charles McAnena	19.3.02	Gallon Upper	Farmer	First school	1915	3
1907	Patrick McGillian	26.5.97	Legfordrum	Farmer	Legfordrum	1908	–
1907	Peter Ward	28.6.98	Legfordrum	Farmer	First school	1908	3
1907	Thomas McDonnell	8.7.92	Legfordrum	Carpenter	First school	1908	6
1907	Patrick J Ward	5.5.94	Legfordrum	Farmer	First school	1908	5
1907	John Ward	13.10.92	Legfordrum	Farmer	First school	1908	6
1908	Charles Bradley	17.6.01	Crosh	Labourer	First school	1911	–
1908	John Bradley	28.8.02	Crosh	Labourer	First school	1911	–
1908	John McAnena	3.7.04	Gallon Upper	Labourer	First school	1915	–
1908	Michael Smith	20.4.03	Legfordrum	Pedlar	First school	1908	–
1908	Robert Reid	19.3.02	Ballynasolus	Cottier	First school	1909	–
1908	Patrick Tracey	19.4.02	Tullyherin	Cottier	First school	1916	4
1908	James Morris	4.6.05	Gallon Sessiagh	Farmer	First school	1914	5
1908	Thomas Brogan	13.6.05	Gallon Upper	Farmer	First school	1916	4
1908	James McGarvey	21.5.05	Gallon Upper	Farmer	First school	1916	4
1908	William J Dolan	14.9.05	Gallon Upper	Cottier	First school	1916	4
1910	Francis McCanny	13.9.07	Glenock	Cottier	Newtown NS	1913	3
1910	Jeremiah McCanny	12.8.03	Glenock	Cottier	First school	1913	–
1910	Peter McCanny	3.4.06	Glenock	Cottier	First school	1913	–
1910	Prancis McGillian	2.2.06	Glenock	Cottier	First school	1918	3
1910	John J Tracey	4.4.05	Glenock	Cottier	First school	1913	3
1911	Patrick Kelly	13.2.04	Gallon Sessiagh	Cottier	First school	1918	6
1911	John Kelly	16.1.05	Gallon Sessiagh	Cottier	First school	1918	6
1911	William Th McConnell	31.1.04	Glenock	Farmer	First school	1919	4
1911	Charles McColgan	5.5.05	Gallon Sessiagh	Farmer	First school	1919	4
1911	John Brogan (Ned)	7.6.08	Gallon Upper	Farmer	Corrick NS	1920	5
1912	James McColgan	2.1.08	Gallon Upper	Farmer	Corrick NS	1925	5
1912	Charles O Hagan	5.7.01	Carnargan	Farmer	First school	1914	3
1912	James Young	6.5.02	Tullyherin	Farmer	First school	1912	–
1912	Michael McAnena	8.4.09	Gallon Upper	Farmer	First school	1923	3

1912	Edward O Hagan	7.5.02	Lisnafin	Farmer	First school	1913	–
1912	John McNamee	16.6.07	Gallon Upper	Cottier	First school	1919	4
1912	John Brogan (John)	17.10.07	Gallon Upper	Cottier	First school	1916	–
1912	Denis McGarvey	13.11.08	Gallon Upper	Farmer	First school	1923	4
1912	Daniel Morris	11.1.09	Gallon Upper	Farmer	First school	1923	–
1912	Joseph M Tracey	30.6.06	Tullyherin	Cottier	First school	1919	–
1913	Patrick McAnena	11.3.07	Gallon Upper	Farmer	First school	–	6
1913	John McAnena	15.3.07	Gallon Lower	Farmer	First school	–	–
1913	Thomas Tracey	14.12.07	Tullyherin	Cottier	First school	–	–
1913	Owen McColgan	–	Gallon Sessiagh	Farmer	First school	–	5
1913	Patrick Morris	–	Tullyherin	Farmer	First school	–	2
1914	Hugh Morris	13.7.10	Gallon Sessiagh	Farmer	First school	1927	4
1914	Daniel McGillian	14.5.08	Carnargan	Cottier	First school	1915	–
1915	Hugh McAnena	10.4.10	Gallon Lower	Farmer	First school	1915	3
1915	Denis McKenna	26.9.13	Gallon Upper	Cottier	First school	1915	–
1916	Patrick O Hagan	13.9.11	Tullyherin	Farmer	First school	1919	–
1916	Daniel Kelly	18.8.11	Sessiagh		First school	1925	4
1916	James Brogan	19.5.11	Gallon Upper	Farmer	First school	1923	4
1916	Bernard Brogan	23.1.13	Gallon Upper	Cottier	First school	1926	5
1916	Bernard McNamee	27.5.13	Gallon Upper		First school	1925	–
1916	James McAnena	25.3.13	Lisnafin		First school	1924	4
1917	Thomas Brogan	27.2.14	Gallon Sessiagh	Cottier	First school	–	5
1918	Edward McLaughlin	–	Shannony East	Cottier	First school	–	3
1918	Francis McLaughlin	–	Shannony East	Cottier	First school	–	4
1919	Patrick Maguire	28.6.13	Lisnafin	Farmer	First school	–	4
1919	John Morris	15.8.14	Tullyherin	Farmer	First school	–	3
1920	James McAnena	10.5.16	Gallon Upper	Farmer	First school	1929	5
1920	Charles Jos McAnena	12.7.16	Gallon Upper	Farmer	First school	1920	–
1921	Hugh Maguire	12.5.16	Gallon Upper	Farmer	First school	1929	6
1921	James McNamee	4.5.16	Gallon Upper	Farmer	First school	1929	5
1921	Charles McNamee	14.5.17	Gallon Upper	Farmer	First school	1929	6
1921	William Charles Judge	3.5.16	Gallon Upper	Labourer	First school	1928	3
1921	Michael Judge	30.10.09	Gallon Upper	Labourer	Newtown NS	1924	–
1922	Patrick McColgan	10.5.15	Gallon Upper	Farmer	First school	1929	6
1922	John? McColgan	11.5.22	Gallon Upper	Farmer	First school	1923	–
1923	Bernard McAnena	18.4.18	Gallon Upper	Labourer	First school	1934	8
1923	Denis Morris	7.6.17	Gallon Upper	Farmer	First school	1933	5
1923	Patrick McAnena	10.7.18	Gallon Lower	Farmer	First school	1931	4
1923	Patrick McCrory	6.6.15	Gallon Upper	Farmer	Plumbridge	1923	–
1923	Emerson McCarron	16.6.14	Gallon Lower	Labourer	Douglas NS	1924	–
1923	Henry O'Brien	25.1.12	Gallon Upper	Labourer	Newtown NS	1926	–
1923	Patrick Jos McNamee	2.4.20.	Gallon Upper	Farmer	First school	–	6
1924	James Brogan	11.7.17	Ballynasolus	Farmer	First school	–	3
1924	Patrick Fr Maguire	20.6.19	Tullyherin	Labourer	First school	–	6
1924	David Devine	1.10.16	Gallon Sessiagh	Farmer	Doorat NS	–	4
1925	Joseph McColgan	8.1.18	Gallon Sessiagh	Farmer	First school	–	6
1925	John J Morris	24.5.21	Gallon Sessiagh	Farmer	First school	–	4
1925	John McAnena	16.2.20.	Gallon Upper	Labourer	First school	–	5
1926	Patrick Brogan	1.5.19	Ballynasolus	Farmer	First school	–	6
1926	John McAnena	7.7.22	Gallon Lower	Farmer	First school	–	3
1926	Arthur McAnena	9.10.23	Gallon Upper	Farmer	First school	–	4
1927	William Jas Maguire	23.10.16	Gallon Upper	Farmer	First school	–	5
1927	Columba Maguire	4.9.16	Gallon Upper	Farmer	First school	–	–
1927	John J Maguire	22.3.21	Lisnafin	Farmer	First school	–	4
1927	Patrick Jos Devine	24.5.21	Lisnafin	Farmer	First school	–	5
1927	James Maguire	22.2.21	Beaghs	Farmer	First school	–	5
1928	Bernard McColgan	24.12.22	Gallon Upper	Farmer	First school	–	4

1928	John McNamee	5.9.21	Shannony East	Labourer	First school	–	5
1928	John Maguire	8.1.17	Glasgow	Labourer	First school	–	–
1928	William Gwynne		Gallon Upper	Labourer	First school	–	–
1929	William Jas McLaughlin	18.8.25	Gallon Lower	Labourer	First school	–	–
1929	George Morris	3.9.24	Gallon Upper		First school	–	–
1930	John Gallagher	6.1.16	Legfordrum	Farmer	First school	–	3
1930	John McAleer	24.11.19	Legfordrum	Farmer	First school	–	5
1930	Gerard McColgan	9.4.26	Gallon Upper	Farmer	First school	–	–
1930	William Morris	15.12.25	Gallon Upper	Labourer	First school	–	–
1930	Cecil O'Neill	16.6.25	Gallon Upper	Farmer	First school	–	–
1931	Barney Maguire	?.3.27	Lisnafin	Farmer	First school	–	–
1931	Michael McNamee	4.4.25	Gallon Upper	Farmer	First school	–	–
1931	Alexander Sproule	25.5.18	Gallon Upper	Farmer	First school	–	4
1931	John Jas Donegan	30.10.25	Tullyherin	Pedlar	First school	–	–
1931	Thomas McNamee	5.3.26	Shannony East	Farmer	First school	–	–
1931	Francis McGillian	31.5.25	Legfordrum	Farmer	First school	–	–
1932	James Morris	21.8.27	Gallon Upper	Labourer	First school	–	–
1932	Patrick McAnena	15.10.26	Gallon Upper	Farmer	First school	–	–
1932	Samuel K Donegan	6.8.26	Gallon Upper	Farmer	First school	–	–
1932	William Maguire	8.10.26	Tullyherin	Farmer	First school	–	–
1932	Daniel McLaughlin	27.6.28	Gallon Lower	Farmer	First school	–	–
1933	Patrick Quinn	21.3.27	Lisnafin	Farmer	First school	–	–
1933	John Coyle	31.1.26	Lisnafin	Farmer	First school	–	–
1934	Anthony Donegan	10.7.29	Tullyherin	Farmer	First school	–	–
1934	George Magure	28.5.34	Tullyherin	Farmer	First school	–	–

NOTES

All the pupils in the register were Roman Catholics, except James McElrea, James Young and Emerson McCarron who were Presbyterian, and William Gwynne who was Church of Ireland. Dates when children are struck off (ie leave the school) or their highest classes are not always accurate

REGISTER OF GALLON PUBLIC ELEMENTARY SCHOOL 1896-1934 (GIRLS)

Entry date	Name	Date of birth	Address	Parent's occupation	Previous school	Struck off	Highest class
1896	Sarah Devlin	8.7.83	Gallon Sessiagh	Farmer	Gallon NS	1897	5
	Rose McGarvey	30.1.84	Gallon Upper	Farmer	Gallon NS	1900	6
	Margaret Kelly	5.7..85	Tullyherin	Cottier		1896	5
	Cassie Boyle	25.7.86	Glenock	Navvy	Gallon NS	–	–
	Jane McCullagh	10.4.85	Glenock	Shopkeeper	Gallon NS	–	–
	Bridget McAnena	7.8.81	Gallon Lower	Farmer	Gallon NS	1897	6
	Eileen Kelly	15.4.83	Tullyherin	Cottier	Gallon NS	1896	5
	Mary A McNamee	3.2.83	Glenock	Farmer	Gallon NS	1896	5
	Bridget Boyle	29.4.83	Glenock	Navvy	Gallon NS	–	–
	Letitia McAnena	20.7.84	Gallon Lower	Farmer	Gallon NS	–	–
	Susan McNamee	7.3.86	Gallon Upper	Farmer	Gallon NS	1899	5
	Catherine McLaughlin	26.12.86	Gallon Upper	Cottier	Gallon NS	1899	4
	Catherine Devlin	9.6.87	Gallon Sessiagh	Farmer	Gallon NS	1899	4
	Rose A Conway	18.10.85	Gallon Sessiagh	Widow	Gallon NS	1898	3
	Teresa McNamee	31.1.86	Gallon Upper	Farmer	Gallon NS	1899	5
	Sara Margt Brogan	12.2.86	Ballynasolus	Farmer	Gallon NS	1899	4
	Mary E McCullagh	19.6.87	Glenock	Shopkeeper	Gallon NS	1898	4
	Catherine A Cochrane	4.11.88	Gallon Upper	Widow	Gallon NS	1901	4
	Margaret McNally	31.12.87	Gallon Upper	Farmer	Gallon NS	1900	4
	Margaret McGarvey	13.10.89	Gallon Upper	Farmer	Gallon NS	–	6
	Margaret McCullagh	29.7.89	Glenock	Shopkeeper	Gallon NS	–	4

Copied from old register

	Bridget McNamee	29.8.89	Gallon Upper	Farmer	Gallon NS	–	4
	Margaret J Devlin	6.5.89	Gallon Sessiagh	Farmer	Gallon NS	–	4
	Matilda Donnelly	9.5.86	Gallon Upper	Shoemaker	Gallon NS	–	2
	Margaret Donnelly	21.7.89	Gallon Upper	Shoemaker	Gallon NS	–	4
	Annie McGillian	11.7.91	Gallon Upper	Cottier	Gallon NS	–	–
	Mary Ellen Brogan	24.1.91	Gallon Upper	Cottier	Gallon NS	–	–
	Ellen Morris	7.97	Gallon Upper	Cottier	Gallon NS	–	4
	Cassie Conway	3.6.90	Gallon Sessiagh	Widow	Gallon NS	1896	–
	Bella A McColgan	4.92	Gallon Sessiagh	Farmer	Gallon NS	1897	6
	Jane Brogan	20.11.92	Glenock	Farmer	Gallon NS	1907	6
	Susan Gormley	17.12.92	Glenock	Cottier	First school	1907	6
	Maggie McAnena	8.8.90		Farmer	Corrick	1901	4
1897	Mary A Devlin	8.90.	Gallon Upper	Farmer	Gallon NS	1905	6
1897	Maggie Bradley	1.12.92	Gallon Lower	Farmer	First school	1905	4
1897	M Agnes Smith	3.92	Gallon Lower	Baker	First school	1898	–
1898	Maggie Morris	8.86	Gallon Sessiagh	Tradesman	Gallon NS	1899	–
1898	Cassie Ellen Brogan	8.94	Gallon Lower	Farmer	Corrick	1909	3
1898	Elizabeth A McClintock	6.7.95	Gallon Upper	Cottier	First school	–	3
1899	Mary McGarvey	–	Gallon Upper	Farmer	First school	1908	6
1899	Ann Eliz Gormley	4.95	Glenock	Labourer	Corrick	1903	6
1899	Alice McCullagh	5.95	Glenock	Shopkeeper	First school	1901	4
1900	Rose E Devlin	1.96	Gallon Sessiagh	Farmer	First school	1909	6
1900	Maggie Devlin	4.96	Gallon Upper	Farmer	First school	1912	3
1900	Margaret Martin	4.84	Gallon Upper	Labourer	First school	1902	–
1900	Sara McNamee	4.90	Gallon Upper		First school	1903	–
1900	Rose Ann Bradley	11.97	Gallon Lower	Widow	First school	1911	–
1900	Sara Ann McGarvey	9.97	Gallon Upper	Farmer	First school	1912	–
1900	Maggie Morris	10.97	Gallon Sessiagh	Farmer	First school	1912	–
1900	Bridget Hood	7.92	Ballynasolus	Farmer	First school	1905	–
1900	Margaret Hood	7.93	Ballynasolus	Farmer	First school	1907	–
1902	Aggie Morris	4.99	Gallon Sessiagh	Cottier	First school	1913	–
1902	Cassie Gormley	7.98	Glenock	Navvy	First school	1903	–
6.02	Annie Brogan	12.98	Tullyherin	Cottier	Glasgow	1911	–
7.02	Matilda Hill (Pres)	2.98	Gallon Lower	Farmer	Legfordrum NS	1906	–
1902	Sara Morris	3.95	Gallon Upper	Cottier	Legfordrum NS	1911	3
1902	Aggie Morris	10.99	Gallon Sessiagh	Farmer	Legfordrum NS	–	4
1902	Cassie McGarvey	3.00	Gallon Upper	Farmer	First school	1913	7
1903	Annie Tracey	5.97	Tullyherin	Cottier	Dergalt NS	1907	–
1903	Maggie Tracey	9.99	Tullyherin	Cottier	First school	1912	–
1904	Isabella Tracey	9.98	Tullyherin	Cottier	First school	1910	–
1905	Anne Jane Bradley	7.3.96	Legfordrum	Farmer	First school	1908	4
1905	Mary Morris	2.9.01	Gallon Sessiagh	Farmer	First school	–	–
1906	Bridget McGillian	29.3.02	Glenock	Farmer	First school	1914	5
1906	Maggie McGillian	29.3.03	Glenock	Farmer	First school	–	5
1906	Anne Dolan	10.1.02	Ballynasolus	Farmer	First school	1908	–
1906	Catherine Conwell	7.6.02	Gallon Upper	Farmer	First school	1907	–
1906	Sara J O Hagan	3.9.02	Gallon Upper	Farmer	First school	1915	–
1907	Maggie Brogan	1.2.03	Tullyherin	Farmer	First school	1915	4
1907	Alice Morris	17.3.03	Gallon Sessiagh	Farmer	First school	1913	–
1907	Susan Morris	20.10.02	Tullyherin	Cottier	Corrick	–	–
1907	Cassie McConnell	13.11.00	Glenock	Labourer	First school	1907	–
1907	Annie McGillian	6.6.99	Legfordrum	Farmer	First school	1908	–
1907	Mary McGillian	19.7.98	Legfordrum	Farmer	First school	1908	3
1907	Cassie Quinn	7.6.94	Legfordrum	Farmer	First school	1908	4
5.08	Mary McColgan	1.1.98	Gallon Upper	Farmer	First school	1909	–
1908	Alice Reid	25.12.97	Ballynasolus	Farmer	First school	1909	3
1908	Annie Reid	13.11.95	Ballynasolus	Farmer	First school	1911	3

1908	Cassie Watson	4.5.98	Gallon Upper	Farmer	First school	1910	–
1909	Mary Tracey	3.4.05	Tullyherin	Cottier	First school	1908	5
1909	Annie Hill	7.6.01	Gallon Lower	Farmer	First school	1911	–
1909	Teresa Brogan	7.5.05	Tullyherin	Cottier	First school	1915	4
1909	Maggie Morris	3.11.05	Tullyherin	Farmer	First school	1915	–
1911	Mary Agnes Gouldrey	12.11.02	Lisnafin	Farmer	First school	1912	–
1911	Maggie McColgan	3.10.04	Gallon Sessiagh	Farmer	First school	1920	4
1911	Lily Morris	3.5.09	Gallon Upper	Farmer	First school	1924	3
1911	Ellen McColgan	5.6.07	Gallon Upper	Farmer	First school	1914	3
1912	Cassie E Kelly	23.2.08	Gallon Sessiagh	Labourer	First school	–	6
1912	Susan Brogan	13.2.09	Gallon Upper	Labourer	First school	1924	5
1912	Maggie O Hagan	3.6.04	Carnargan	Farmer	First school	1919	3
1912	Bridget McNamee	2.1.09	Gallon Upper	Cottier	First school	1923	6
1913	Maggie Kelly	20.2.08	Gallon Upper	Cottier	First school	1922	4
1913	Cassie McAnena	10.7.07	Gallon Upper	Farmer	First school	1920	3
1913	Catherine A O'Hagan	15.8.07	Carnargan	Farmer	First school	–	3
1914	Jennie Kelly	16.5.09	Gallon Upper	Cottier	First school	1923	4
1914	Mary A McGillian	23.6.06	Glenock	Farmer	First school	1915	–
1914	Christina McConnell	13.5.08	Glenock	Farmer	First school	1923	–
1914	Mary McKenna	10.7.05	Glenock	Cottier	Glasgow	1915	–
1914	Sara McKenna	16.9.08	Glenock	Cottier	First school	1915	–
1916	Jeannie Morris	13.5.10	Tullyherin	Farmer	Newtown NS	1916	–
1916	Cassie Brogan	1.4.12	Gallon Upper	Farmer	First school	1924	–
1916	Hannah McAnena	20.2.14	Gallon Lower	Farmer	First school	1925	–
1916	Rose McColgan	4.4.19	Gallon Sessiagh	Farmer	First school	1926	–
1916	Rose McAnena	5.3.14	Lisnafin	Labourer	First school	1927	–
1918	Maggie Quinn	13.5.13	Gallon Upper	Labourer	First school	1927	6
1918	Lizzie Scott	12.5.15	Gallon Upper	Labourer	Douglas NS	1919	–
1918	Cassie Maguire	14.5.13	Gallon Lower	Farmer	Douglas NS	1927	3
1918	Mary Ag Maguire	17.6.14	Gallon Lower	Farmer	Corrick NS	1928	5
1918	Susan McAnena	3.1.15	Lisnafin	Labourer	Corrick NS	1928	7
1919	Mary Kelly	28.7.14	Gallon Upper	Labourer	First school	1928	4
1919	Rose O Hagan	14.6.14	Carnargan	Farmer	First school	1920	–
1920	Eliz McAnena	15.6.13	Gallon Upper	Farmer	Chicago	1920	–
1920	Annie McLaughlin	10.5.15	Gallon Upper	Labourer	First school	1927	–
1920	Mary E McColgan	11.5.15	Gallon Upper	Farmer	First school	1928	4
1921	Jeannie McMenamin	1.4.15	Gallon Upper	Labourer	First school	1922	–
1921	Lizzie McLaughlin	6.4.13	Gallon Upper	Labourer	First school	1923	–
1921	Eileen McLaughlin	4.4.17	Gallon Upper	Labourer	First school	1931	7
1921	Rose Judge	1.1.14	Gallon Upper	Labourer	First school	1926	3
1922	Annie McColgan	14.1.17	Gallon Upper	Farmer	First school	1932	7
1922	Cassie Maguire	19.4.21	Lisnafin	Farmer	Legfordrum	1932	5
1923	Rose McColgan	1.10.19	Gallon Upper	Farmer	Newtown NS	1934	7
1923	Maggie Judge	4.4.20	Lisnafin	Cottier	First school	1930	2
1923	Maggie Morris	17.8.19	Gallon Upper	Farmer	First school	1932	5
1923	Emily McCarron	14.1.11	Gallon Lower	Farmer	First school	1932	–
1923	FannyMcCarron	7.10.13	Gallon Lower	Farmer	First school	1924	–
1923	Grace Devenny	1.4.15	Corrick	Labourer	First school	1924	–
1923	Rebecca Devenny	4.4.13	Corrick	Labourer	Glasgow	1924	–
1924	Rose E Brogan	1.7.18	Ballynasolus	Farmer	First school	1930	4
1924	Mary McAnena	3.7.19	Gallon Upper	Labourer	First school	1933	5
1924	Catherine Brogan	14.1.14	Gallon Upper	Farmer	First school	1928	4
1924	Mary Jane Brogan	7.10.15	Gallon Upper	Farmer	First school	1928	4
1924	Margaret Brogan	26.2.17	Gallon Upper	Farmer	First school	1928	3
1925	Margaret Doherty	15.8.12	Gallon Upper	Farmer	First school	1925	–
1925	Mary Kat McLaughlin	7.8.19	Gallon Upper	Labourer	First school	1933	6
1925	Alice Morris	26.2.20?	Gallon Upper	Farmer	First school	1932	4

1925	Bella McColgan	27.3.21	Gallon Upper	Farmer	Garvagh NS	1930	–
1925	Rosaleen McLaughlin	16.7.21	Gallon Upper	Labourer	Legfordrum NS	1931	3
1925	Bridget Maguire	12.19	Gallon Upper	Farmer	First school	1927	–
1927	Nellie McLauglin	1.8.21	Gallon Upper	Labourer	First school	1635	–
1927	Bessie McLaughlin	28.2.17	Gallon Upper	Labourer	Douglas NS	1931	–
1927	Kathleen McLaughlin	1.3.15	Gallon Upper	Labourer	Douglas NS	1929	–
1927	Bridget T McLaughlin	4.4.23	Gallon Lower	Labourer	First school	1937	–
1927	Rose Reid	6.3.17	Gallon Upper	Housekeeper	First school	1927	–
1928	Mary Brogan	5.22	Ballynasolus	Farmer	First school	1935	–
1928	Maggie Maguire	23.11.19	Tullyherin		First school	1928	–
1928	Annie M McNamee	11.10.22	Gallon Upper	Farmer	First school	1936	–
1928	Mary McGillian	9.12.21	Shannony East		First school	1935	–
1928	Lily McAnulla	16.5.23	Lisnafin	Farmer	First school	1937	–
1929	Lily McGillian	7.4.23	Tullyherin		First school	1938	–
1929	Maggie Brogan	16.6.24	Ballynasolus	Farmer	First school	1936	3
1929	Lily McNamee	27.12.23	Shannony East	Farmer	First school	1938	–
1929	Magt Mary Bradley	18.10.24	Lisnafin	Farmer	First school	1935	3
1929	Bridget McAnena	19.5.26	Gallon Upper	Farmer	First school	1937	–
1930	Mary B McKenna	20.9.19	Gallon Lower	Farmer	First school	1930	3
1930	Mary McAleer	30.6.22	Beaghs	Farmer	First school	1936	–
1931	Teresa S McNulty	31.5.26	Gallon Upper	Labourer	First school	–	–
1931	Kathleen Bradley	23.5.26	Gallon Sessiagh	Farmer	First school	1939	–
1931	Mary A Sproule	11.5.20	Gallon Upper	Farmer	First school	–	3
1931	Kathleen Sproule	18.12.21	Gallon Upper	Farmer	First school	–	–
1931	Alice Donegan	27.8.24	Tullyherin	Pedlar	First school	1937	–
1931	Annie McNulty	9.12.27	Gallon Upper	Labourer	First school	1933	–
1931	Rosaleen McGillian	4.2.23	Legfordrum	Farmer	First school	1932	–
1931	Alice McGillian	6.10.20	Legfordrum	Farmer	First school	1932	–
1931	Agnes McGillian	1.4.18	Legfordrum	Farmer	First school	1932	–
1932	Jean Flynn	26.9.28	Gallon Upper	Labourer	First school	1933	–
1933	Rose Bradley	11.4.28	Lisnafin	Farmer	First school	1942	–
1933	Margt Mary Bradley	26.11.27	Gallon Lower	Farmer	First school	1941	–
1933	Mary Quinn	1.7.28	Lisnafin	Farmer	First school	1940	–
1933	Alice M McNamee	9.8.28	Shannony East	Farmer	First school	1941	–
1934	Teresa Bradley	18.2.30	Gallon Lower	Farmer	First school	1943	–

Note: All the pupils were Roman Catholic, except Matilda Hill, Anne Hill, Lizzie Scott, Emily McCarron and Fanny McCarron who were Presbyterian, and Mary Sproule and Kathleen Sproule who were Church of Ireland.

REGISTER OF GALLON PUBLIC ELEMENTARY / PRIMARY SCHOOL 1923-1951 (BOYS)

Note: All pupils were Roman Catholic except John Jos. Sproule, William Gray and Ronald Gray: Church of Ireland – James Baxter: Presbyterian.

Roll no.	Amd date	Pupil's name	Address	Occupation of parent	Previous school / class	When struck off	Destination (if known)
1	1925	John James Morris	Gallon Upper	Farmer	First school	Sep-36	St Columb's
2	1926	John McAnena	Gallon Lower	Farmer	First school	Jun-36	Work at home
3	1926	Arthur McAnena	Gallon Upper	Farmer	First school	Sep-36	Work at home
4	1927	John James Maguire	Lisnafin	Farmer	First school	Mar-35	Home
5	1927	Patrick Joseph Devine	Lisnafin	Farmer	First school	May-37	Work at home
6	1927	James Maguire	Beaghs	Farmer	First school	Jan-35	
7	1928	Bernard McColgan	Gallon Upper	Farmer	First school	Jan-37	
8	1928	John McNamee	Shannony East	Farmer	First school	Sep-35	
9	1929	William Js McLaughlin	Gallon Lower	Labourer	First school	Sep-39	work
10	1929	George Morris	Gallon Upper	Labourer	First school	Jul-35	Work to farmer
11	1930	Gerald McColgan	Gallon Upper	Farmer	First school	Apr-40	Work at home
12	1930	William Morris	Gallon Upper	Labourer	First school	Mar-41	Work at home
13	1930	Cecil O'Neill	Gallon Upper	Labourer	First school	Jul-39	Work
14	1931	Bernard Maguire	Lisnafin	Farmer	First school	Mar-41	Work at home
15	1931	Michael McNamee	Gallon Upper	Farmer	First school	Apr-40	Work at home
16	1931	John James Donegan	Tullyherin	Labourer	First school	Jan-37	Newtown NS
17	1931	Thomas McNamee	Shannony East	Farmer	First school	Feb-40	Work at home
18	1932	James Morris	Gallon Upper	Labourer	First school	Oct-41	
19	1932	Patrick McAnena	Gallon Upper	Farmer	First school	Nov-40	Work at home
20	1932	Kevin Donegan	Tullyherin	Labourer	First school	August-41	
21	1932	William Maguire	Tullyherin	Farmer	First school		
22	1932	Dan McLaughlin	Gallon Lower	Labourer	First school		
23	1933	Patrick Quinn	Gallon Sessiagh*	Farmer	First school	August-39	Illness
24	1933	John Coyle	Lisnafin	Farmer	Magheracolton	May-40	Work
25	1934	Arthur Donegan	Tullyherin	Labourer	First school	Jul-43	
26	1934	George Maguire	Tullyherin	Farmer	First school	Jul-42	
27	1934	William Chas McAleer	Beaghs	Labourer	First school	Nov-38	Legfordrum NS
28	1935	Michael Gallagher	Legfordrum	Farmer	Legfordrum	Oct-36	
29	1935	Charles McNamee	Gallon Upper	Farmer	First school	Jun-42	
30	1935	Vincent McNamee	Gallon Upper	Farmer	First school	Jul-43	Work at home
31	1935	Thomas K McConnell	Carnargan	Domestic	Corrick	Dec-42	Work at home
32	1935	Neal McNamee	Gallon Upper	Farmer	First school	May-45	Work at home
33	1936	Patk Jos McConnell	Carnargan	Domestic	First school	May-44	Work at home
34	1936	Arthur Leo Maguire	Lisnafin	Farmer	First school	Mar-45	Work at home
35	1936	John James McGillian	Gallon Upper	Labourer	First school	May-45	Work at home
36	1937	Edward J Bradley	Gallon Lower	Farmer	First school	August-45	Work at home
37	1937	John Jos. Sproule	Gallon Upper?	Labourer	First school	Feb-44	Invalid mother
38	1937	James Coyle	Lisnafin	Farmer	Magheracolton	Feb-45	Work at home
39	1937	Patrick Jos Coyle	Lisnafin	Farmer	Magheracolton	Jan-42	Work at home
40	1937	Patk Francis Maguire	Legfordrum	Farmer	First school	Mar-45	Work at home
41	1938	Thomas Tracey	Gallon Upper	Labourer	First school	Apr-39	Left the district
42	1938	John James Tracey	Gallon Upper	Labourer	First school	Apr-39	Left the district
43	1938	James Brogan	Gallon Lower	Farmer	New York	May-41	Work at home
44	1938	Pat Frances McLaughlin	Gallon Lower	Labourer	Ayr, Scotland	Dec-38	Left the district

45	1938	Michael McCone	Gallon Upper	Labourer	Legfordrum	Jun-40	Work at home
46	1939	Joseph McCone	Gallon Upper	Labourer	Legfordrum	Dec-42	
47	1939	Charles Coyle	Ballymullarty	Labourer	First school	Jun-47	
48	1939	William McGillian	Tullyherin	Labourer	First school	Oct-40	Corrick PES
49	1939	Denis Devenney	Gallon Upper	Labourer	Magheracolton	August-44	Work at home
50	1939	Patrick Devenney	Gallon Upper	Labourer	Magheracolton	Sep-42	Work at home
51	1939	Bernard McNamee	Gallon Upper	Farmer	First school		
52	1939	Joseph Gallagher	Lisnafin	Domestic	First school		
53	1939	Gerald Maguire	Beaghs	Domestic	First school		
54	1939	Michael J Donegan	Gallon Lower	Labourer	First school		
55	1940	William Reid	Lisnafin	Co Council	Camus		
56	1940	James Reid	Lisnafin	Co Council	Camus		
57	1940	Robert J McClure	Gallon Upper	Labourer	First school		
58	1940	John Bradley	Lisnafin	Farmer	First school		CBS Omagh
59	1941	James O'Hagan	Lisnafin	Farmer	Camus		
60	1941	John J McCallion	Gallon Upper	Labourer	Liscrevaghan		
61	1941	Thomas McCallion	Gallon Upper	Labourer	Liscrevaghan		
62	1941	Joseph McCallion	Gallon Upper	Labourer	Liscrevaghan		
63	1941	Ronald Gray	Gallon Upper	Soldier	Gortin		
64	1941	William Gray	Gallon Upper	Soldier	Gortin		
65	1942	Andrew Caldwell	Gallon Upper	Labourer	Legfordrum		
66	1942	Kieran O'Hea	Gallon Lower?		Derry		
67	1942	Daniel Caldwell	Gallon Upper	Labourer	First school		
68	1942	John J Hood	Beaghs	Farmer	Never		
69	1942	William McNamee	Gallon Upper	Farmer	First school		
70	1942	Hugh Ray Coyle	Lisnafin	Farmer	First school		
71	1943	Charles Boyle	Carnargan	Widow	Rockfield, Donegal		
72	1943	Archibald Bain	Lisnafin	Soldier	Glebe		
73	1943	Edward H Donegan	Lisnafin	Labourer	First school		
74	1943	John Boyle	Carnargan	Widow	Rockfield		
75	1943	Brendan McName	Shannony East	Farmer	First school		
76	1943	Francis Boyle	Carnargan	Widow	Rockfield		
77	1943	Patrick Boyle	Carnargan	Widow	Rockfield		
78	1944	William J Patton	Gallon Upper	Farmer	First school		
79	1944	James Baxter	Gallon Lower	Labourer	First school		
80	1944	David G Devenney	Gallon Lower	Labourer	First school		
81	1945	John Morris	Gallon Upper	Factory worker	First school	Jan-51	Gone to Glasgow
82	1945	James Arth McAleer	Gallon Upper	Housekeeper	First school	Dec-45	Died
83	1946	James McColgan	Gallon Upper	Labourer	Cloghcor	Jun-50	Left the district
84	1947	Thomas Js Patton	Gallon Upper	Farmer	First school	Sep-52	Left the district
85	1947	James Jos McCallion	Gallon Upper	Labourer	First school	Mar-55	Work
86	1947	William John Bradley	Gallon Lower	Farmer	First school	Jul-55	CBS Grammar
87	1948	John James Morris	Gallon Upper	Labourer	First school	Nov-51	Left the district
88	1950	Patrick Reamon Patton	Gallon Upper	Labourer	First school	Sep-52	Left the district
89	1950	David Luke Caldwell	Gallon Upper	Labourer	First school	Sep-55	Gone to England
90	1950	William John Morris	Gallon Sessiagh	Farmer	First school	Jul-59	
91	1950	Joseph McMenamin	Ballymullarty	Labourer	Newtown NS	Oct-58	Work
92	1951	John Fr Tracey	Gallon Upper	Labourer	First school	Jul-59	Intermediate sch
93	1951	James Morris	Ballymullarty	Farmer	First school	Jul-59	Intermediate sch
94	1951	Thomas McNamee	Shannony East	Farmer	First school	Jul-59	Intermediate sch

REGISTER OF GALLON PUBLIC ELEMENTARY / PRIMARY SCHOOL 1923-1951 (GIRLS)
* Addresses were given as Lisnafin.

Roll no.	Amd date	Pupil's name	Address	Occupation of parent	Previous school / class	When struck off	Destination (if known)
1	1923	Rose McColgan	Gallon Upper	Farmer	First school	Jun-34	Work at home
2	1927	Nellie McLaughlin	Gallon Upper	Farmer	Newtown PES	August-35	
3	1927	Bridie McLaughlin	Gallon Lower	Labourer	First school	Sep-37	Strabane Tech
4	1928	Mary Brogan	Ballynasolus	Farmer	First school	Jun-35	Work at home
5	1928	Annie McNamee	Gallon Upper	Farmer	First school	Sep-36	Work at home
6	1928	Mary McGillian	Gallon Upper	Labourer	First school	Dec-35	Work
7	1928	Lily McAnulla	Gallon Sessiagh	Labourer	First school	Oct-37	Left district
8	1929	Lily McGillian	Gallon Upper	Labourer	First school	Jan-38	Newtown PES
9	1929	Maggie Brogan	Ballynasolus	Farmer	First school	Oct-36	Work
10	1929	Lily McNamee	Shannony East	Farmer	First school	Jan-38	Work at home
11	1929	Margt Mary Bradley	Gallon Sessiagh*	Farmer	First school	Nov-35	Beltany PES
12	1930	Brigid McAnena	Gallon Upper	Farmer	First school	Jun-35	Work at home
13	1930	Mary McAleer	Beaghs	Labourer	First school	Sep-36	Work at home
14	1931	Kathleen Bradley	Gallon Sessiagh*	Farmer	First school	Sep-39	Loreto Grammar
15	1931	Alice Donegan	Tullyherin	Labourer	First school	Jan-35	Other school
16	1933	Rose Bradley	Gallon Sessiagh*	Farmer	First school	Sep-42	Work at home
17	1933	Margt Mary Bradley	Gallon Lower	Farmer	First school	August-41	Loreto Grammar
18	1933	Mary Quinn	Gallon Sessiagh	Farmer	First school	Jun-42	Work at home
19	1933	Alice Mary McNamee	Shannony East	Farmer	First school		
20	1934	Teresa Bradley	Gallon Lower	Farmer	First school	May-35	Strabane Tech
21	1935	Josephine Bradley	Gallon Sessiagh*	Farmer	First school	Sep-42	Secondary Sch
22	1935	Elizabeth Smith	Gallon Upper	Labourer	First school	Jan-40	Left district
23	1935	Gertrude McConnell	Carnargan	Domestic	Corrick PES	Nov-40	Work at home
24	1935	Agnes McConnell	Carnargan	Domestic	Corrick PES	Apr-39	Work
25	1935	Rose Mary McLaughlin	Carnargan	Domestic	Corrick PES	Apr-39	Work
26	1935	Jeannie McAnena	Gallon Upper	Farmer	First school	Apr-44	Work at home
27	1936	Susan Maguire	Tullyherin	Labourer	Glasgow	Sep-36	Left district
28	1936	Monica J McLaughlin	Gallon Lower	Labourer	First school	Feb-45	Work at home
29	1936	Annie Quinn	Gallon Sessiagh	Farmer	First school	Jan-44	Work at home
30	1936	Susan Quinn	Gallon Sessiagh	Farmer	First school	Jun-48	Work Drumquin
31	1936	Mary McClure	Gallon Upper	Labourer	First school	May-45	Work at home
32	1937	Margaret P Coyle	Lisnafin	Labourer	Magheracolton	Jul-37	Work at home
33	1937	Lena Maguire	Tullyherin	Farmer	First school	Jul-44	Work at home
34	1937	Teresa P Bradley	Lisnafin	Farmer	First school	August-45	Loreto Grammar
35	1937	Agnes McNamee	Shannony East	Farmer	First school	August-45	Loreto Grammar
36	1937	Rose Ellen Coyle	Lisnafin	Farmer	Magheracolton	Nov-41	
37	1937	Clare McLaughlin	Gallon Lower	Labourer	First school	Mar-42	
38	1938	Annie McClure	Gallon Upper	Farmer	First school	Feb-47	Work in Sion Mills
39	1938	Josephine McAnena	Gallon Upper	Farmer	First school	Jun-47	
40	1938	Kathleen V McConnell	Carnargan	Domestic	First school	Apr-47	
41	1938	Catherine Brogan	Gallon Lower	Farmer	New York	Sep-42	Work at home
42	1938	Bernadette Brogan	Gallon Lower	Farmer	New York	Sep-42	Secondary sch
43	1939	Brigid McCone	Gallon Upper	Labourer	Legfordrum	Feb-41	
44	1939	Rose E Bradley	Gallon Lower	Farmer	First school	August-47	Strabane Tech
45	1939	Bridie McNamee	Shannony East	Farmer	First school	August-47	Strabane Tech

46	1939	Sara Devenney	Gallon Upper	Labourer	Magheracolton	Mar-40	Work at home
47	1940	Philomena McLaughlin	Gallon Lower	Labourer	First school	Jun-47	Trainee nurse
48	1941	Pearl McCallion	Gallon Upper	Labourer	Liscreevaghan PS		Nov-41
49	1941	Sheila Stamp	Gallon Upper	Shipyard wkr	Belfast	Jun-41	Left the district
50	1941	Sadie Stamp	Gallon Upper	Shipyard wkr	Belfast	Jun-41	Left the district
51	1941	Gladys Stamp	Gallon Upper	Shipyard wkr	First school	Jun-41	Left the district
52	1941	Maureen McNamee	Gallon Upper	Farmer	First school	Jul-48	Loreto Grammar
53	1941	Susan T Coyle	Ballymullarty	Labourer	First school	Jan-49	
54	1941	Brigid McCallion	Gallon Upper	Labourer	First school	Nov-41	
55	1941	Rose Morris	Gallon Upper	Labourer*	First school	Jun-45	Glasgow
56	1942	Elizabeth Gilchrist	Gallon Upper	Labourer	First school	Jun-43	Jul-48
57	1942	Catherine B Bradley	Gallon Lower	Farmer	First school	Jul-48	Loreto Grammar
58	1942	Elizabeth Gray	Gallon Upper?	Soldier	First school	Jun-42	Left the district
59	1942	Charolotte Gray	Gallon Upper?	Soldier	First school	Jun-42	Left the district
60	1942	Betty Gray	Gallon Upper?	Soldier	First school	Jun-42	Left the district
61	1942	Pauline McClure	Gallon Upper	Labourer	First school	Jan-51	
62	1943	Brigid P Patton	Shannony East	Labourer	First school	Sep-50	
63	1943	Frances Ashenhurst	Gallon Upper	Labourer	Aldoughal	Sep-49	
64	1943	Charlotte M Bain	Gallon Lower	Soldier	Glebe NS	Mar-43	Left the district
65	1943	Sarah P Patton	Gallon Lower	Soldier	First school	Feb-51	Strabane Tech
66	1943	Mary K Patton	Gallon Lower	Soldier	First school	Jul-51	Work
67	1943	Margaret Morris	Gallon Upper	Farmer	First school	Nov-50	
68	1943	Barbara Kelly	Crosh	Docker	Greenock	Sep-43	Newtownstewart
69	1943	Mary Kath Kelly	Crosh	Docker	Greenock	Sep-43	Newtownstewart
70	1943	Susan Jane Bradley	Gallon Lower	Farmer	First school		Loreto Grammar
71	1944	Kath Eliz T Caldwell	Gallon Upper	Labourer	First school		
72	1944	Rebecca Ashenhurst	Gallon Upper	Labourer	First school		
73	1944	Sheila Donegan	Gallon Upper	Labourer	First school		
74	1944	Philomena Fr Patton	Gallon Lower	Soldier	First school		
75	1944	Maureen Patton	Gallon Upper	Labourer	First school		
76	1944	Patricia A Bradley	Gallon Lower	Farmer	First school		
77	1944	Mary Maguire	Lisnafin	Farmer	First school		
78	1945	Kath Vera Caldwell	Gallon Upper	Labourer	Newtown PES		
79	1945	Mary Patricia Caldwell	Gallon Upper	Labourer	First school		
80	1945	Brigid Melaugh	Gallon Upper	Housekeeper	Newtown PES	Jun-45	Left the district
81	1945	Sara Melaugh	Gallon Upper	Housekeeper	Newtown PES	Jun-45	Left the district
82	1945	Agnes Vera Bradley	Gallon Sessiagh*	Farmer	First school	Sep-52	Loreto Grammar
83	1945	Serena McClure	Gallon Upper	Labourer	First school	Jul-54	
84	1945	Susan Jos McNamee	Shannony East	Farmer	First school	Sep-54	Strabane Tech
85	1945	Kathleen Eliz Maguire	Glenock	Farmer	First school	Sep-54	Strabane Tech
86	1945	Noreen McAleer	Gallon Upper	Housekeeper	First school	Jan-48	Left the district
87	1945	Brigid McConnell	Carnargan	Housekeeper	First school	Apr-53	Home
88	1945	Mary (Una) Boyle	Carnargan	Housekeeper	First school	Sep-52	Strabane Tech
89	1946	Mary Vera Caldwell	Gallon Upper	Soldier	First school	Jan-48	Cabra School
90	1947	Anna Patton	Gallon Lower	Labourer	First school	Jul-56	Strabane Tech
91	1947	Mary Brigid McCallion	Gallon Upper	Labourer	First school	Sep-56	Home
92	1947	Margaret Isobel Patton	Gallon Upper	Labourer	First school	Sep-52	Left the district
93	1947	Nora Cecelia Caldwell	Gallon Upper	Labourer	First school	Sep-55	Left the district
94	1947	Philomena Bradley	Gallon Lower	Farmer	First school	Jul-50	Strabane Tech
95	1947	Eileen V Donegan	Gallon Lower	Pedlar	First school	Oct-49	Left the district
96	1948	Kathleen McNamee	Gallon Upper	Farmer	First school	Mar-58	
97	1948	Bernadette McConnell	Carnargan	Housekeeper	First school	Jul-56	Home

98	1948	Rose Pat Caldwell	Gallon Upper	Labourer	First school	Sep-48	Cabra School
99	1948	Mary Jo Maguire	Gallon Lower	Labourer	First school	Mar-59	Home
100	1949	Rose Tracey	Gallon Upper	Labourer	First school	May-57	Strabane Tech
101	1950	Kathleen R Parkinson	Gallon Lower	Machinist	First school	May-53	Left the district
102	1950	Grace Mary Ashenhurst	Gallon Upper	Labourer	First school	Jul-59	Home
103	1950	Rose Pat McNamee	Gallon Upper	Labourer	First school	Jul-59	Intermediate sch
104	1950	Susan Jos Tracey	Gallon Upper	Labourer	First school	Jul-59	Intermediate sch
105	1950	Nora McCallion	Gallon Upper	Labourer	First school	Jul-59	Intermediate sch
106	1950	Ellen McMenamin	Ballymullarty	Labourer	Newtown PES	Jul-59	Intermediate sch
107	1950	Kathleen McMenamin	Ballymullarty	Labourer	First school	Jul-59	Intermediate sch
108	1951	Margaret R McCallion	Gallon Upper	Labourer	First school	Jul-59	Intermediate sch
109	1951	Margaret T Maguire	Gallon Lower	Labourer	First school	Jul-59	Intermediate sch
110	1951	Brenda Coyle	Beaghs	Labourer	First school	Jul-59	Intermediate sch

Note: All the pupils were Roman Catholic, except Sheila, Sadie & Gladys Stamp and Elizabeth, Charolotte & Betty Gray: Church of Ireland.

REGISTER OF GALLON PRIMARY SCHOOL 1952-1969 (Boys and Girls)

Roll no.	Adm date	Pupil's name	Parent's name	Address of parent	Previous school / class	When struck off	Destinat'n (if known)
1A	1952	Mary McSorley	Daniel	Glenock	Liscable PS	Jul-59	
2A	1952	Elizabeth McCallion	Elizabeth	Gallon Upper	First school	Jul-59	
3A	1952	Alice Morris	Hugh	Ballymullarty	First school	Jul-59	
4A	1952	Philip Caldwell	Andrew	Gallon Upper	Strabane Convent PS	Jul-59	
5A	1952	Bernadette Patton	James	Gallon Lower	First school	Jun-54	
6A	1952	Eileen McLaughlin	James	Lisnafin	Threemilehill PS	Sep-56	
7A	1952	John J McLaughlin	James	Lisnafin	Threemilehill PS	Mar-57	
8A	1952	Hugh McLaughlin	James	Lisnafin	Threemilehill PS	Mar-57	
9A	1952	Pamela McLaughlin	James	Lisnafin	Threemilehill PS	Mar-57	
10A	1953	Anne Maguire	Patrick	Glenock	First school	Mar-57	
11A	1953	Philip McNamee	John	Gallon Upper	First school	Jul-59	
12A	1953	Rosemary O'Brien	Henry	Gallon Upper	First school	Jul-60	
13A	1953	Kathleen O'Brien	Henry	Gallon Upper	First school	Jul-60	
14A	1953	Cecilia Nora McSorley	Daniel	Glenock	First school	Jul-59	
15A	1954	John (Sean) McNamee	John	Gallon Upper	First school	Jul-61	
16A	1954	Hugh Morris	Hugh	Ballymullarty	First school	Jul-59	
17A	1954	Kenneth Caldwell	David	Gallon Upper	First school	Jul-55	
18/A	1954	Elizabeth Morris	Hugh	Ballymullarty	First school	Jul-60	
19A	1954	Ignatius Connolly	William	Deerpark	Newtownstewart PS	May-58	
20A	1955	Annie Mulhern	John	Legfordrum	Legfordrum PS	Mar-55	
21A	1955	Hugh Mulhern	John	Legfordrum	Legfordrum PS	Mar-55	
22A	1955	Matilda Mulhern	John	Legfordrum	Legfordrum PS	Mar-55	
23A	1955	Anne Teresa O'Brien	Henry	Gallon Upper	First school	Jul-61	
24A	1955	Margaret C Caldwell	Andrew	Gallon Upper	First school	Jul-61	
25A	1955	Eugene McNamee	John	Gallon Upper	First school	Jul-62	
26A	1955	Margt Rose Tracey	John	Corrick	Plumbridge PS	Jul-59	
27A	1955	Michael Tracey	John	Corrick	Plumbridge PS	Jul-59	
28A	1955	John Conway	John	Lisnafin	First school	Jul-61	
29A	1955	Patrick Maguire	Patrick	Gallon Lower	First school	Jul-61	
30A	1955	John Joseph McConnell	Gertrude	Gallon Upper	First school	Jul-60	
						Jul-61	
31A	1955	Brigid McLaughlin	James	Shannony East	First school	Jul-61	
32A	1956	Michael Conway	John	Lisnafin	First school	Jul-62	
33A	1956	Francis Tracey	John	Corrick	First school	Jul-59	
34A	1956	Brendan McNamee	John	Gallon Upper	First school	Jul-63	
35A	1956	Elizabeth McColgan	John	Beaghs	First school	Jul-61	
36A	1956	Patricia McLaughlin	James	Shannony East	First school	Jul-62	
37A	1956	Brigid Morris	Hugh	Ballymullarty	First school	Jul-63	
38A	1956	Liam O'Doherty	John W	Strabane Rd, Nts	First school	Nov-57	
39A	1956	Anthony Maguire	Patrick	Gallon Lower	First school	Jul-64	
40A	1956	Bernadette McNamee	Charles	Gallon Upper	First school	Oct-58	
41A	1957	Mary McNamee	John	Gallon Upper	First school	Jul-65	
42A	1958	Arthur Francis McLaughlin	James	Shannony East	First school	Jul-64	
43A	1958	John Gerard McSorley	Daniel	Glenock	First school	Jul-64	
44A	1958	Patrick Anthony Tracey	Patrick	Gallon Upper	First school	Nov-59	
45A	1958	Bridget R Connolly	John	Garvagh Pullans	Laght PS, C'derg	Sep-58	
46A	1958	Thomas Kevin Tracey	John James	Corrick	First school	Jul-59	
47A	1958	John James McColgan	Margaret	Beaghs	First school	Jul-63	
48A	1958	Th McMenamin	Thomas	Ballymullarty	First school	Jul-65	
49A	1959	Frances Patrick Lynch	John James	Ballymullarty	Strabane	Jun-59	

50A	1959	Terence McNamee	John	Gallon Upper	First school	Jul-65
51A	1959	Marian J McAnena	Arthur	Tullyherin Upper	First school	Jul-65
52A	1959	Brendan Devine	David	Gallon Upper	First school	Jul-65
53A	1959	Oliver P Morris	Hugh	Ballymullarty	First school	Jul-64
54A	1959	Mary McLaughlin	James	Shannony East	First school	Jul-65
55A	1959	Mary Morris	Hugh	Ballymullarty	First school	Jan-66
56A	1959	Michael A Lynch	John James	Ballymullarty	Camus PS	Jan-60
57A	1960	Hugh J Maguire	Patrick	Gallon Lower	First school	May-65
58A	1960	Kevin McNamee	John	Gallon Upper	First school	August-66
59A	1960	Norah McSorley	Daniel	Glenock	First school	Mar-66
60A	1960	Patricia O'Brien	Henry	Gallon Upper	First school	Jan-63
61A	1960	Thomas David Devine	David	Gallon Upper	First school	
62A	1960	Kevin Patk McLaughlin	James	Shannony East	First school	
63A	1960	Mary Bridget Devine	David	Gallon Upper	First school	
64A	1960	James McMenamin	Thomas	Ballymullarty	First school	
65A	1961	Gerard Patk McAnena	Arthur	Tullyherin Upper	First school	
66A	1961	Philomena McColgan	Margaret	Beaghs	First school	
67A	1961	Patricia Ann Devine	David	Gallon Upper	First school	
68A	1961	Charles Eugene Doherty	Anthony	BFPO 17	First school	
69A	1961	Annie Teresa Doherty	Anthony	BFPO 17	First school	
70A	1961	Mary Bridget Doherty	Anthony	BFPO 17	First school	
71A	1962	Anthony Conway	John	Lisnafin	First school	
72A	1962	Bridget McAnena	Arthur	Tullyherin Upper	First school	
73A	1962	Regina A McNamee	John	Gallon Upper	First school	
74A	1962	Bernadette M Maguire	Eileen	Gallon Lower	First school	
75A	1962	Ann Patricia McNamee	Thomas	Gallon Upper	First school	
76A	1962	Monica A McLaughlin	James	Shannony East	First school	
77A	1962	Martin F Devine	David	Gallon Upper	First school	
78A	1962	Geraldine McNamee	Neil	Gallon Upper	First school	
79A	1963	Kieran McNamee	Thomas	Gallon Upper	First school	
80A	1963	Daniel G Morris	Hugh	Ballymullarty	First school	
81A	1963	Declan G McNamee	John	Gallon Upper	First school	
82A	1963	Gerard Kevin McNamee	David	Gallon Upper	First school	
83A	1964	Christopher Patton	Mary	Glenock	First school	
84A	1964	Geraldine Maguire	Eileen	Gallon Lower	First school	
85A	1964	Kathleen Maguire	Bernard	Lisnafin	First school	
86A	1964	Rose P McNamee	Neil	Gallon Upper	First school	
87A	1964	Damien F McNamee	Thomas	Gallon Upper	First school	
88A	1964	Isobel Agnes Browne	Jean	Gallon Upper	First school	
89A	1964	Marian Browne	Jean	Gallon Upper	Newtown PS	
90A	1964	Anthony McLaughlin	James	Shannony East	First school	
91A	1964	Stephen Morris	Hugh	Ballymullarty	First school	
92A	1965	Jacqueline Devine	David	Gallon Sessiagh	First school	
93A	1965	Frances McGarvey	Thomas	Ballymullarty	First school	
94A	1965	Bernadette McGarvey	Thomas	Ballymullarty	First school	
95A	1965	John McNamee	Neil	Gallon Upper	First school	
96A	1965	Anthony Maguire	Bernard	Lisnafin	First school	
97A	1965	Anthony Conway	Vincent	Glenock	First school	
98A	1965	William McSorley	Daniel	Gallon Sessiagh	First school	
99A	1965	Carmel McNamee	Thomas	Gallon Upper	First school	
100A	1965	Brenda Doherty	Anthony	Gallon Upper	Plumbridge PS	
101A	1965	Anthony Doherty	Anthony	Gallon Upper	Plumbridge PS	
102A	1966	Angela Devine	David	Gallon Sessiagh	First school	
103A	1966	Liam McLaughlin	James	Shannony East	First school	

104A	1966	Dawn McClure	Robert	Gallon Upper	First school
105A	1966	Madge B McNamee	Neil	Gallon Upper	First school
106A	1967	Mairead M Bradley	John	Lisnafin	First school
107A	1967	Geraldine Brown	Michael	Gallon Upper	First school
108A	1967	Jennifer Devine	David	Gallon Sessiagh	First school
109A	1967	Martina G Conway	Vincent	Glenock	First school
110A	1967	Bernadette Ann Maguire	Bernard	Lisnafin	First school
111A	1967	William John McClure	Robert	Gallon Upper	First school
112A	1967	Liam Thomas McNamee	William	Shannony East	First school
113A	1967	Gerard McNamee	William	Shannony East	First school
114A	1967	Sean Arthur McAnena	Arthur	Tullyherin Upper	First school
115A	1967	Deirdre T McNamee	Thomas	Gallon Upper	First school
116A	1967	Geraldine McLaughlin	James	Shannony East	First school
117A	1967	Geraldine Mgt McNamee	William	Shannony East	First school
118A	1968	Brian McColgan	Bernard	Gallon Upper	First school
119A	1968	Patrick John Maguire	John James	Gallon Sessiagh	Legfordrum PS
120A	1968	Martin Maguire	John James	Gallon Sessiagh	Legfordrum PS
121A	1968	Daniel K McNamee	Neil	Gallon Upper	First school
122A	1968	Dermot John McNamee	Thomas	Gallon Upper	First school
123A	1968	Patricia Doherty	Anthony	Shannony East	Mountfield
124A	1968	Andrew Doherty	Anthony	Shannony East	Mountfield
125A	1968	Fidelma Devine	David	Gallon Sessiagh	First school
126A	1968	Siobhan McNamee	Vincent	Gallon Upper	First school
127A	1968	Park Eugene Brown	Michael	Gallon Upper	First school
128A	1968	Noel Chas McLaughlin	James	Shannony East	First school
129A	1968	Raymond McNamee	William	Shannony East	First school
130A	1969	Rose Mary McColgan	Bernard	Gallon Upper	First school
131A	1969	Thomas Doherty	Anthony	Shannony East	First school
132A	1969	Rosemarie McClure	Robert	Gallon Upper	First school
133A	1969	Clare McLaughlin	James	Shannony East	First school

APPENDIX E: CLASS LISTS FROM SELECTED YEARS

GALLON SCHOOL: CLASS LISTS FROM SELECTED YEARS 1918/19 – 1968/69

1918/19

Infants
Bernard Brogan
Hugh McAnena
Bernard McNamee
James McAnena
Thomas Brogan
Edward McLaughlin
Hannah McAnena
Rose McColgan
Rose McAnena
Maggie Quinn
Lizzie Scott
Cassie Maguire
Mary Maguire
Susan McAnena

First Standard
James Brogan
Daniel Kelly
Patrick O'Hagan
Patrick Morris
Hugh Morris
Daniel Morris
Cassie Brogan
Jeannie Morris
Lily Morris

Second Standard
Michael McAnena
Owen McColgan
Thomas Tracey
Michael Tracey
Jeannie Kelly
Maggie Kelly

Third Standard
Denis McGarvey
James McColgan
John Tracey
Francis McGillian
Cassie McAnena
Susan Brogan
Christina McConnell
Cassie O'Hagan
Maggie O'Hagan
Teresa Brogan
Maggie McColgan

Fourth Standard
Pat McAnena
John Brogan
John McNamee

1923/24

Infants
Charles McNamee
Bernard McAnena
Patrick McAnena
Denis Morris
Joseph Brogan
Pat J Mc Namee
Rose McColgan
Cassie Maguire
Maggie Morris
Rose Ellen Brogan
Maggie Judge

First Standard
Hugh Maguire
James McNamee
Patrick McColgan
Emerson McCarron
William Judge
John Morris
Henry O'Brien
Mary McColgan
Eileen McLaughlin
Annie McColgan
Fanny McCarron

Second Standard
James McAnena
Thomas Brogan
Bernard McNamee
Patrick McGuire
Hugh McAnena
Annie McLaughlin
Rose Judge
Mary Kelly

Third Standard
Edward McLaughlin
Mary Maguire
Cassie Maguire
Susan McAnena
Emily McCarron
Hannah McAnena
Lily Morris

Fourth Standard
Bernard Brogan
Hugh Morris
James McAnena
Rose McColgan
Rose McAnena
Maggie Quinn

1929/30

Infants under six.
William J McLaughlin
George Morris
Lily McGillian
Maggie Brogan
Lily McNamee

Infants over six years
Bernard McColgan
John McAnena
Arthur McAnena
Bridget McLaughlin
Lily McAnulla
Annie M McNamee
Mary Brogan

First Standard
John James Maguire
James Maguire
Patrick J Devine
John McNamee
John McAnena
William Guynne
Mary McGillian
Rosalind McLaughlin
Bella McColgan
Nellie McLaughlin

Second Standard
Patrick Brogan
Patrick McNamee
John McColgan
Mary K McLaughlin
Maggie Judge
Elizabeth McLauglin

Third Standard
Patrick McAnena
William J Maguire
Wm Charles Judge
Patrick F Maguire
Joseph Brogan
Rose McColgan
Mary McAnena
Cassie Maguire
Kath McLaughlin
Maggie Brogan
Maggie Maguire

Fourth Standard
Bernard McAnena
Charles McNamee

34/35

Infants under six
Dan McLaughlin
Anthony Donegan
Teresa Bradley

Infants over six
George Maguire
Wm Chas McAleer
Kevin Donegan
James Morris
Patrick Quinn
Bernard Maguire
William Maguire
Thomas McNamee
Mary Quinn
Alice McNamee
M Mary Bradley

Second Standard
Patrick McAnena
Gerald McColgan
Cecil O'Neill
Rose Bradley

Third Standard
William Morris
William J McLaughlin
John Coyle
Brigid McAnena
Lily McGillian
Lily McAnulla

Fourth Standard
John J Donegan
George Morris
Michael McNamee
Kathleen Bradley
Alice Donegan
Lily McNamee
Mary McAleer

Fifth Standard
John McAnena
John Jas Maguire
M Mary Bradley
Maggie Brogan
Mary McGillian

Sixth Standard
Bernard McColgan
Arthur McAnena
John J Morris

1940/41

Infants under six
Philomena McLaughlin
Maureen McNamee
Brigid McCallion

Infants over six
John Bradley
Robert J McClure
Rose E Bradley
Bridid McNamee
Susan T Coyle

First Standard
Bernard McNamee
Michael Donegan
William McGillian
Charles Coyle
Joseph Gallagher
Gerald Maguire
Joseph McCallion
Josephine McAnena
Pearl McCallion
Sheila Stamp

Second Standard
Joseph McGone
James O'Hagan
Thomas McCallion
Patricia McLaughlin
Annie McClure
Kathleen McConnell

Third Standard
John McGillian
Edward J Bradley
James Coyle
Patrick Maguire
Neal McNamee
John J Sproule
Denis Devenney
Agnes McNamee
Lena Maguire
Sadie Stamp

Fourth Standard
Patrick Devenney
Anthony Maguire
Patrick McConnell
James Reid
John J McCallion
Teresa P Bradley
Susan Quinn
Mary McClure
Monica McLaughlin
Annie Quinn

Fifth Standard
Vincent McNamee

William McConnell
James Morris
Cassie Kelly
Bridget McNamee
Maggie O'Hagan
Teresa Brogan
Maggie McColgan

Fifth Standard
James Morris
James McGarvey

Sixth Standard
Patrick Kelly
John Kelly

Seventh Standard
Minnie Tracey

Teachers
Mr James Crampsey
Miss Mary McAnena

Fifth Standard
Owen McColgan
Daniel Kelly
Cassie E Brogan

Sixth Standard
James McColgan

Teachers
Mr James Crampsie
Miss Mary McAnena

David Devine
John Maguire
Rose E Brogan
Annie McColgan
Mary Kelly
Mary E McColgan

Fifth Standard
James McNamee
Hugh Maguire
Mary Jane Brogan
Eileen McLaughlin

Sixth Standard
Patrick McColgan
James McAnena
Mary Maguire

Teachers
Mr Cornelius O'Donnell
Miss Mary McAnena

James Maguire
Bridie McLaughlin
Annie McNamee
Nellie McLaughlin

Seventh & Eighth Stds
Mary Brogan
Rose McColgan

Teachers
Mr Cornelius O'Donnell
Miss Mary McAnena

Anthony Donegan
Dan McLaughlin
Bernadette Brogan
June McAnena
Frances J Bradley
Teresa Bradley
Elizabeth Smith
Rose E Coyle
Gladys Stamp
Sixth Standard
Charles McNamee
George Maguire
Thomas McConnell
Patrick Coyle
William Reid
James Morris
Alice McNamee
Kathleen Brogan
Seventh Standard
James Brogan
Kevin Donegan
Mary Quinn
Mary Bradley
Rose Bradley
Gertrude McConnell
Eighth Standard
William Maguire
Patrick McAnena
William Morris
Agnes McConnell

Teachers in 1940/41
Mr Con O'Donnell
Miss Mary McAnena (to Sep 1941)
Miss Annie Doherty (from Oct 1941)

1946/47
Infants under six
Thomas J Patton
Anna Patton
Mary B McCallion
Pearl Patton
Noreen McAleer
Nora Caldwell
Philomena Bradley
Eileen T Donegan

Infants over six
James McColgan
James McCallion
Kathleen Maguire
Serena McClure
Maureen Patton
Mary Vera Caldwell

First Standard
Ruby Ashenhurst
Susan McNamee
Bridget McConnell
Teresa Caldwell
Mary Maguire
Mary Phil Caldwell

1952/53
Infants under six
Philip McNamee
Bernadette Patton
Anne Maguire
Rosemary O'Brien
Kathleen O'Brien
Cecilia N B McSorley
Elizabeth McCallion
Alice Morris
Bernadette Patton

Infants over six
John Tracey
Hugh J McLaughlin
Brenda Coyle
Pamela McLaughlin

First Standard
Thomas McNamee
Jomes Morris
Philip Caldwell
Margaret Maguire
Margaret McCallion
Kathleen McMenamin
Mary McSorley

1958/59
Primary One
Chris T McMenamin
Patrick Anth Tracey
John Gerard McSorley
Arthur Fr McLaughlin
Kevin Tracey
John James McColgan

Primary Two
Anthony Maguire
Mary McNamee
Bernadette McNamee

Primary Three
Brendan McNamee
Michael Conway
Eugene McNamee
Francis Tracey
Brigid Morris
Patricia McLaughlin

Primary Four
Patrick Maguire
John Conway
John Joe McConnell

1964/65
Prmary One
John P McNamee
Stephen Morris
Damien McNamee
Anthony McLauglin
Christopher Patton
Daniel Morris
Gerard K Devine
Isobel Agnes Browne
Rose McNamee
Kathleen Maguire
Geraldine Maguire
Jacqueline B Devine

Primary Two
Kieran McNamee
Declan McNamee
Martin Devine

Primary Three
Anthony Conway
Thomas D Devine
Geraldine McNamee
Bridget McAnena
Regina McNamee

1968/69
Primary One
Thomas Doherty
Raymond McNamee
Noel Ch McLaughlin
Daniel K McNamee
Dermot McName
Andrew Doherty
Eugene Browne
Brian H McColgan
Clare McLaughlin
Rosemarie McClure
Rosemary McColgan
Siobhan McNamee
Fidelma Devine
Geraldine McNamee
Geraldine McLaughlin

Primary Two
Sean McAnena
William McClure
Gerard McNamee
Liam McNamee
Liam McLaughlin
Deirdre Mc Namee
Jennifer Devine

Una Boyle
Kathleen V Caldwell
Patricia Bradley
Vera Bradley
Philomena F Patton
Sheila Donegan

Second Standard
Daniel Caldwell
Brendan McNamee
William Patton
Edmund H Donegan
Sara Patton
Margaret Morris
Mary K Patton

Third Standard
Hugh Coyle
Bridget Patton
Susan J Bradley

Fourth Standard
William McNamee
Andrew Caldwell
Pauline McClure

Fifth Standard
John Hood
Tessie Coyle
Catherine Bradley
Maureen McNamee
Philo McLaughlin

Sixth Standard
Bernard McNamee
Patrick Boyle
Charles Coyle
Robert J McClure
Rose Bradley
Frances Ashenhurst
Bridie McNamee

Seventh Standard
John Bradley
Michael Donegan
Gerald Maguire
Joseph Gallagher
Francis Boyle
Josephine McAnena
Kathleen McConnell

Eighth Standard
John Boyle
Clare McLaughlin

Teachers
Mr Sean Doherty
Miss Annie Doherty

Nora McCallion
Gracey Ashenhurst

Second Standard
Raymond Patton
Luke Caldwell
Joe McMenamin
William John Morris
John J McLaughlin
Kathleen Parkinson
Rose McNamee
Josephine Tracey
Kathleen McNamee

Third Standard
Mary J Maguire
Rose Tracey
Maisie McCallion

Fourth Standard
John Bradley
Thomas Patton
James McCallion
Pearl Patton
Bernadette McConnell
Noreen Caldwell

Fifth Standard
Anna Patton
Philomena Bradley
Ellen McMenamin
Eileen McLauglin

Sixth Standard
Kay Maguire
Serena McClure
Maureen Patton
Frances Patton
Ruby Ashenhurst
Josephine McNamee
Tess Caldwell
Bridie McConnell

Seventh Standard
Patricia Bradley
Vera Bradley
Vera Caldwell
Una Boyle
Mollie Maguire
Cissie Patton

Teachers
Mr Sean Doherty
Miss Mary Bradley

Sean McNamee
Veronica McLaughlin
Elizabeth McColgan
Elizabeth Morris

Primary Five
Philip McNamee
Anne T O'Brien
Claire Caldwell
Kathleen O'Brien
Bridget Connolly

Primary Six
John Tracey
Hugh Morris
Jack Tracey
Rosemary O'Brien
Rose Tracey
Elizabeth McCallion

Primary Seven
Anne Maguire
Bernadette Patton
Cecilia McSorley
Alice Morris
Margaret McCallion
Brenda Coyle
Nora McCallion

Primary Eight
James Morris
Thomas McNamee
Philip Caldwell
Wm John Morris
Joe McMenamin
Kathleen McMenamin
Gracey Ashenhurst
Margaret Maguire
Rose McNamee
Maureen McSorley
Josephine Tracey
Mary Jo Maguire

Teachers
Mr James Grant
Miss Mary Bradley

Ann Patricia McNamee
Monica McLaughlin
Bernadette Maguire
Patricia Devine

Primary Four
Gerard P McAnena
Kevin P McLaughlin
James McMenamin
Mary Phil Morris
Frances McGarvey
Bernadette McGarvey

Primary Five
Kevin McNamee
John Hugh Maguire
Mary K McLaughlin
Bridget Marian Browne
Mary Bridget Devine

Primary Six
Brendan Devine
Noreen McSorley
Marian McAnena

Primary Seven
Terence McNamee
Mary McNamee

Teachers
Mr John Bradley
Miss Mary Bradley

Patricia Doherty

Primary Three
Geraldine Browne
Martina Conway
Madge McNamee
Dawn McClure
Angela Devine

Primary Four
Anthony Doherty
Anthony Conway
Anthony McLaughlin
Anthony Maguire
Patrick Maguire
John McNamee
Carmel McNamee

Primary Five
Damien McNamee
Declan McNamee
Gerard Devine
Christopher Patton
Isobel Browne
Jacqueline Devine

Primary Six
Keiran McNamee
Martin Devine
Rose McNamee
Brenda Doherty

Primary Seven
Bridget McAnena
Regina McNamee

Teachers
Mr Wm John Bradley
Miss Mary Bradley

APPENDIX F

ESTATE OF CHARLES EDGAR MATURIN-BAIRD Land Purchase Commission Record no NI626
Mon 10 July 1933. Date of commencement of purchase annuity: 1 May 1930

GALLON LOWER

Annuity	Name	Address	Occupat	Area a.r.p	Money advanced	Folio nos
£3.9.4	James McAneny	Gallon Lower	Farmer	15.3.30 9.0.0 (S)	£72.19.8	8, 8A, 8B, 8C, 9
£3.9.4	Michael McAneny	Gallon Lr	farmer	14.2.30 9.0.0 (S)	£72.19.8	7, 7A, 7B, 7C, 9
£3.3.10	Joseph McAnena	Gallon Lr	farmer	21.1.20	£67.3.10	5
£3.13.4	Henry E Bradley	Gallon Lr	farmer	24.1.38	£77.3.10	10, 10A, 10B
£3.13.4	Sarah Maguire	Gallon Lr	farmer	24.2.35	£77.3.10	11, 11A, 11F

GALLON UPPER

Annuity	Name	Address	Occupat	Area a.r.p	Money advanced	Folio nos
£7.2.2	Mary McColgan	Gallon Upr	widow	20.3.0	£149.13.0	30
£1.7.8	Mary McColgan	Gallon Upr	widow	4.1.33	£29.2.5	28, 28A-28G30
£6.16.10	Mary A McNamee	Gallon Upr	spinster	20.1.6	£144.0.8	27
£4.2.10	Margt McNally	Gallon Upr	widow	13.2.19	£87.3.10	29, 29A-C
£3.8.4	Thomas Brogan	c/o Mrs Hood	farmer	9.3.11	£71.18.7	25A, 25B
£3.8.4	John J Brogan	Tullyherin	farmer	9.1.9	£71.18.7	26A, 26B
£3.19.10	John McGarvey	Gallon Upr	farmer	16.3.27	£84.0.8	17A-C
£6.8.8	Sarah McGarvey	Gallon Upr	widow	26.0.8	£135.8.9	18, 18A-R
£2.13.4	Michael McGarvey	c/o Mrs Hood	farmer	9.0.28	£56.2.10	20-20M
£0.19.10	Patrick O Brien	Gallon Upr	farmer	5.1.4	£20.17.7	21-21F
£3.14.0	Patrick J McGarvey	Gallon Upr	farmer	22.1.5	£77.17.11	22-22M
£0.14.4	Neil Kelly	Gallon Upr	farmer	1.2.19	£15.1.9	23-23A
£5.13.4	John McGarvey	Gallon Upr	farmer	23.3.23	£119.6.0	10-10A
£2.10.2	Bernard McNamee	Gallon Upr	farmer	11.2.34	£52.16.2	11-11B
£2.17.4	Robert Monteith	Gallon Upr	farmer	12.3.0	£60.7.0	12-12B
£0.18.0	Charles McAnena	Gallon Upr	farmer	3.2.16	£18.18.11	13-13B
£0.15.10	Charles Quinn	Gallon Upr	farmer	5.2.12	£16.13.4	6
£5.3.2	Neil McAnena	Gallon Upr	farmer	21.3.2	£108.11.11	9

£6.19.8	Denis, John James	Gallon Upr	farmers	41.0.23	£147.0.4	1
	Margaret & Alice Morris	Gallon Upr	spinsters			
£2.17.6	James Brogan	Gallon Upr	farmer	18.3.2	£60.10.6	5-5B
£2.17.6	Henry McAleer	Gallon Upr	farmer	21.2.21	£60.10.6	4-4D
£2.17.8	Arthur Devlin	27 Oakbank Place	farmer	22.0.12	£60.14.0	3-3D
£2.1.2	John McNamee Jr	c/o Mrs Hood	farmer	11.2.15	£43.6.8?	
£7.9.8	Bernard McColgan	Gallon Upr	farmer	43.3.24	£157.10.11?	

NOTES ON THE LAND PURCHASE COMMISSION RECORD NO N1626
Gallon Upper and Gallon Lower belonged to the Maturin Baird estate from 1854. In the early years of 20th Century, the British government bought out all landlords.Farmers henceforth had legal title to their lands on payment of a annuity. Notice that not all farms are listed, perhaps because some had been bought out under a previous scheme. This list deals with lands formerly comprising parts of the Maturin-Baird estate, so Gallon Sessiagh is not included.

INDEX